A SUMMER FOR HEROES

A SUMMER FOR HEROES

DEREK WOOD WITH DEREK DEMPSTER

Based on the book *The Narrow Margin*
by the same authors

specialtypress

Based on the book *The Narrow Margin*.
Copyright © Derek Wood and Derek Dempster, 1961.
© Derek Wood with Derek Dempster, 1969.

This edition © Derek Wood with Derek Dempster, 1990.

First published by Hutchinson & Co. (Publishers) Ltd., 1961.
Second impression, 1963.
Published by Arrow Books, 1969.
Revised, illustrated edition, Arrow Books, 1969.
New revised, illustrated edition, Tri-Service Press, 1990.

Introduction © Barry Wheeler, 1990.
This edition published in the USA 1990 by Speciality Press, Minnesota.

ISBN 0 933424 54 X

Designed by Mick Keates.
Typeset by Florencetype, Kewstoke, Avon.
Printed in Great Britain by Butler & Tanner Ltd., Frome and London.

Half title page *Liberally sprayed by the fire section, this Spitfire of 92 Squadron came to grief at Biggin Hill during the September battle.*

Title page *Leader of the 'Big wing' protagonists, Sqn Ldr Douglas Bader is shown fourth from the right with some of his pilots from 252 Sqn on October 4th. Under the cockpit is his rank pennant while just visible on the nose is his personal motif showing a boot kicking a figure of Hitler.*

Below *A Spitfire of 92 Squadron taxies across a southern airfield during the Battle.*

CONTENTS

INTRODUCTION

"Please convey my warmest congratulations to the Fighter squadrons who, in recent days, have been so heavily engaged in the defence of our country. I, like all their compatriots, have read with ever-increasing admiration the story of their daily victories. I wish them continued success and the best of luck."

> His Majesty The King George VI
> August 15th, 1940

The victory gained by the Royal Air Force over the German Luftwaffe in the summer of 1940 was the first and probably the most decisive of all air battles. On the skill and bravery of rather more than 1,000 young airmen, rested the future of the United Kingdom and ultimately the rest of Europe. The German defeat of England would have eliminated the remaining opposition to Hitler's plans for a Thousand Year Reich and prevented the islands from becoming a springboard for any future invasion of Europe, an event that was to take place just four years later!

War between Britain and Germany was inevitable following Hitler's attack on Poland on September 1st, 1939. The subjugation of the Poles took just 27 days, with the outnumbered Polish Air Force of 900 front-line aircraft fighting a courageous defensive battle against the Luftwaffe force of nearly 2,000. Despite the propaganda of the time, not all went well for the Germans, who lost 743 airmen and 285 aircraft including 109 bombers.

The collapse of Poland was followed by a period known as the 'Phony War', which was broken in April 1940 by Germany's attack on Denmark and Norway. His northern flank secure, Hitler turned west, and on May 10th his mechanised armour supported by the Luftwaffe rolled into France, Belgium and Holland in a *Blitzkrieg* (Lightning War) to defeat the Allied armies which stood between him and total German domination of mainland Europe. So-called impregnable defensive positions, including the famous Maginot Line, crumbled. The elements of the BEF (British Expeditionary Force) on the left of the line withdrew to Dunkirk where they were plucked from the beaches by an armada of small boats. The 'miracle' of Dunkirk resulted in the safe evacuation of no less than 338,226 troops, men who would turn the tide of defeat into victory in the coming years. For the RAF, more than 900 aircraft had been sacrificed in the effort to stem the German onslaught.

With the fall of France, Hitler controlled most of Europe – and all achieved in a mere nine months. It was a triumphant enemy who now stood on the southern shore of the English Channel and eyed the chalk-white cliffs at Dover just 21 miles away. The expectation was that England would sue for peace; the alternative was an invasion by sea and air.

THE DEFENDERS

In June 1940 the RAF began preparing for what Air Chief Marshal Sir Hugh Dowding, the far-sighted C-in-C of Fighter Command, believed would be a concentrated series of heavy air attacks on the British Isles. To ensure a safe passage across the Channel for the German Army, the Luftwaffe had to gain mastery of the skies by destroying the RAF. Dowding's armoury contained three main fighter aircraft, the Hawker Hurricane, Supermarine Spitfire and Boulton Paul Defiant. The first two were single-seat monoplanes, each powered by the latest Rolls-Royce Merlin engine and armed with eight machine guns in the wings. The Defiant on the other hand, was a two-seater, also powered by a Merlin but having four guns mounted in a turret behind the pilot. This provided excellent defence rearwards but none forwards or underneath, and that was the weakness the Luftwaffe was to exploit with tragic results, forcing the withdrawal of this aircraft from day fighter use.

As well as the fighters and their young pilots, Dowding had a further weapon – Radar, or Radio Direction and Ranging. Britain had perfected the use of this form of early warning only a few years before and had erected a series of tall lattice masts around the coast known as Chain Home Low stations. These masts were widely believed to be navigation aids, but their true purpose as a vital part of Britain's defence system would not be fully revealed for some years. In addition, RAF fighter airfields had undergone extensive modernisation during the late 1930s, with main sector bases such as Kenley and Biggin Hill having protected operations rooms, underground fuel tanks, dispersed aircraft revetments and all the infrastructure needed to maintain command and control links with Fighter Command headquarters during battle. Also established was a visual and aural reporting system run by the Observer Corps, consisting of more than 1,000 posts manned by volunteer personnel.

Between the fall of France and the initial combats in July, Dowding was given a month's much-needed respite to hone his defences into shape. He had at his disposal 48 squadrons of fighters, from which he could put some 600 aircraft into the air; he also had 1,253 pilots.

THE ATTACKERS

Across the Channel and North Sea, Luftwaffe units with more than 3,000 aircraft were moving into occupied airfields to prepare for operations against Britain. Under Reichsmarschall Hermann Göring, the German Air Force had few doubts about its ability to bring to combat and then destroy the RAF's fighter force. Unlike the British, the Germans fielded only one type of single-seat monoplane fighter during the Battle and that was the famous Messerschmitt Bf 109, identified hereafter by its better-known wartime designation Me 109. Bloodied in combat during the Spanish Civil War, this nimble little fighter had gained a formidable reputation, mainly in combat with foes flying underpowered, ill-equipped aircraft. Against the Spitfire, the Me 109 met its match!

Another fighter was fielded by the Luftwaffe, but this was a two-seat twin-engined aircraft, the Me 110, which had been designed as a long-range Zerstörer or destroyer. However, in the British skies it was to prove extremely vulnerable against single-seat fighter opposition, and the Me 110 units suffered heavy casualties.

To carry their offensive to the fighter airfields around London, the Germans employed four types of bomber aircraft. The relatively short-range Stuka, or Junkers Ju 87, was the smallest of the four and had gained notoriety during the early campaigns for its dive-bombing attacks on refugees as well as military targets. Its early success in the Battle was short-lived and the RAF exacted a heavy toll from the Stuka units, forcing the type's withdrawal from operations over England. The three other bombers were all twin-engined, the Dornier Do 17, Heinkel He 111 and – the most modern of the trio – the Junkers Ju 88. Without heavy fighter protection, these bombers were to meet considerable difficulty in reaching their designated targets unscathed. Their design for tactical operations in support of the Army highlighted their meagre defensive armament, limited range and comparatively small bomb-loads. Pre-war theorists stated that the bomber would always 'get through': the RAF was about to rewrite the textbooks!

So the stage was set for one of the most significant battles in history. On its outcome would be determined the future of the civilised world. Command of the air by day was crucial for Hitler's invasion of England, Operation Sealion, and Göring had pledged that his powerful air fleets would soon destroy the RAF. Air Chief Marshal Dowding and the other British leaders, however, had other ideas!

The following account of the Battle has been divided into the five separate phases over which it was fought by the Germans, each phase detailing the daily operations flown by both sides. Naturally, most of the RAF were ignorant of the Luftwaffe's operational plans, and it was left to the Fighter Command planners who had more of an overview to realise the changes in tactics when they took place.

Each daily entry is prefixed with a brief summary of the targets against which the Luftwaffe operated during the day and at night. The all-important weather summary is also included, for it was only the days of heavy cloud and rain that gave the RAF some breathing space from the steady pounding that the Germans gave it on the bright sunny days through August and September. Details of each day's operations have been extracted from a number of sources, principally official RAF and Luftwaffe reports compiled at the time, squadron and unit records and eyewitness acounts from individuals.

With hindsight, it is all too easy to reflect that the battle of Britain lasted in total just four months, after which the German offensive faded and the RAF had won the day. At the time things were different, and no one on the British side could predict just how long the steady attrition that the RAF was taking would go on.

BARRY WHEELER

FIRST PHASE

JULY 10 – AUGUST 7

With France out of the war, Britain in July 1940 no longer had thoughts for anything but her immediate defence against an almost certain assault. Anything that could help to hinder the success of an attack had to be turned into a weapon. Barbed wire and minefields were planted around the south coast, trenches were dug behind them, civilians drew Home Guard uniforms, armed themselves with pikes and pitchforks and set about erecting obstructions on every field a glider could use. On the aircraft industry's airfields old cars salvaged from the unlikeliest rubbish-heaps lined the runways ready to be rolled into the paths of invading aircraft.

At Fighter Command attention had been focused on building up the squadrons. Before Dunkirk the pilot strength of most averaged about seventeen; by the second week in June they had about twenty.

Left: The 'heroes' of that tense summer pose for a Press photographer at a 32 Sqn dispersal at RAF Hawkinge, Kent, in July 1940. Five wear Mae West lifejackets and all are in No 1 Service Dress, the standard RAF flying kit of the period. Left to right, PO R. F. Smythe, PO K. R. Gillman, PO J. E. Proctor, Flt Lt P. M. Brothers, PO D. H. Grice, PO P. M. Gardner and PO A. F. Eckford. Surprisingly, given the casualties, only PO Gillman was lost in action during the Battle. Behind is a Hawker Hurricane Mk I with a Trolley Accumulator plugged in for a quick start.

Simultaneously the tasks fighter pilots were called upon to do were amplified; they were not merely to repulse raids levelled at the coasts of Britain, they were to fly special patrols over occupied areas of Belgium and France, and even to reconnoitre the continental coasts by day.

By June 30th Göring had detailed the preparatory work the Luftwaffe would have to undertake to fulfil the Nazis' objectives against England.

Two Fliegerkorps were assigned to establish air superiority over the Channel and close it to British shipping: General Lörzer's II Flieger-

korps based on the Pas de Calais and General Richthofen's VIII Fliegerkorps near Le Havre.

Clearing the Straits of Dover seemed such a simple task that Lörzer did not consider it necessary to commit his whole force. A small battle group under Johannes Fink, Kommodore of the Do 17-equipped Kampf-geschwader 2 based at Arras, was accordingly given the job.

In addition to the Dornier bombers, Fink had at his disposal two Stuka Gruppen and two Me 109 Jagdgeschwader based on the Pas de Calais. The fighter component was distinguished by the fact that JG26 was led by

Major Adolf Galland and JG53 by Major Werner Molders.

The battle group numbered in all about seventy-five bombers, sixty or more Stukas and about 200 fighters. To achieve air superiority over the English Channel Fink was given the impressive title of Kanalkampf-führer, or Channel Battle Leader.

Fink established his command post in an old bus near a statue of Louis Blériot erected to commemorate the pioneer's conquest of the Channel in 1909. It stood on top of the cliffs at Cap Blanc Nez and from its windows Fink could follow the progress of his units. In good visibility he could watch the British through powerful binoculars.

Among the first officers to be sent to the Calais area that June was General Major Kurt von Döring. He also set up headquarters on the cliffs near Wissant with a W/T station. One of von Döring's other assignments was to supervise the installation of a maritime radar observation system — Freya — but it was not until the end of July that it came into opera-tion on the cliffs of Wissant to detect Channel shipping.

Richthofen did not dispose of any twin-engined bombers but his Stukas, supported by fighters, were presumed to be capable of establishing air superiority and clearing shipping from the area between Portsmouth and Portland.

On July 2nd the German Air Force Supreme Command issued instructions for the cam-paign against Britain. By the following day the effect was apparent. Small groups of bombers, covered from above by roving fighter patrols, were out hunting for ships.

On July 3rd a Dornier suddenly dived out of cloud and attacked No 13 EFTS at Maiden-head. One man was killed and half a dozen injured, while six Tiger Moths were destroyed and twenty-five damaged.

On the 4th twenty Ju 88s bombed Portland and two enemy aircraft penetrated as far as Bristol — one of these being shot down by 92 squadron from Pembrey.

One pilot of 601 squadron shot down a Dornier 17 on July 7th and reported that when about 100 yards from the bomber some

The massive 350 ft. high transmitter masts of a typical Chain Home (CH) radar station in 1940

20 metal boxes, about 9 inches cube and attached to wires, were thrown out behind. The fighter was hit by the boxes, but remained serviceable.

The Luftwaffe's first few incursions over the Channel made it clear that the British radar network was not able to pick up the German aircraft soon enough for the defending fighters to intercept. From July 4th a flight from each R.A.F. sector station was dispatched to operate from its forward landing grounds.

On July 8th Flying Officer Desmond McMullen leading a section of three No. 54 Squadron Spitfires ran into trouble tackling a formation of Me 110s which crossed the coast at Dungeness. The Spitfires were about to intercept when they were attacked from above by Me 109s.

Two of the Spitfires were shot down and the third was damaged. There were no casualties, but one, FO Coleman, was wounded and put out of action for several weeks.

The Spitfire pilots were caught napping because they were still employing formations and tactics taught before the war and because the lessons learnt at Dunkirk had not been fully digested.

Before the war R.A.F. squadrons flew compact formations based on tight elements of three planes and the tactics employed were standardised in what were known as 'Fighting Area Attacks'. There were five different forms of attack and a flight commander ordered them in combat as he saw fit.

In terms of flying discipline and spectacle they were excellent. They were worthless tactically and when related to effective shooting. There was never enough time to get the sights on the target since the business of keeping station was the prime requirement.

Following the command 'F.A.A. Attack No. 1 – Go', for example, the fighters would swing into line astern behind the leader, follow him in an orderly line up to the bomber, fire a quick shot when their turn came in the queue and then swing gracefully away after the leader again, presenting their bellies to the enemy gunner. They were all based on the belief that modern aircraft, especially fighters, were too fast for the dogfight tactics of World War I.

Fighting Area attacks were disastrous and it was not long before the British were imitating the Germans.

With war came the blackout and air raid precautions. Here an A.R.P. warden sets a black-out clock at an A.R.P. post near London in 1939

By flying their loose formations the Germans found these advantages: they could maintain their positions more easily, they could keep a better look-out and by flying at separated heights they could cover each other and scan a greater area of sky.

The perfect fighter formation was devised by the Germans. It was based on an element of two planes which they called the *rotte*. About 200 yards separated a pair of fighters and the main responsibility of the wingman, or number two, was to cover the leader from quarter or stern attack. The leader looked after navigation and covered his wingman.

The *schwarme* consisted of two pairs, and it was this formation the R.A.F. adopted. The British called it a *finger-four* because each plane flew in a position corresponding to the finger-tips seen in plan view.

In this formation the leader is represented by the longest finger, the number two by the index. Numbers three and four take up the positions of the third and little finger-tips. Number two always flies on the sun side of the leader scanning down-sun. And he positions himself slightly below so that the other pilots can see him well below the glare. That leaves two pairs of eyes stepped-up down-sun of the leader scanning the danger area.

While these lessons were still being learned Fighter Command found itself on July 10th fighting the opening phase of the Battle of Britain.

Pilots of 151 Squadron, North Weald, in July. Fourth from the left is Squadron Leader E. M. Donaldson. On the previous day he had been shot down off Boulogne but was later picked up by a R.A.F. high-speed launch. Fifth from the left is Wing Commander F. V. Beamish, North Weald Station Commander, who flew many sorties during the Battle

RAF Hornchurch, June 27, 1940. Flt Lt 'Al' Deere, a New Zealander of 54 Sqn, receives a well-merited Distinguished Flying Cross from King George VI. Next to the King stands Air Chief Marshal Hugh Dowding, AOC-in-C Fighter Command. Al Deere survived an extraordinary number of incidents and crashes, shot down four German fighters during the Battle and finally retired from the RAF as an Air Commodore.

Dispersed from their sector airfield at Biggin Hill, officer and NCO pilots of 610 'County of Chester' Sqn lounge in the sun at RAF Hawkinge waiting for the next call to scramble. The date is early July. Behind can be seen a Spitfire carrying the code of the squadron (DW) on the fuselage.

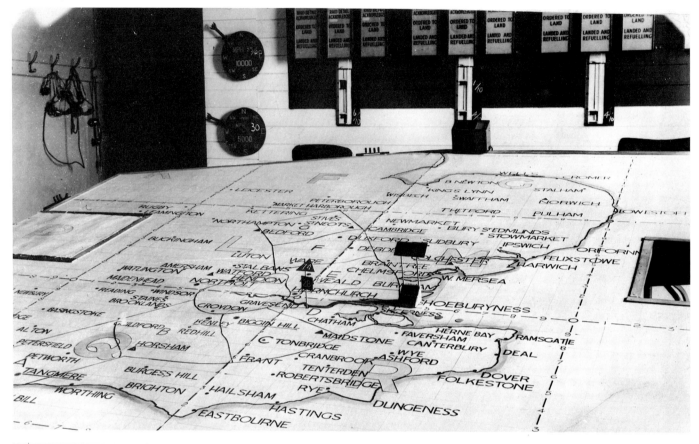

JULY 10

Day Convoy raids off North Foreland and Dover.
Night The east coast, home counties and western Scotland attacked.
Weather Showery in south-east England and Channel. Continuous rain elsewhere.

The first plots to appear on the operations room table indicated that the Luftwaffe were following routine procedure. Skirting the west of England, weather reconnaissance aircraft steered for the Atlantic. Radar tracked them for part of their course but they gave the R.A.F. few opportunities to intercept.

After sunrise a Spitfire from the Coltishall Sector, Suffolk, was directed to a suspect plot. Despite the morning haze it engaged a reconnaissance machine.

Apart from a few other skirmishes the morning was uneventful but activity showed signs of increasing.

A new procedure adopted by No. 11 Group nominated a whole squadron instead of a flight for dawn deployment to forward airfields. The squadron would return home in the evening.

Shortly before 1.30 p.m. radar blips showed a substantial build-up behind Calais. As a west-bound convoy streamed past Dover guarded by six Hurricanes from Biggin Hill about twenty Do 17s escorted by thirty Me 110s and twenty Me 109s arrived.

Within half an hour the Hurricanes were joined by elements of four squadrons from neighbouring sectors, including Hurricanes of No. 56, based at North Weald, but operating from Manston.

A photograph taken before the war of the operations room table at No. 11 Fighter Group, Uxbridge. The 11 Group sectors are outlined and the 100 km. squares of British Grid system. In the background is the bottom of the 'Tote Board' showing squadrons and their states of readiness

Near Newhaven a train was attacked, the driver being killed and the guard injured.

The fight cost the Luftwaffe four fighters. Three Hurricanes were lost, one of them, belonging to No. 111 Squadron, losing a wing after hitting a bomber. Only one small ship was sunk.

Meanwhile seventy German bombers attacked Swansea and Falmouth killing thirty people and damaging shipping, a power station and railways. The Royal Ordnance Factory at

Pembrey was hit and seventeen bombs fell on Martlesham.

The most significant event of a day in which Fighter Command flew 609 sorties was the promptness with which Me 110s went into a defensive circle when they were attacked by Hurricanes. It was a clear indication that this long-range fighter needed as much protection as a bomber.

An anti-aircraft battery on the south coast claimed a record by shooting down a 109 in thirty seconds with only eight shells. The battery log-book reads: '1312 hrs. – enemy aircraft seen at 8,000 feet. 1314 hrs. – opened fire on E/A; range 7,000 yards. 1314½ hrs. – cease fire. Enemy had disappeared. 1325 hrs. – enemy reported in the sea.'

Thirteen German aircraft failed to return. Six British fighters were destroyed.

JULY 11

Day Convoys attacked off Suffolk. Portland harbour raided.
Night Activity over south-west England, East Anglia, Yorkshire coast and Portsmouth.
Weather Channel overcast. Cloud base 5,000 feet. Visibility fair. Thunderstorms and bright intervals in the midlands and north.

At 7.30 a.m. two Luftflotte 3 formations operating from Cherbourg peninsula were detected by radar heading for a convoy steaming eastwards across Lyme Bay. Six Spitfires and six Hurricanes from Warmwell in the Middle Wallop Sector were scrambled, the Spitfires to patrol the convoy, the Hurricanes to meet the German formations.

The Hurricanes intercepted ten Stukas and about twenty Me 109s shortly before eight o'clock. One Hurricane was shot down almost immediately.

Spitfires arrived as the Stukas were preparing to dive on the convoy. Three Spitfires

In the early evening of July 11th Heinkel 111's of KG55 raided Portsmouth. They were intercepted by R.A.F. fighters and this bomber crashed on the beach between Selsey and Pagham, Sussex. Two of the crew were killed and three injured. As the aircraft burns local inhabitants look on – including two firemen with magnificent Victorian-style helmets

positioned themselves to attack the dive-bombers while the other three stood by to cover from the rear. Two were shot down when the 109s broke through the rearguard. No ship was sunk.

No. 54 Squadron at Manston flew continuous convoy patrols throughout the day. 'B' Flight, led by Air Commodore A. C. Deere, then a flight lieutenant, ran into trouble on the fourth scramble. It had just crossed the coast at Deal when Deere spotted a silver-coloured seaplane with Red Cross markings flying at wave-top height. Behind it were a dozen Me 109s in loose formation.

There was a fierce fight during which Deere collided head-on with a 109. His engine dead and the propeller blades bent horizontal, he glided back to a crash-landing five miles from Manston, badly bruised, but otherwise unhurt. Two Spitfires were shot down for two Me 109s. The seaplane force-landed.

If the Me 109 pilot came down in the Channel he was probably picked up. The German air-sea rescue organisation was then better than the British.

The Germans used about thirty Heinkel 59 seaplanes to rescue their pilots from the water. Luftwaffe air crews were provided with inflatable rubber dinghies and a chemical that stained the sea around them a bright and conspicuous green.

The British system was not fully organised until after the formation of the Directorate of Air-Sea Rescue in the middle of February 1941. Before that R.A.F. crews had to rely on luck, the Navy, the coast-guards or a passing convoy, although Park, by the end of July, had succeeded in borrowing some Lysander aircraft to work with the launches and other craft.

Once located, R.A.F. naval high-speed launches or lifeboats of the Royal National Lifeboat Institution did the rescuing. These vessels were under the operational control of the local naval authorities. They formed a chain round the coast with an important centre at Dover, where a rescue service had been working since May.

Around midday on the 11th fifteen Luftflotte 3 Stukas joined thirty to forty 110s over the Cherbourg peninsula and set course for Portland. Thirty minutes later they surprised six Hurricane pilots of No. 601 Squadron, scrambled from Tangmere to intercept what they thought would be a single aircraft. The controllers of Nos 10 and 11 Groups sent off more fighters. None intercepted until the Stukas were bombing.

Being up-sun from the Germans, the 601 Squadron Hurricanes exploited the situation by diving on the Stukas and shooting down two before the Me 110s could intervene.

While the R.A.F. was fighting in the skies above, the call to civilians on the ground was for scrap aluminium to build more aircraft. Here is A.R.P. post C 2/3 at Canterbury in July, collecting pots and pans of all shapes and sizes

The shattered cockpit of a Dorner Do 17Z, coded 3Z+GS, from KG77 which careered across a hop field at Horsmonden, Kent on July 3rd after a raid on RAF Kenley and combat with Hurricanes of 32 Sqn.

A running battle quickly developed.

Luftflotte 3's next raid did not come as such a surprise. Radar warned of a big attack and No. 601 were again sent forward to intercept. As predicted, the Hurricanes found twelve He 111s escorted by twelve Me 110s over the Isle of Wight heading for Portsmouth.

The Hurricanes split into two sections, the first to tackle the bombers and the other to climb and take on the fighters. In confused fighting the Luftwaffe lost eleven aircraft during the day and the R.A.F. four in the course of 432 sorties. At night 30 bombers raided Portsmouth, killing nine and injuring fifty.

JULY 12

Day Attacks on convoy off Norfolk-Suffolk coast, shipping off the Isle of Wight and Aberdeen.
Night South Wales and Bristol areas.
Weather Mainly cloudy with early-morning fog in the Channel. Thunderstorms in many districts.

Formation of early-morning fog in the Channel hampered the Germans, and until 8.50 a.m. activity was slight. Several plots were then picked up heading for the convoys 'Agent', off North Foreland, and 'Booty', twelve miles north-east of Orfordness.

The heavier attack was aimed at 'Booty', and sections from Nos. 242, 17, 85 and 264 squadrons were scrambled by No. 12 Group to cover the convoy. No. 151 Squadron from No. 11 Group intercepted.

Later that morning No. 603 Squadron shot down a He 111 belonging to 2./KG26 off Aberdeen, and during the afternoon several more German aircraft were destroyed – among them one off the Isle of Wight. Poor visibility made interception difficult and by nightfall these had become impossible. German losses by midnight totalled eight. In the course of 670 sorties the R.A.F. lost six.

The death of two pilots in the seaplane engagement on the 11th had brought No. 54 Squadron's casualties up to six killed and two injured in ten days. The squadron was now down to twelve pilots and eight aircraft, thirteen Spitfires having been lost or damaged in that time.

Before Dunkirk, squadron strengths averaged seventeen pilots. The lull throughout June had enabled most units to train pilots and give newly appointed section leaders an opportunity to obtain experience. Even at this early stage some squadrons were beginning to run short of pilots.

The need for additional fighter pilots was fully realised by Flying Training Command. As early as June the A.O.C.-in-C., Air Marshal L. A. Pattinson, said the command's '. . . main contribution to the defence of this country is the maximum training output up to the required standards, and that some risks in local defence must be faced in order to meet the main responsibility'.

To the Luftwaffe, who had started serious planning for an all-out assault on Britain only on July 11th, British defences were still an unknown quantity, and it was to probe these defences and train new crews, particularly in navigation, that the Germans increased their activities at night. They were to encounter difficulties.

R.A.F. intelligence had found out before the war that the Germans were using normal broadcasting stations as navigational beacons. All the B.B.C.'s transmitters in Britain were in or near target areas, so a system of synchronising their transmissions was worked out to confuse or deny the Luftwaffe navigators the bearings they needed.

As soon as the operations room at Fighter Command saw that a hostile aircraft had got to within reach of a good bearing from a transmitter, the B.B.C. were warned and that station was closed down. Broadcasting services were not interrupted, however. Transmissions were continued by the other stations in the particular group concerned.

In the event of all but one station in a group

Right: A Heinkel 59 seaplane high and dry on the beach at Deal after being forced down on July 9th. The British Government refused to grant immunity to these seaplanes when operating in the battle area

Inset: An overshoot during the Battle. A Hurricane of 56 Squadron ends up in a hedge on the Epping road after attempting a landing at North Weald in July

Inset far right: During the fighting over Dunkirk at the end of May and the offensive patrols in June/July the R.A.F. committed its Spitfire force for the first time. This Spitfire of 64 Squadron crashed in a beet field in France, providing a source of particular interest for locally based Luftwaffe personnel

being closed down, the remaining station was also closed and broadcasting was continued on alternative frequencies used by other groups or stations. Thus, unless hostile aircraft were inside relatively restricted areas broadcasting could continue. Under war conditions the scheme was entirely successful and the Germans were unable to use the B.B.C.'s broadcasting stations as beacons.

JULY 13

Day Shipping attacks off Dover and Portland.
Night Minelaying in Thames Estuary.
Weather Early-morning fog in southern England clearing by mid-morning.

Before the battle Park and Brand expressed the view that once the Germans began their offensive it would be as much as they could do to provide enough planes to guard the convoys. The first three days confirmed their fears.

Dowding resisted the temptation to strengthen the south-east sectors at the expense of the others, foreseeing that to do so would invite a flank attack he would be ill prepared to meet. Such changes as he did make were designed chiefly to strengthen the West Country and No. 11 Group's right flank rather than its more obviously threatened centre. Thus he moved No. 152 Squadron with Spitfires from Acklington, Northumberland, to Middle Wallop, Hampshire, on July 12th, and a flight of No. 247 Squadron's Gladiators from Sumburgh in the Shetland Islands to Roborough, Devon, on July 18th.

Roborough, a small grass airfield on the outskirts of Plymouth, was too small for Spitfires and Hurricanes, but it was no problem to the biplane Gladiators whose main task was the local defence of Plymouth.

Park and Brand therefore had to make do with what they had – Park with seven Spit-

The heart of radar operations in 1940 – the filter room at Bentley Priory. The operations map shows the East and south coasts of England and the network of all-important C.H. and C.H.L. radar stations. On the wall is the 5 minutes colour change clock which was standard throughout all R.A.F. and Observer Corps operations rooms

fire, thirteen Hurricane and three Blenheim squadrons, Brand with two Spitfire and two Hurricane squadrons and a flight of Gladiators directed from No. 10 Group's new headquarters at Rudloe Manor, Box, Wiltshire, inaugurated on this day.

German generals had by now reached Berchtesgaden to confer with Hitler who was still baffled by the British. Wrote General Halder in his diary: 'The Führer is obsessed with the question why England does not want to take the road to peace.'

Hitler, he said, was reluctant to smash Britain because it would lead to the disintegration of the Empire which would benefit America, Japan and other countries at a cost to them only of German blood.

That evening Hitler wrote to Mussolini, declining that Duce's offer to send Italian troops and aircraft for the invasion of Britain.

Pressure on the two groups was much reduced on the 13th owing to a deterioration in the weather. German bombers were, however, out after shipping, and two convoys were attacked off Harwich. There were two air engagements off Dover in which the Germans claimed two Spitfires and six Hurricanes and admitted the loss of five. In fact one British fighter was destroyed while the Germans lost seven aircraft including a FW 200 of I/KG40. At this time pilots reported being fired on by 'old and dirty' Hurricanes which bore no roundels or lettering and had two blade wooden airscrews. No official records exist but it is possible that the Luftwaffe used one or two Belgian Hurricanes repaired after the fighting in May.

JULY 14

Day Shipping attacks off Dover and Swanage.
Night Bristol area, Isle of Wight, Kent and Suffolk raided.
Weather Fair all day.

German forces attacked the airfield at Ramsgate and a convoy off Dover. To the west, a destroyer off Swanage was ineffectually bombed, and during the afternoon an attack was directed against the convoy 'Bread'. The Germans inflicted some damage on the convoy, which was guarded by a No. 11 Group patrol. Fighter Command tried to

counter every incursion and flew 593 sorties in the attempt. Four Hurricanes were lost in a fight off Deal. German losses totalled two.

Two days had now elapsed since the Heinkel sea-plane had been forced down and beached near Deal. The Government decided that they could not recognise the right of He 59s to bear the Red Cross, since it was probable that the planes were being used to report movements of British convoys. On the 14th British pilots were instructed to shoot them down.

JULY 15

Day Shipping attacked off Norfolk coast and the Channel.
Night Minelaying.
Weather Low cloud.

Each day German reconnaissance planes would fly at least two patrols, but the use to which the information was put leads to the conclusion that the Germans had too much faith in their intelligence efficiency. Had they fully reconnoitred the airfields, aircraft

Early in July Fighter Command intelligence reports noted that Ju 87 dive bombers had appeared off Portland carrying long-range fuel tanks under the wings to extend their radius of action. The two long-range Ju 87Rs shown here were from III/St.G.2 'Immelmann'. Use of long range tanks, however, made no difference to the fate of the Ju 87 in the Battle as, due to heavy losses, the type was mainly withdrawn in August

factories and other vital targets in Britain in July and August they would have been able to concentrate more of their attacks on important objectives instead of wasting time on training stations like Detling.

The British, on the other hand, owed their small but efficient Photographic Reconnaissance Unit to the brilliant work of a few individuals like the adventurous and unorthodox Mr. F. S. Cotton. Based at Heston, Middlesex, the P.R.U. was equipped with special high-altitude Spitfires as well as other aircraft, including Lockheed Hudsons. These planes ranged over the whole of the German-held coastal areas from Spain to Norway. Between July and October the Photographic Reconnaissance Unit flew over 600 sorties sustaining a loss of only seven of it's Spitfires.

Luftwaffe activity on this Monday morning was devoted entirely to reconnaissance. Alerted to some intense shipping movements in the Channel, however, II Fliegerkorps decided to brave the low cloud and heavy rain. They sent fifteen Do 17s of KG2 into action.

The Dorniers reached the convoy 'Pilot' at 2.13 p.m., but their attacks were thwarted by Hurricanes of Nos. 56 and 151 Squadrons. The Hurricanes did not score.

While the Dorniers were busy in the Channel a small force of Luftflotte 3 bombers flew to the Westland Aircraft Works at Yeovil, Somerset, and other targets in the west of England and Wales. A hangar and the runway at Yeovil were slightly damaged. Bombs also fell on the railway at Avonmouth and on the airfield at St. Athan.

The R.A.F. flew 449 sorties and lost a Hurricane from No. 213 Squadron.

Pilot Officer Holland of No. 92 Squadron attacked a Ju 88 and used all his ammunition trying to shoot it down. All he would claim on returning to Pembrey was a 'probable'. II/LG1 lost a Ju 88 in that area.

The Germans lost three machines, including a He 111 of 2./KG26 off the Scottish coast.

JULY 16

Day Very little activity.
Night Minelaying off the north-east coast.
Weather Fog in northern France, the Straits and south-east England.

In his 'Directive No. 16' Hitler said of the invasion: 'The landing operation must be a surprise crossing on a broad front. . . .'

As with all his plans, the Führer chose to ignore the obvious – that a clandestine crossing of the Channel was impossible. Or did his statement reflect Göring's conviction that the R.A.F. would be destroyed before the invasion fleet set sail?

Later on the 16th the weather cleared sufficiently to release a few aircraft. Again they went for shipping, and again the R.A.F. attempted to beat them off. It was not until 4 p.m. that the first successful interception took place – twenty-five miles east of Fraserburgh, Scotland,

where an He 111 of III/KG26 was shot down. Two hours later No. 601 Squadron from Tangmere destroyed a Ju 88. It went into the Solent where the one surviving member of the crew took to a dinghy.

Fighter Command flew 313 sorties and lost two aircraft. German losses totalled five.

JULY 17

Day Search for shipping off Scottish and east coasts.
Night Targets attacked in south-west. Minelaying.
Weather Dull with occasional rain.

Early reconnaisance patrols were impeded by the weather but it cleared sufficiently later for operations against shipping to begin.

The scale of these operations was small. Fighter Command flew 253 sorties, during which one fighter was lost and a Ju 88 and an He 111 were shot down.

By nightfall Fliegerdivision IX minelayers were flying to the Thames Estuary, Cardiff and Swansea.

In Germany the Army High Command allocated the forces for Sealöwe and ordered thirteen picked divisions to embarkation points on the Channel coast for the first wave of the invasion. The Army Command completed detailed plans for a broad front landing on the south coast of England. General von Brauchitsch told Admiral Reader the whole operation would be relatively easy and over in a month.

JULY 18

Day Shipping off south and east coasts attacked.
Night Very little activity.
Weather Occasional rain in southern districts. Straits of Dover cloudy. Cool.

Sporadic raids against the Channel ports and shipping kept Fighter Command busy. Only one major dog-fight developed – off Deal, where fifteen Spitfires engaged twenty-eight Me 109s. Three British fighters were destroyed in the course of the day, but two Ju 88s, one Do 17 and a Me 109 were lost to the Germans. Between 11 a.m. and 1 p.m. the coast guard station at St Margaret's Bay was bombed and the Goodwin lightship sunk.

In the north No. 232 Hurricane Squadron stationed at Wick detached a flight to Sumburgh in the Shetlands to replace No. 247 Squadron Gladiators sent to Plymouth.

This was not in the general sense a busy day but for one pilot a lot was involved. In a letter from Middle Wallop, Flight Lieutenant Howell wrote:

Bags of excitement here – almost too much. The other day [July 18], Red Section was sent up to 18,000 over Portland. It was a mucky day, and we had to go up through two layers of cloud. Control gave us a bearing to fly on and said that we ought to meet a jerry, possibly two which were in the vicinity. He had hardly finished speaking when out of the cloud loomed a Ju 88. Whoopee! I told Nos. 2 and 3 to look out for enemy fighters while I made an almost head on attack at it. I don't think he liked that one little bit because he turned over and went split arse for the sea, releasing four large bombs, and doing over 350 m.p.h. I got in another attack, and got his port motor. I was going to do a third when I saw the other chaps screaming down at him. So I let them have a go being a generous chap! Just then I smelt a nasty smell! An 'orrid smell! I looked at the dials and things, and saw that the coolant temperature was right off the clock – about 180°c., and the oil temperature at 95° and going up. The bugger had shot me in the radiator! White fumes began pouring back into the cockpit, so I thought that that was not really good enough. The poor old motor began to seize up, groaning pitifully. I called up Bandy and said 'Hello Bandy Control, Red 1 calling – I am going to bale out 4 miles off Poole!' The silly C at the other end of course couldn't hear me and asked me to repeat. Bah. Still, I still had 5,000 feet so I told him again and wished him a very good afternoon, and stepped smartly from the aircraft.

I read something somewhere about pulling a ripcord so had a grope – found same – pulled same, and sat up with a jerk but with no damage to the important parts.

Everything was lovely – quiet as a church, a lovely day – a spot of sun – 3 ships 2 miles away who would be bound to see me! Found myself still holding the handle, so flung it away – chucked my helmet away but kept the goggles! Undid my shoes, blew up my Mae West, and leaned back and admired the scenery. The water quite suddenly came very close – a swish, and then I began my final swim of the season. I set out with a lusty crawl for Bournemouth, thinking I might shoot a hell of a line staggering up the beach with beauteous barmaids dashing down the beach with bottles of brandy – instead the current was taking me out to sea, and I was unceremoniously hauled on board a 12 ft. motorboat. Still the Navy pushed out a boat and the half tumbler of whisky went down with a rush!

JULY 19

Day Dover raided. Defiant squadron largely destroyed.
Night Some activity between Isle of Wight and Plymouth, Thames Estuary and Harwich.
Weather Showery with bright intervals in most cases. Channel winds light – fair.

No. 141 Squadron, newly arrived from Edinburgh with their Defiant two-seater turret-fighters took off from Hawkinge on their first patrol at 12.32. They were assigned to a height of 5,000 feet on a line south of Folkestone

The nine Defiants had not long been airborne when they were attacked by twenty Me 109s diving out of the sun. Within minutes five Defiants had gone into the Channel. A sixth crashed at Dover. The remaining three would have shared the same fate but for the timely intervention of No. 111 Squadron with Hurricanes.

The Germans claimed twelve Defiants shot down. They lost one Me 109 in the engagement. The remains of No. 141 were removed to Prestwick, in Ayrshire, where they could still do good work against unescorted bombers. The other Defiant squadron, No. 264, moved temporarily to Kirton-in-Lindsey and then to Ringway for the defence of Manchester.

Inexplicably, No. 264 was later sent to the Hornchurch sector and for a few days was in the thick of the day fighting.

Radar warned of a big gathering of aircraft over Calais at 4 p.m. on the 19th. Dover was their objective, and Nos. 64, 32 and 74 squadrons were scrambled to intercept. Outnumbered nearly two to one, the thirty-five British fighters did not score.

Fighter Command was more heavily committed than ever before; 701 sorties were flown. Total losses for the day were eight

C.H.L., or Chain Home Low, a rotating aerial radar used in 1940 to search for low-flying raiders. The C.H.L. network was built up in a very short period of time and the sets were based on a 1½ metre aerial array developed for coastal defence

machines. The Germans lost two – a recon-naissance Do 17 and a He 111 bomber – the ratio of victories contributing to German confidence as Hitler made his 'last appeal to reason' speech at the Reichstag.

JULY 20

Day Convoys and shipping at Dover attacked.
Night Widespread minelaying from the Needles, Isle of Wight, to Land's End; Bristol Channel and eastern coastal waters.
Weather Occasional thunderstorms. Straits of Dover cloudy clearing to bright intervals.

There was now so much activity around Dover that it was beginning to get the nickname 'Hellfire Corner'.

In the afternoon a convoy appeared off Dover guarded by two sections of No. 32 Squadron Hurricanes taking turns at escort duty. At 5.40 p.m. it was attacked by Stukas escorted by Me 109s. Two Hurricanes were lost and two damaged.

An hour later forty-eight Messerschmitts clashed with about forty Hurricanes and Spitfires. There was again a lively engagement.

In operations round Britain the R.A.F. lost three and the Germans nine. The Luftwaffe losses included five Me 109s, a Ju 88, a Do 17 and a four-engined FW200, the latter north of Ireland.

The following was the strength of the Luftwaffe on July 20th:

LUFTFLOTTEN 2 AND 3	Available	Serviceable
Bombers	1131	769
Dive-bombers	316	248
Single-engine fighters	809	656
Twin-engine fighters	246	168
Long-range reconnaissance	67	48

LUFTFLOTTE 5	Available	Serviceable
Bombers	129	95
Single-engine fighters	84	69
Twin-engine fighters	34	32
Long-range reconnaissance	67	48

KG 40 of Luftflotten 2 and 3 is not included but of its eleven planes only two were serviceable for mine-laying. KGr. 100 with twelve serviceable aircraft out of forty-two is also not included. Though subordinated to Luftflotte 2 it had moved out of the area.

JULY 21

Day Raids on Convoys in Channel and Straits of Dover.
Night Targets chiefly at Merseyside.
Weather Fine and fair early, clouding over during the morning. Fair in the evening.

The morning of the 21st followed the usual pattern until after 9 a.m. when three British squadrons intercepted twenty German planes over the convoy 'Peewit'. An Me 109 was shot down.

Later a Hawker Hector biplane was shot down by a Me 110 which, in turn, was destroyed by No. 238 Squadron.

Fighter Command sorties numbered 571, and their losses six. German losses totalled seven.

Control rooms were largely dependent on the W.A.A.F. In the heat of battle they were brave and their services were invaluable.

When the fighting began to get tough and the language of the pilots started to match it, senior officers tried moving the girls beyond earshot of the control room loud-speakers. It was not idle swearing, however, but the voices of men fighting for their lives. The girls refused to leave their jobs and said they did not mind the language as much as the men thought.

JULY 22

Day Shipping off the south coast attacked.
Night Minelaying the whole length of eastern seaboard.
Weather Straits fair; Channel cloudy. Light westerly winds in both. Bright intervals between showers in the east.

Although British fighters flew 611 sorties, hostile aircraft were elusive and in the course of the day only one was shot down. The score was even.

At Wick, Sea Gladiators of No. 804 Squadron Fleet Air Arm flew their first Battle of Britain sortie under the control of No. 13 Group.

Spoils of war. Caught by three Hurricanes of Red Section of 238 Sqn, this Me 110C-5 of 4 Staffel Aufkl.Gr.14 was on a daylight reconnaissance mission over southern England on July 21st and made a forced landing at Goodwood. Comparatively undamaged, it was salvaged and assessed by Technical Intelligence, subsequently being repainted and given the RAF serial AX772 for flight trials. The original German code 5F+CM can just be discerned on the fuselage. This picture was one of a number taken on October 28th, 1941 when the aircraft was on the strength of 1426 Flight, the RAF's 'circus' of captured Luftwaffe equipment.

JULY 23

Day East coast shipping raided.
Night Minelaying from Dover to the Tyne and Forth Estuary.
Weather Slight haze in Straits of Dover. Cloudy with occasional rain in other districts.

With prospects of a hard fight ahead, a new situation had arisen as a result of the abolition of the western approaches and the transfer of the country's main trade artery to the North Channel. The result of this (Dowding said in a letter to the Chief of the Air Staff) was that convoys would be navigating around the entire coast of Great Britain.

During the winter months, when it would only be necessary to protect convoys on the east coast, the resources of Fighter Command would be strained to the limit in providing standing patrols, even at section strength for these convoys.

At that time, attacks were made by one or two bombers at the most and a section was an ample escort.

It was the policy for the Germans to attack convoys with strong formations of bombers escorted by fighters whenever possible. Defensive measures had to be on a much larger scale if they were not to have sections frequently overwhelmed by sudden attacks in greatly superior numbers.

Bearing in mind the fact that enemy bombers were active almost every night and that units were detailed in every sector for night flying, it appeared that three squadrons per sector were about the minimum requirement to safeguard the passage of convoys off the east coast of England, and that this number would be inadequate north of the Tay and west of the Isle of Wight.

Dowding had about twenty sectors, not counting Northolt, Sumburgh and Coltishall (the latter because he was already counting the sectors behind); and on this basis he should have had about sixty squadrons to cover the coast from the Orkneys to the north shore of the Bristol Channel.

He had now to expand from St. David's Head to Greenock besides meeting a possible demand for five squadrons in Ireland.

In addition to the above, he could not afford to distribute his squadrons evenly along the front but had to keep some extra strength in the neighbourhood of London to guard against the possibility of invasion in East Anglia or Kent.

It became obvious, then, that the creation of new squadrons should be pressed on with as rapidly as possible to guard against the possibility of invasion.

The Admiralty, said Dowding, had to co-operate with him if any but casual protection was to be afforded to the convoys. They had to start their journeys at definite times and

channels had to be swept as close as possible to the coast-lines.

Since it was impossible for some time to be strong everywhere he would have to consider some form of additional mobility within groups so that a sector opposite whose front a convoy was travelling at any time might be temporarily strengthened for the occasion.

German activity during this day was reduced. Concentration being centered on shipping off the east coast. Fighter Command flew 470 sorties and destroyed three enemy machines at no cost to itself.

JULY 24

Day Convoys and shipping in the channel attacked.
Night Nil.
Weather Channel and Straits of Dover cloudy. Coastal and hill fog in western districts spreading east. Rain in most districts.

A sudden break in the weather brought a co-ordinated attack by two bomber formations heavily escorted by fighters – the first against a convoy steaming into the Thames Estuary, and the other against one off Dover.

It was 8.15 a.m. when No. 54 Squadron were scrambled from Rochford. They climbed to 20,000 feet and were just about to intercept the first raid when Deere, leading Red Section, was warned of the second

> This formation [he said], the largest I had seen up to that time, consisted of about 18 Dorniers protected by a considerable number of escort fighters weaving and criss-crossing above and behind the bombers. I reported the unpleasant facts to control and requested immediate assistance.

Heavily outnumbered, the squadron split – half taking on one raid, the other half taking on the next. In the fierce fighting one pilot was killed.

There were several more engagements that day and at the end of it eight German and three British aircraft were destroyed. Fighter Command flew 561 sorties.

Among the targets attacked in Britain that day was Brooklands. A Ju 88 circled it for seven minutes, and then, after lowering its undercarriage, followed several friendly machines going in to land. The moment it was over the airfield buildings it dropped twelve bombs and flew off. Despite the ruse, there was surprisingly little damage.

While only five French pilots took part in the Battle of Britain the Free French Air Force was beginning to appear at St. Athan, Wales. There, a number of French pilots were given clearance to keep in practice with the aircraft in which they had escaped from France, subject to British markings being carried and the planes being painted yellow underneath. The aircraft were two Potez 63, three Dewoitine D 520s, three Caudron Simoun, a Caudron 440 and a Farman F222.

JULY 25

Day Convoys and shipping in the Channel raided.
Night Minelaying in Firth of Forth and Thames Estuary. Reconnaissance over Bristol and Channel area.
Weather Fine day with haze in the Straits of Dover. Winds north-westerly and light.

The Luftwaffe concentrated again on shipping and in one attack sank five small vessels and damaged another five in the same convoy. The bombers numbered about sixty and they co-ordinated their efforts with nine E.boats which were engaged by the British destroyers *Boreas* and *Brilliant*.

The two destroyers were dive-bombed and one had to be towed into Dover.

Because the Germans were operating from bases close to their objectives, they were much better placed than the defending squadrons to concentrate their planes above any target, for the British fighters had to rely on continuous patrols in small numbers to find the enemy before calling for reinforcements. These patrols invariably attacked on their own without waiting for help which took some time to arrive.

Fighter Command squadrons flew 641 sorties on the 25th, and destroyed sixteen raiders and lost seven fighters. A curious claim in German records was for a French Breguet 690!

Charred and fragmented wreckage of a Dornier Do 17M photo-reconnaissance aircraft of Stab StG 1 that crashed at East Fleet Farm, Fleet, Dorset on July 25th. The victors were Spitfire pilots PO Holmes and Sgt Walton of 152 Sqn.

During the night of July 25th–26th mines were laid along the south and east coasts. One raid penetrated to the Forth Bridge and some bombs were dropped in raids on northern Scotland.

JULY 26

Day Shipping off south coast attacked.
Night Minelaying in Thames Estuary and off Norfolk coast. Bristol area.
Weather Heavy cloud with rain and poor visibility.

Fliegerkorps VIII took the initiative with attacks on shipping near the Isle of Wight. Two of the convoy raiders were shot down near Portland in the course of 581 sorties by British fighter planes. Two British planes were destroyed. The motor lifeboats *Rosa Wood* and *Phyllis Lunn* went out after survivors of three steamers sunk in the Channel.

The pattern of German flying during the night pointed to mine-laying in the Thames Estuary, Norfolk and the Bristol Channel.

JULY 27

Day Raids on shipping and naval units in Dover harbour and Straits.
Night Attacks on south-west England.
Weather Fair Straits, cloudy in Channel. Slight rain in the midlands and the North Sea.

Richthofen's Fliegerkorps started operations at 9.45 a.m. with an attack on a convoy off Swanage. Simultaneously two convoys off the estuary and Harwich were bombed. The destroyer H.M.S. *Wren* was sunk.

In two attacks on Dover four high-explosive bombs dropped on the harbour and five fell on the barracks. In the second attack the destroyer *Codrington* was hit. A second destroyer was sunk off the east coast and another was damaged, with the result that the Admiralty applied the policy of withdrawing the target. Dover was abandoned as an advanced base for anti-invasion destroyers which relieved Fighter Command of the burden of protecting them. This meant, however, that the defence of the Straits now depended more than ever on the R.A.F. One of the Dover attacks was carried out by six

During the battle Göring confers with, left, the Commander of Luftflotte 3, Generalfeldmarschall Hugo Sperrle and, centre, the Commander of Luftflotte 2, Generalfeldmarschall Kesselring

Me 109Es carrying bombs on centre-section racks. This was the first report of 109s being used in this role.

German attacks on Dover were becoming so serious that the Air Ministry issued special instructions to Fighter Command to engage them approaching the port with superior forces whenever possible. To secure this concentration in the south-east meant increasing the number of squadrons to twenty-eight and making more use of Hawkinge and Manston.

Accidents were putting a strain on the repair organisation. To reduce them Dowding ordered the posting of two flying disciplinary flight lieutenants to each station to keep an eye on aircraft handling. At the same time he ordered that pilots were not only to take physical exercise, but to take at least eight hours off a day and twenty-four hours' leave a week.

Early that afternoon Belfast was raided and at about 6 p.m. planes were reported near Wick and Plymouth. The weather deteriorated to such an extent in the south-east of England, however, that those fighters protecting the convoy 'Agent' had to be recalled. Nine Thames barrage balloons were struck by lightning.

During the night several raids were flown over the Bristol Channel and there was some minelaying between Portland and the Lizard, and along the east coast.

By midnight British fighters had flown 496 sorties and destroyed four raiders at a cost of one fighter.

JULY 28

Day Shipping attacked off Dover and south coast ports.
Night Minelaying from Thames Estuary to Humber. Scattered raiders over England and Wales.
Weather Fine early. Fair for the rest of the day, clouding over in the evening.

Luftwaffe activity was mainly confined to the Channel and east coasts. At 12 a.m. a large raid set course for Dover, but it turned back when halfway across the Straits and dispersed. At 2 p.m. more than 100 machines approached

and were engaged by No. 11 Group in the Straits. There were fifty fighters and fifty bombers in the formation. No bombs were dropped.

Four No. 11 Group squadrons were involved in harassing the Germans – Nos. 74, 41, 257 and 111. They lost four Hurricanes. Fighter Command flew 758 sorties and shot down fifteen. Five British planes were destroyed during the day.

German minelaying aircraft were so active during the night that it was impossible to distinguish all the tracks in the operations room. Other raiders were plotted at Nottingham, Edinburgh, Perth, the Tyne, Newcastle-under-Lyme, Hungerford, Manchester, the Mersey and Plymouth. Some bombs were dropped but with little effect.

JULY 29

Day Convoy off Dover raided.
Night Activity on reduced scale over land.
Weather Fair all over Britain. Thames Estuary and Dover hazy.

After weeks of deliberation over an He 59 Red Cross seaplane forced down on July 1st off Hartlepool, the Air Ministry issued this communique:

. . . enemy aircraft bearing civil markings and marked with the Red Cross have recently flown over British ships at sea and in the vicinity of the British coast, and that they are being employed for purposes which His Majesty's Government cannot regard as being consistent with the privileges generally accorded to the Red Cross.

His Majesty's Government desire to accord to ambulance aircraft reasonable facilities for the transportation of the sick and wounded, in accordance with the Red Cross Convention, and aircraft engaged in the direct evacuation of the sick and wounded will be respected, provided that they comply with the relevant provision of the Convention.

His Majesty's Government are unable, however, to grant immunity to such aircraft flying over areas in which operations are in progress on land or at sea, or approaching British or Allied territory, or territory in British occupation, or British or Allied ships.

Ambulance aircraft which do not comply with the above requirements will do so at their own risk and peril.

The first indication of a raid showed on radar at 10.20 a.m. It was intended to surprise Dover. No. 11 Group controllers were quick off the mark, however, the thirty Stukas and fifty Me 109s being intercepted at levels from 5,000 to 15,000 feet before they could line up for an accurate bombing run.

The fighting was fierce and it was made the more dangerous for the British pilots by the heavy anti-aircraft fire of the Dover gunners who, however, hit two Stukas.

At 5 p.m. twenty raiders attacked near Harwich. Seventy-four fighters scrambled to intercept but only No. 151 Squadron engaged. The Germans lost six machines for a loss by the British of three. Sorties flown by the R.A.F. numbered 758.

JULY 30

Day Raids on convoys off Orfordness, Clacton and Harwich.
Night South Wales and midlands.
Weather Unsettled, with drizzle and low cloud.

Flying was largely restricted by the weather, but by noon the Germans were hunting in the Channel and the North Sea. At 11 a.m. Ju 88s attacked a convoy without success. Drizzle hampered R.A.F. efforts, but Fighter Command flew 688 sorties and shot down five German machines without loss. One of the raiders, a He 111, was destroyed by No. 603 Squadron south-east of Montrose.

JULY 31

Day Widespread attacks on shipping in south, south-east and south-west coastal waters. Dover balloon barrage.
Night South Wales and Thames raided.
Weather Fair all over the country with temperatures slightly above average. Channel and Straits hazy.

Thick haze made flying for both air forces difficult. German aircraft attacked convoys at

11. a.m. At 12.50 p.m. the Luftwaffe was active with reconnaissance planes off the Lizard and between 1 and 4 p.m. flew a number of isolated raids over the North Sea. At 5 p.m. fifteen Me 109s went for Dover, and although five squadrons were sent after them only No. 74 was able to engage.

Fighter Command flew only 365 sorties, shot down five enemy machines and lost three themselves.

A large proportion of the night raiders were mine-layers, and they operated in the Tyne, Humber, Harwich, Thames Estuary and Dover areas. Some scattered raids were flown against random targets in the south-east and East Anglia.

Dover under fire on July 29th, 1940. Ju 87s can be seen banking away after dropping their bombs on the convoy in the harbour. The sky is peppered with bursting anti-aircraft shells

Throughout July the Germans probed and sparred with little achievement. They sank eighteen small steamers and four destroyers, and shot down 145 British fighters for the loss of 270 planes.

For the R.A.F. the planes lost were more than replaced by one week's output from the factories. Only the shortage of pilots, who now numbered 1,434, gave cause for concern.

So far as the system was concerned, July gave Fighter Command ample opportunity of putting it to the test. Experience produced confidence, but the defences were not yet fully tried in the face of a heavy onslaught.

targets as far apart as Bristol, Southend and Montrose.

In addition to carrying high explosives and incendiaries, planes raiding the West Country scattered Hitler's 'Last Appeal to Reason', a turgid document printed on green-and-yellow paper. The German air crews could scarcely have chosen a less receptive readership, for the majority fell among the grazing cattle of Hampshire and Somerset.

Fighter Command squadrons flew 659 sorties and destroyed five hostile aircraft for the loss of one Hurricane. A sixth, shot down in the vicinity of Mablethorpe by a No. 12 Group plane, was later identified as a Battle belonging to No. 1 Group.

AUGUST 1

Day East and south coast shipping attacked.
Night South Wales and midlands targets. Minelaying in Thames Estuary and north-east Scottish coast.
Weather Fair in most districts with Straits and Channel overcast. Low cloud dispersing during the day. Warmer.

Shortly before 1 p.m. Church Fenton sector controllers were alerted to two plots approaching the east coast convoys 'Agent' and 'Arena'. Nos. 616 and 607 Squadrons were scrambled and they intercepted a Do 17 and a Ju 88, but without definite results. Cloud base was down to 1,000 feet and this enabled the raiders to escape.

In the south a No. 145 Squadron section operating from Westhampnett, Sussex, intercepted two raids off Hastings and reported shooting down a Hs 126 and damaging a Ju 88. They lost a Hurricane and its pilot. Simultaneously an attack was developing on Norwich, where a factory, a timber yard and a goods yard were hit. Fire gutted the timber yard.

Minelayers were active again during the night and twelve raids were flown on

AUGUST 2

Day Shipping attacked in Channel and east coast.
Night South Wales and the midlands.
Weather Mainly fine in the north but cloudy in the east. Channel cloudy. Drizzle in Dover Straits.

After early-morning reconnaissance and weather sorties by German aircraft an east coast convoy was attacked and a trawler sunk. R.A.F. fighters intercepted several hostile raids in the course of 477 sorties but claimed no victories although four of the planes they damaged failed to reach home. No R.A.F. fighters were lost.

The steamship *Highlander* shot down two He 111s and steamed into Leith harbour with one of the victims on the deck.

Minelayers were active again during the night and eighty were plotted from the Orkneys to Dungeness, together with raids on the R.A.F. Technical College at Halton, the airfields of Catterick, Farnborough and Romford and the Forth Bridge.

AUGUST 3

Day Mainly shipping reconnaissance in Channel.
Night South Wales, with some raids continuing to Liverpool, Crewe and Bradford area.
Weather Mainly dull with bright patches. Cloud base 4,000 feet. Visibility two to five miles.

Hostile activity in the morning was largely confined to shipping reconnaissance. Five

Left: A line-up of Spitfires of No. 65 Squadron at Hornchurch in July 1940. The censor of the period has scratched out the serial number of the first aircraft in the line to avoid identification by German intelligence

Inset: A typical summer scene at a fighter airfield in 1940. Pilots of 92 Squadron relax on the grass at Bibury, a station in No. 10 Group. The pilot on the left is Flight Lt. C. B. F. Kingcombe. In the background is a Spitfire with the trolley accumulator plugged in

raids developed in the south-west, but activity was slight except for the occasional pack of about a dozen aircraft over the Channel against which 415 sorties were flown by Fighter Command at no cost to themselves. Four German planes were destroyed in the twenty-four hours.

Minelayers were active again during the night and bombers from Luftflotte 5 attacked the Orkneys and the Firth of Forth. In the south a dozen raids were flown on Harwich, and six each were reported from the Tyne and the Humber. At Gravesend a bomb put an Observer Corps post out of action and incendiaries in Essex set fire to some cornfields.

One enterprising raider dropped a large bundle of leaflets to which was attached an explosive charge; the whole assembly fell in the right place – a sewage farm near Tonbridge.

AUGUST 4

Day Reconnaissance along the south coast and Bristol Channel.
Night Little activity.
Weather Fine to fair early. Cloudy with bridge intervals at midday, clearing in the evening.

Sunday, August 4th, gave Fighter Command a respite. A few reconnaissance sorties were flown over the Channel and as far as the west of England, but otherwise the R.A.F. had little to contend with in the course of 261 sorties during which neither side scored.

AUGUST 5

Day Shipping in Straits attacked.
Night Minelaying between the Wash and the Tay.
Weather Temperatures high. Fine with slight haze in the Channel.

In a sharp clash with Spitfires of No. 65 Squadron on patrol over the Straits of Dover a Me 109 was damaged at 8 a.m.

At 2 p.m. No. 41 Squadron with Spitfires and No. 151 Squadron with Hurricanes engaged between thirty and forty Germans hunting for shipping in the Channel. Because of the haze the interception was only partially successful, but a Me 109 went down in the fighting.

Fighter Command flew 402 sorties. Six German planes were destroyed for two British machines.

AUGUST 6

Day Little activity.
Night Minelaying off east and south-east coasts.
Weather Generally cloudy with fairly strong winds. Cloud ceiling 3,000 to 5,000 feet.

Only seven hostile planes reached the English coast although there was some activity in the Channel against which Fighter Command flew 416 sorties. At the end of the day neither side had suffered any losses on operations.

AUGUST 7

Day Convoy reconnaissances. Convoy off Cromer attacked.
Night Widespread raids from Thames Estuary to Aberdeen and from Poole, Dorset, to Land's End and Liverpool.
Weather Mainly fair with cloud and thunderstorms in eastern districts. South-eastern districts cloudy. Winds variable.

In the light of subsequent events it is not surprising that German operations were so light, and why they were largely confined during the daylight hours of August 7th to convoy reconnaissance. Preparations were being made for Adlerangriff. Fighter Command squadrons flew 393 sorties, destroying one hostile plane at no cost to themselves. Bomber Command destroyed or damaged seven Me 109s in a raid on Haamsteede.

Broadcasting to the German people on this day, General Sander hinted at the measures to be taken against Britain and indicated that the main weapon would be the bomber. The dawn of Adler Tag was near.

Hurricanes of No. 56 Squadron take off from North Weald for a patrol in July. Another aircraft from 56 stands at dispersal

The photograph above shows a typical scene by a British country road in 1940; an A.13 2-pounder gun cruiser tank of the 2nd Royal Tank Regiment with branches for camouflage.

Left: Originally someone's 'pride and joy'! A 1934 Alvis 'Speed 20' after it had been doctored by the King's Lynn Home Guard. The chicken-wire-lined 'roof' was designed to keep out enemy hand grenades

Below: At first sight a street in Chicago during prohibition, but in fact a Home Guard-modified Railton Terraplane motor car at Maidenhead, Berkshire. In the sunshine roof is a Home Guard with an American P.17 rifle while similar weapons protrude from the side windows

SECOND PHASE

AUGUST 8 – 23

While the Luftwaffe operations staff anxiously awaited a good weather forecast for the opening of the Adler-angriff, it was not yet committed to an all-out attack on the R.A.F. fighter defence system. For Fighter Command across the Channel a new and serious phase of the battle opened on August 8th when bombing was intensified. Fierce air fighting developed with higher losses to both sides and a month of attrition began in which the British system was strained to the utmost.

To Göring the day held no great significance as he waited impatiently for the belt of high pressure from the Azores which would give him the fine weather required to gain air superiority in 'four days'. He was convinced this aim could be achieved, and outwardly the convoy attacks of July had done nothing to change his views. On the contrary the operations staff and intelligence reports showed heavy British shipping and fighter losses without prohibitive cost to the Germans.

The Reichsmarschall could not know that Dowding on the other side of the Channel was holding his forces in check, and refusing to commit large numbers of fighters to a battle over water where warning time was short, and the enemy usually had the advantage.

Left: One of the few air-to-air photographic sorties flown during the Battle resulted in this shot of nine Spitfire Mk Is of 610 Sqn based at Biggin Hill.

After an initial success due to surprise, the Boulton Paul Defiant two-seat turret fighter proved very vulnerable. Units equipped with the type were withdrawn to the north. In the autumn Defiant squadrons returned to southern airfields in a night fighter role. These Defiants of No. 264 Squadron were airborne from Kirton-in-Lindsey on August 9th

By husbanding his resources, Dowding could show a moderate but steady build-up in personnel and surprising increases in aircraft strength and reserves. On August 3rd he had 708 fighters available for operations, and 1,434 pilots, a marked improvement over June 30th, when the respective figures were 587 and 1,200.

On July 10th Fighter Command possessed fifty-two squadrons, but by August 8th three more had been added and six others were under training including No. 1 R.C.A.F. During July the three new squadrons formed were 302 Polish, 303 Polish and 310 Czech.

Most units in the groups rotated through satellite airfields for short periods and the 609 Squadron diarist Flying Officer Dundas recorded:

By the beginning of August 609 were working to a settled operational programme with 238 and 152 Squadrons – 609 and 238 Squadrons being based at Middle Wallop, 152 at Warmwell. The routine went as follows – a day on 15 minutes availability at Wallop – a day of release off camp. A day of readiness at Warmwell where

we kept a servicing party of thirty airmen under Flight-Sergeant Agar and Sergeant Fitzgerald.

At this time Warmwell possessed, though in rather irregular proportions, the two chief characteristics of a forward station – action and discomfort. Every third day at mid-day the pilots were to set off from Wallop in squadron formation, their cockpits bulging optimistically with sponge-bags, pyjamas, and other articles of toilet which they got very little opportunity of using.

Sleeping accommodation was provided for visiting squadrons in the sergeants' quarters, but after some experience of this pilots preferred to accommodate themselves as best they could in the dispersal tent, which was furnished with beds, dirty blankets, and an assortment of unreliable telephones.

AUGUST 8

Day Three major attacks on a Channel convoy.
Night Small raids and minelaying.
Weather Showers and bright intervals. Channel cloudy.

The weather in the morning was well suited to German tactics, with visibility six to eight miles and clouds at 2,000 feet giving good cover for enemy aircraft operating from the coast only thirty miles distant.

On the previous night Convoy C.W.9, code-name 'Peewit', had sailed from the Thames Estuary with twenty ships. Its passage did not, however, go unnoticed by operators

of the Freya radar set on the cliffs near Wissant, and steps were speedily taken to deal with it. Before dawn on the 8th a pack of E-boats attacked, sinking three ships and damaging others.

At nine o'clock a force of Stukas from Fliegerkorps VIII escorted by Me 109s from JG27 approached from Cherbourg, but was successfully intercepted and broken up by five squadrons from No. 11 Group and one from No. 10 Group.

The bombing was resumed by fifty-seven Ju 87s on a twenty-mile front at 12.45 when the scattered ships were steaming east of the Isle of Wight. Casualties were caused despite the intervention of four and a half British fighter squadrons. Some ships survived, and were duly noted by the departing aircraft. The orders were to sink the convoy completely, if possible, and so a further raid of eighty-two escorted Stukas from Cherbourg moved into the Swanage area at 5 p.m.

Fully alerted, Nos. 10 and 11 groups between them were able to put up seven squadrons, several of which found themselves in excellent positions for attack.

Squadron Leader J. R. A. Peel, commanding No. 145 Hurricane Squadron from Westhampnett, Sussex, reported:

We climbed to 16,000 feet, and, looking down, saw a large formation of Ju 87s approaching from the south with Me 109s stepped up behind to 20,000 feet. We approached unobserved out of the sun and went in to attack the rear Ju 87s before the enemy fighters could interfere. I gave a five-second burst to one bomber and broke off to engage two Me 109s. There was a dogfight. The enemy fighters, which were painted silver, were half rolling, diving and zooming in climbing turns. I fired two five-second bursts at one and saw it dive into the sea. Then I followed another up in a zoom and got him as he stalled.

A flight-commander of the same squadron brought down two Ju 87s although his own engine had stopped. Despite the engine failure he dived on one Ju 87 which crashed into the sea. His engine re-started and he proceeded to attack another 87 which, instead of bombing a ship, went straight on into the water. After this the engine stopped completely and he glided back to base. No. 145 Squadron was in action three times over the convoy and with No. 43 Squadron caused most of the enemy's losses.

The remains of the battered convoy ploughed its way on, having lost four merchantmen sunk, six badly damaged, with six armed rescue vessels damaged during the day, and three ships sunk by the E-boats. It was the greatest effort made against a single convoy during the whole battle.

While the raids had been going on, German reconnaissance aircraft concentrated on airfields and harbours, the former including Lee-on-Solent, Gosport and Farnborough, and the latter Portsmouth, Portland and Dover. The photographs brought back from these flights and the ensuing four days led to the heavy raids on Lee and Gosport on the 16th and 18th.

The R.A.F. claimed twenty-four German bombers and thirty-six fighters shot down, while the Luftwaffe decided they had shot down forty-nine British fighters. In the upshot the actual losses were nineteen R.A.F. (and one at night) and thirty-one German. These were the highest figures on both sides since the Battle started on July 10th, and Churchill was moved to send a congratulatory message to the Secretary of State for Air.

At night, Fliegerdivision IX laid mines in the Thames Estuary and off the east coast, while small numbers of bombers dropped their loads on Cardiff, Hull, Liverpool, Middlesbrough, Birmingham and the Bristol Aeroplane Company's factory at Filton.

AUGUST 9

Day Quiet. Isolated raids and attacks on the east coast shipping.
Night Minelaying and attacks off east coast.
Weather Cloud and rain showers. Some bright intervals. Channel cloudy.

The Luftwaffe Command staff were pre-occupied with the date for Adler Tag. After some discussion, and with Göring's approval, preliminary orders were issued for the commencement of large-scale operations on the 10th. By nightfall, however, these had been cancelled and the action postponed pending the arrival of better weather.

After the dog-fights off the Isle of Wight the previous day, the 9th was quiet. One enemy aircraft reached Sunderland and dropped bombs on the shipyard, causing some damage. Scattered raids were made by Fliegerkorps X on east coast convoys, and two Me 109s attempted to destroy balloons of the Dover barrage without success. Over Plymouth a Ju 88 from 2./LG1 was shot down, also an He 111 from 7./KG26 off the north-east coast.

During the day Fighter Command flew 409 sorties, many of them against 'X' or unidentified raids, which turned out to be mainly reconnaissance patrols. Three R.A.F. fighters were lost (and one at night); five German machines were destroyed. After dark mine-laying continued in the same areas as the previous night. Bombers from the Continent hit targets in East Anglia and north of London while Luftflotte 5 attempted to interfere with east coast convoys.

AUGUST 10

Day Shipping and overland reconnaissance.
Night Minelaying.
Weather Squally and thundery, some bright intervals. Channel cloudy.

German activity was limited to shipping reconnaissance off the south and east coasts, eleven bombs from a Dornier 17 falling near West Malling, and a surprise raid being made on Norwich. Fighter Command searched for the elusive raiders in the course of 116 patrols but made no interceptions. There were no

losses on either side, although some raiders had tried to find the Boulton Paul factory at Norwich and others flew over Odiham.

Once again at night Fliegerdivision IX laid mines, extending its activities from Harwich and the Thames Estuary to the Bristol Channel. A raid was sent to the Rolls-Royce works at Crewe, but did not find the target.

AUGUST 11

Day Heavy attack on Portland, feints by fighter formations over Dover. Convoy attacks in Thames Estuary and off East Anglia.
Night Harassing attacks on Merseyside. Minelaying.
Weather Fair in morning. Cloudy most of day.

Compared with the lull on the 10th, this Sunday morning started with considerable activity. From 7 to 10.30 a series of probing attacks developed against Dover. First two formations of fifteen + fighters and Me 110 fighter bombers from Gruppe 210 attacked the Dover balloon barrage, followed by a threat to Channel convoys at 8.30 a.m. No sooner had this died down than thirty + of the enemy returned to Dover and were engaged by anti-aircraft fire and by fighters from Nos. 74, 32, 54 and 64 squadrons. The German formation was not looking for action and only served to draw off British aircraft.

The Luftwaffe plan was to attract as many fighters as possible to the Dover area, while the main strike was delivered much farther west, at Portland. This operation being laid on in place of the mass Adler Tag assault, which had again been postponed.

While three squadrons were hotly engaged over Dover, the radar stations, in particular Ventnor, picked up a large raid heading for the Weymouth area, and Nos, 145, 238, 152, 213, 609 and 187 Squadrons were scrambled to intercept. They found some 150 aircraft, Ju 88s and He 111s escorted by Me 109s and Me 110s. Fierce dog-fights developed as the bombers pressed home their high-level and dive-bomber attacks against docks, oil-tanks, barracks and gasworks at Weymouth and Portland. A resident of one of the houses attacked described the formations as being 'like a swarm of bees in the sky. I counted up to fifty and then stopped.'

When the situation maps showed Portland

clear, more fighters appeared off Dover to shoot at balloons from the long-suffering No. 961 Balloon Squadron. A further force attacked the convoy 'Booty' off the Norfolk coast and seriously damaged two ships. A destroyer and two minesweepers off Margate were attacked. They put up a spirited defence but one minesweeper suffered several casualties and the ship was finally beached under the North Foreland.

A typical example of the work of the fighter squadrons involved on the 11th was No. 74 at its forward base at Manston.

The squadron took part in no less than four separate combats from dawn to 2 p.m. and accounted for a number of German aircraft with the loss of only two pilots. The first operational order was received at 7.49 a.m. to intercept a hostile raid approaching Dover. The squadron with twelve aircraft, led by Squadron Leader Malan, climbed to 20,000 feet, and surprised approximately eighteen Me 109s flying towards Dover. Pilot Officer Stevenson's aircraft was hit by enemy fire and he baled out and came down in the sea. He attracted the attention of a motor torpedo-boat by firing his revolver. The second combat took place between 9.50 and 10.45 when twelve aircraft again took off to intercept enemy fighters approaching Dover. Several small groups of Me 109s were sighted in mid-Channel. Owing to R/T difficulties, part of the squadron did not engage.

The third combat started at 11.45 when eleven aircraft took off to patrol the convoy 'Booty' about twelve miles east of Clacton. Forty Me 110s were sighted approaching the convoy from east in close formation just below cloud base. Enemy aircraft formed a defensive circle on sighting the fighters, but Pilot Officer Freeborne led the squadron in a dive into the middle of the circle. Aircraft landed back at Manston at 12.45. The squadron took off for the fourth time at 1.56 with eight aircraft, to patrol Hawkinge at 15,000 feet and subsequently north-east of Margate where enemy raids were reported. Ten Ju 87s were sighted passing through cloud at 6,000 feet and twenty Me 109s at 10,000 feet. Fighters attacked the 109s, who dived for cloud and a dog-fight ensued.

No. 604 Squadron found a Heinkel 59 rescue seaplane afloat off the French coast with its engines running, and destroyed it, despite interference from the Me 109 escort.

An Me 110 flying along the Sussex coast near Bexhill during one of the August raids

The rest of the afternoon was quiet and that night a few harassing attacks were aimed at Merseyside and more mines were laid in the Bristol Channel.

In the confused fighting, the honours of the day were nearly even – thirty-eight German and thirty-two British losses. This was not the kind of tally sheet which 11 Group liked, or could afford. Fighters had clashed heavily with fighters and thirteen Me 109s had been destroyed (six from JG2) and ten Me 110s. Of the latter two were from the fighter-bomber unit Epr.Gr.210 operating off Harwich.

AUGUST 12

Day Sharp raid on Portsmouth. Convoy in Thames Estuary, radar stations and coastal airfields attacked.
Night Widespread harassing raids.
Weather Fine except for mist patches.

To the harassed staff of the O.K.L., Göring's headquarters, the 12th was an important day. The meteorological forecast showed the first

movement of a high-pressure belt in the Azores which would give good clear weather over the United Kingdom on the following day. The operations branch, IA, issued orders to Luftflotten 2 and 3 to be ready for the big attack at 7 a.m. on the 13th.

In preparation for this the 12th was to be devoted to the first raids on British fighter airfields and radar stations while maintaining pressure against shipping and harbours. The battle area now moved forward over the island itself, and Fighter Command had its most intensive day since the war began.

The attacks were divided into five phases moving pendulum fashion backwards and forwards along the south coast. Feints began over Dover at 7.30 a.m., and at nine o'clock five radar stations were attacked. Dunkirk radar had two huts destroyed and a 1,000 lb. bomb near the concrete transmitting block moved it inches. No vital damage was done and plotting continued.

At Dover the aerial towers were slightly damaged and huts inside the compound were smashed, while at Rye all huts were destroyed,

but miraculously the transmitting and receiving blocks and the watch office were unharmed. A stand-by diesel put the station back on the air by noon. At Pevensey eight 500 kg. bombs were dropped and damage included a cut in the electric main. The airfield at Lympne was also bombed.

After an hour's respite the second phase opened with a formation of Ju 87s attacking convoys 'Arena' and 'Agent' in the Estuary, while Ju 88s from Luftflotte 3, with heavy escort, were flying in towards the Southampton area. Some aircraft diverted to bomb convoys 'Snail' and 'Cable', but the main target was Portsmouth, which received a heavy attack, despite the concentrated fire of every ship and landborne A.A. gun in the harbour. At Margate the lifeboat crew were sitting watching a film of the B.E.F. evacuation from Dunkirk in the town hall when the siren sounded. The crews hurried to their station and the motor lifeboat *J. B. Proudfoot* was launched in time to pick up the survivors of two Admiralty trawlers, *Pyrope* and *Tamarisk*, which had been sunk.

This Junkers Ju 88A-1 of Stab II/KG54 being dismantled by RAF technicians force-landed on Portland Head following an attack by a Hurricane of 213 Sqn. The German aircraft was part of the large raid on Portland on Sunday August 11th.

The enemy had approached the target by flying up the Channel in a westerly direction from Spithead and then turned through the gap in the balloon barrage formed by the harbour mouth. Several fires were started in the docks and the city itself, and the harbour station was burnt out. As they saw no fighters over the A.A. area, the citizens of Portsmouth felt that the Germans had been allowed too liberal a use of their air-space.

While Portsmouth was being hit, fifteen Ju 88s dive-bombed the long-range C.H. radar station at Ventnor on the Isle of Wight. Fires were started, and because of lack of water on the site most of the buildings were destroyed and other serious damage done. A German reconnaissance later in the day noted 'craters in the vicinity of the wireless station masts,

The Sector Station at Middle Wallop, Hampshire, in August. On the left, a 609 Squadron Spitfire is wrecked and on fire. In the right-hand picture, three Spitfires of 609 Squadron are seen scrambling to intercept a raid

and the station quarters on fire'.

Shortly after this the coastal airfield at Manston received the first of many raids. A formation of Dorniers came in low at 1.25 p.m. and dropped about 150 high-explosive bombs, pitting the airfield with craters, destroying the workshops and damaging two hangars, all in the space of five minutes. Only one casualty was recorded, but the airfield was unserviceable until the 13th.

No. 54 Squadron had striven to deflect the bombers from Manston, but could not penetrate the heavy escort. On the ground No. 65 Squadron's Spitfires were taxiing out for take-off when the first bombs hit. Most of them managed to get into the air and joined in the mêlée of 109s and No. 54 Squadron aircraft above. When the Dornier formation from KG2 turned for home it was without its main escort and came in for a determined attack by the Hurricanes of No. 56 Squadron.

Hawkinge, another advance airfield on the coast, was seriously damaged by Ju 88s which smashed two hangars, destroyed the station workshops and damaged stores. Despite twenty-eight craters on the airfield, Hawkinge was not completely unserviceable and became fully operational again on the morning of the 13th. Four aircraft had been badly damaged, five people killed and seven seriously injured.

Lympne, which had received 141 bombs in the morning, was the subject of a second attack in the fifth phase of the day commencing at 3 p.m. Two hundred and forty-two bombs were dropped in two runs and the airfield rendered unserviceable, although seventy of the bombs fell into surrounding fields. The remainder of the force from Luftflotte 2 bombed Hastings and Dover.

As evening came, the Luftwaffe were jubilant. German radio stations spoke of very heavy damage on the British mainland and claimed seventy-one R.A.F. aircraft, including the whole of No. 65 Squadron at Manston. The German headquarters report of the 13th claimed that forty-six Spitfires, twenty-three Hurricanes and one Morane 406 had been destroyed on the 12th. In fact the Germans had lost thirty-one machines and the R.A.F., in the course of 732 sorties, had suffered twenty-two casualties.

The attacks had been severe and they provided a foretaste of the main August battle pattern. Of the six radar stations attacked, only one had been knocked out, Ventnor, but this was not apparent to German intelligence.

These initial strikes at radar had brought out two important points. First, the aerial towers themselves consistently deflected dive-bombing attacks away from the vital operations rooms underneath. Second, the W.A.A.F. plotters showed courage of the highest order under fire and the ability to keep on reporting a raid until it bombed their own station.

The airfields received many tons of bombs but survived. While it was clear to the R.A.F. that very heavy concentration at frequent intervals would be required completely to wreck a particular field, the Luftflotten staffs in France had already begun the foolhardy process of deleting units and stations on the map after each attack.

That night widespread harassing raids developed overland in addition to the normal crop of minelaying. Small numbers of aircraft dropped bombs on many towns and villages, including Stratford-upon-Avon.

Right: A German target photograph of the Ventnor Chain Home radar station on the Isle of Wight taken on August 12th, 1940. This was the day when 15 Ju 88's caused severe damage to the site. The caption to the picture reads: Radio Station with warning capability 1. 3 transmitter masts 2. 4 small transmitter masts 3. Low-level defences 4. Special fuel installation 5. Anti-aircraft position; additional buildings under construction

GB *9623 bc*

Maßstab etwa 1: 11 000

500 | 0 | 500 | 1000 | m

(1cm = 110 m)

Ventnor (Insel Wight)
Funkstation mit Sonderanlage

G B *9623 bc*
Geheim

Bild:
933 SG / 177 (v)

vom
12.8.40.

Karte GB/ E
1:100 000
Blatt 38

Länge
(*westl.*Greenw.):
1 ° 11 ' 45 "
Nördl. Breite :
50 ° 36 ' 07 "
( )

Mißweisung:
- 11 ° 6 '
(Mitte 19 38)

Zielhöhe
über NN 240 m

1634

Sept. 40

Insel Wight

Ventnor

○   23   Funkstation mit Sonderanlage: 1) 3 Sendemasten (Richtstrahler); 2) 4 kleine Sendemaste; 3) Futteranlagen; 4) Sonderbetriebsgebäude; 5) Luftschutzanlagen; Erweiterungsanlagen sind im Ausbau.

AUGUST 13

Day Opening of 'Eagle Day' misfires. Heavy raid on Eastchurch followed by afternoon raids on Portland, Southampton and airfields in Hampshire and Kent. 1,485 German sorties.
Night Light raids on midlands, Wales and the west.
Weather Mainly fair, early-morning mist and slight drizzle in places. Channel, some cloud.

Luftflotten 2 and 3 were keyed up for the great attack and at dawn all was ready for the opening of the air battle which would crush Britain. Airfield, harbour and shipping targets had been minutely detailed, and the air fleet staffs had worked overtime producing up-to-date photographic maps from films brought back by the reconnaissance groups. Unfortunately, some very poor analyses were made and certain photographic aircraft were shot down, with the result that coverage was not complete. Fleet Air Arm, Training Command and Coastal Command airfields were included as fighter stations and many attacks were made on them, the results being overestimated and attributed to Fighter Command.

Typical of the poor reconnaissance interpretations made was contained in the O.K.L. situation report for August 13th. In covering the naval air stations at Ford, Gosport and Lee, twenty-four Hawker Demons and ten Spitfires were identified although no such aircraft were based there. Tangmere was credited with no less than fifty-five Hurricanes at the dispersals, a considerable exaggeration.

The incorrect assessment of British control and radio techniques by Schmid at Intelligence IC had resulted in the assumption that mass attacks would confuse the defences as much as multi-pronged raids over a wide area.

In the morning, formations began to take off to execute the plan, but at the last moment a personal signal from the Reichsmarschall postponed Adlerangriff until the

Top left: A Dornier Do 17Z of KG2, based at Cambrai, delivers its load over an English target. The fuselage bay could accommodate 20 110lb SD50 bombs or four 551lb SD250s.

Left: Dornier 17Zs of Stabstaffel/KG3 head out across the Channel for southern England

afternoon, when the weather would clear. Three units were, however, already on their way above the cloud-base of 4,000 feet, one headed for the Eastchurch area, another for Odiham, and the third to provide a diversion off Portland.

The main force, seventy-four Dornier 17s from KG2, at Cambrai and St Leger, lost its escort of Me 110s over the coast shortly after 5.30 a.m. Kesselring's headquarters had been frantically radioing instructions to cancel the operation following Göring's message, but only the Me 110s picked it up, and returned to base.

In two separate formations, KG2 made for Eastchurch aerodrome and Sheerness. Because of poor estimating on the part of radar operators and difficulty in plotting by the Observer Corps due to low cloud, the assessments of strength were wrong and insufficient fighters were put up.

No. 74 Squadron, from Hornchurch, found the Dorniers over Whitstable at 7 a.m. as they emerged from cloud. A fierce fight developed with this, the rear formation, but the leaders with General Fink, the commodore of KG2 in command, went on unmolested to East-church. The bombing there was very heavy with a direct hit on the operations room, five Blenheims of No. 35 Squadron destroyed by incendiary bullets, 12 people killed and 40 injured. The Luftwaffe claimed 10 Spitfires destroyed on the ground.

Nos. 111 and 151 squadrons joined in the fight just after Eastchurch had been hit and between them the three squadrons shot down four Dorniers and damaged four more as they dodged between the clouds. Eastchurch had been severely damaged and was written off by Luftflotte 2 as a fighter airfield destroyed. In fact it belonged to 22 Group Coastal Command, and housed a composite anti-shipping force of fighters and light bombers. It was operational again ten hours after the raid, despite wrecked buildings, broken communications and fifty bomb craters.

To the west, the Ju 88s of KG54 headed for the airfield at Odiham and the Royal Aircraft Establishment, Farnborough, in Hampshire, in two sections with escort. They were engaged over the coast by No. 43 Squadron and a section from Northolt, these being shortly joined by Nos. 601 and 64 Squadrons. Harried by fighters and disorganised by thick

Blenheim IF twin-engined fighters were outpaced by German fighters and in certain cases even by Luftwaffe bombers. Despite this, Blenheim-equipped units fought hard; they also bore the brunt of fighting before the advent of the Beaufighter. Shown here is a Blenheim 1 of 604 Squadron based at Middle Wallop

cloud, the two attacks missed their targets.

At 11.40 radar picked up twenty + raiders about eight miles distant and they were tracked in towards Portsmouth.

The raid on Portland by KG 54 completely misfired as the bombers did not put in an appearance and their escort of Me 110s were picked up by radar over Cherbourg. They were hotly engaged by two R.A.F. squadrons, who dived on them and destroyed six in the space of five minutes, the remainder going flat out for the protection of the French coast.

The real opening thrust of the 'Attack of the Eagles' developed in the afternoon, despite continued poor weather. Mass attacks were made from 3.45 to 5 p.m. on Portland, Southampton, Kent and the Thames Estuary.

After the incursions of the morning, No. 10 Group prepared to put up strong forces to meet formations of 20+, 50+, 30+ which showed up on the radar screens as coming in from Jersey. No. 152 from Warmwell was over the coast and was joined by Nos. 238 and 213 from Middle Wallop and Exeter respectively, while No. 609 Squadron

from Warmwell patrolled over Weymouth. Tangmere sector provided No. 601 Squadron to cover the Isle of Wight.

German bomber formations in three waves were drawn from Lehr Geschwader 1 in the Orléans Bricy area with Ju 88s and Flieger-korps VIII with Ju 87s. First on the scene was a heavy forward sweep of German fighters which became involved in a fight with Nos. 231 and 152 squadrons, while No. 238's Hurricanes fell in with a force of Me 110s supposedly guarding Ju 87s.

Most of the Ju 88s got through to South-ampton where serious damage was done and large fires started in the warehouses and docks.

No. 609 Squadron found a golden opportunity and took it. Thirteen Spitfires found a formation of Ju 87s below them with half the escort well above, and the other half deeply involved with No. 238.

Attacked out of the sun, the Stukas made a perfect target. On the way the Spitfires dived through five Me 109s, breaking them up, Pilot Officer D. M. Crook sending one spinning down into a field on fire. The whole Stuka formation broke up with several falling in flames or with the crews dead. For once the Spitfires had altitude, position and surprise and they used it to deadly effect. One member of the squadron remarked that he rather missed the 'Glorious Twelfth' this year – 'but the glorious thirteenth was the best day's shooting I ever had'.

The remaining Ju 87s missed their main target, Middle Wallop, and scattered their bombs over three counties. They hit Andover airfield, but this was not a fighter station and little damage was done.

Away to the east the other prong of the divided German attack was coming in in waves from Luftflotte 2 with Detling (near Maidstone) and Rochester as its main targets. The bombers were heavily escorted, and while No. 65 Squadron was engaged with the fighters, a bomber force slipped through and got to Detling. Due to cloud, Rochester was not discovered and as the force for this target returned home they were caught by No. 56 Squadron from Rochford and bomb loads were jettisoned over Canterbury. Other bombs fell on Lympne and Ramsgate.

At Detling the commanding officer was killed by dive-bombing and the hangars set on fire. The operations room, the messes and the cookhouse were all destroyed, but essential services, including communications, were working by noon on the 14th.

At the end of a day of severe fighting on both flanks of 11 Group the final score was thirteen R.A.F. fighters lost on 700 sorties and forty-five German aircraft brought down, a definite victory for Fighter Command to which the vulnerable Ju 87 contributed in no small measure.

The Luftwaffe had flown its greatest number of sorties to date – 1,485 – and it claimed that seventy Spitfires and Hurricanes and eighteen Blenheims had been destroyed, exaggeration by nearly 700 per cent.

At night while thirty-six British bombers flew 1,600 miles to bomb the Fiat and Caproni works at Turin and Milan, German aircraft from Luftflotte 5 raided northern Scotland and machines from the Continent flew to Wales, the West Country, the midlands and Norwich. The main target was the Spitfire shadow factory at Castle Bromwich where eleven bombs were dropped. One of the British bombers returning from Italy crashed in the Channel in the early morning following. A fishing boat picked up two of the crew and a third was rescued by a Miss Prince who rowed out in a small canoe.

Shot down by Spitfires of 92 Sqn on August 14th, this He 111 of 9./KG27 lies wrecked beside a road in the Mendip Hills near Cheddar. Its target was Cardiff Docks.

AUGUST 14

Day Targets, south-east England, airfields and communications. Airfields in the west.
Night Little activity.
Weather Mainly cloudy with bright patches. Channel cloudy.

After their efforts of the previous day, the Luftwaffe put in a third the number of sorties with ninety-one bombers and 398 fighters.

O.K.L.IA staff had issued orders to Luft-flotten 2 and 3 for attacks on aircraft industry and R.A.F. ground organisation targets. Accordingly at 11.40 formations of bombers and escorts built up over Boulogne and Calais in full view of the coastal radar stations. By noon the attack had developed over Dover and the Kentish airfields in successive waves, mainly consisting of fighters looking for combat. At 1 p.m. a dozen Me 110 fighter bombers from 210 Gruppe slipped through, while Spitfires were occupied with a feint

off Dover, and bombed Manston airfield destroying four hangars but losing two machines, one to an Army Bofors gun and one to an R.A.F. aircraft-type Hispano cannon temporarily fitted to a ground mounting.

Three and a half squadrons of 11 Group fighters were in the area, but mainly above cloud dealing with Me 109s and 110s, the Me 109s coming from JG26. Shortly afterwards the main enemy force, which had held back, came in over Folkestone and Dover, shooting down eight barrage balloons and sinking the Goodwin Light Vessel.

In the afternoon it was the turn of Luft-flotte 3 and Sperrle's policy was to send in small raids over a wide area in the hope of upsetting the defences. Eight airfields and various railway lines were the main targets.

At Middle Wallop sector station a dive-bombing raid by three machines set on fire the No. 609 Squadron hangar and killed three airmen, while offices were hit and ten airmen at the station headquarters injured. The

The railways suffered continuously right through the Battle of Britain and the Blitz. Here workers repair the down-line at St. Denys, Southampton, after one of the afternoon trains had been bombed on August 14th

Luftwaffe, however, reported that it had bombed Netheravon.

Maintenance Command had its first share of the battle at 30 M.U. Sealand, Cheshire, when a Heinkel 111 flew in at 1,000 feet and dropped eight high-explosive bombs and one incendiary in a line, but caused no serious damage. A second Heinkel followed up to more purpose, smashing the sergeants' mess and causing one fatal casualty. Despite water failure and a cut in the main high-tension cable, the station reported a full working day 'with two hours' overtime' on the 15th. Colerne was also attacked but to no good effect. Of the railways, the worst hit was Southampton where the main line was blocked by debris.

Despite hits on various airfields and the

problems of bad weather, 10 and 11 Group could show a ratio of over 2:1 in their favour as regards losses, with nineteen German aircraft down against eight R.A.F. fighters.

Although the operational training units were not involved in the struggle, No. 7 O.T.U. at Hawarden, Flintshire, formed a battle flight to deal with emergencies. On the 14th, after hearing explosions and machine-gun fire in the vicinity, Wing Commander Hallings-Pott accompanied by Squadron Leader J. S. McLean and Pilot Officer P. V. Ayerst, took off in Spitfires and intercepted a Heinkel 111, shooting it down near Chester.

Night brought the usual series of small raids over the south of England and Wales. The defences were keyed up for a heavy attack following interception of German radio massages threatening a raid on Liverpool, but nothing developed.

The first week of the second phase had now passed although Fighter Command had no inkling of it and could only see a vista of continued attacks perhaps for six months or more. There were no decisive highs or lows, only more or less fighting.

As the controllers watched the last raids out and awaited first light, they did not know that the morning would bring the combined strength of three Luftflotten against Britain and that all four fighter groups would be in action to score probably the most notable victory of the whole battle.

AUGUST 15

Day Decisive; heavy raids by all three Luftflotten, their greatest effort of the battle. Seventy-five German aircraft main target. Airfields main target.
Night Little activity.
Weather Ridge of high pressure over Britain. Fine, warm weather. Some cloud over Channel.

With clear weather forecast the Luftwaffe exerted its greatest effort of the campaign, throwing in every available fighter, and major portions of its bomber forces.

Left: Worn out, Sgt. G. Booth, of No. 85 Squadron, fast asleep after a day's operations in August. He is still wearing his Mae West and his air maps are stuffed into the top of his boot. Sgt. Booth was shot down later in the Battle and died of his wounds in February 1941

The German plan of attack – outlined in a command paper of the previous day – was to produce a series of raids on a wide front – aimed at wrecking airfields and radar and bringing as many British fighters into battle as possible. Luftflotte 5 was to use most of its force to attack targets in the north-east, where it was presumed that fighter defences had been greatly weakened in order to reinforce the south.

The whole perimeter of the German line from Norway to Brittany was a hive of activity at first light, with final briefings, bombing up, and last minute adjustments to engines and equipment.

In Britain the early hours seemed quiet enough apart from reconnaissance flights but from eleven o'clock onwards five main attacks developed.

First about 100 enemy aircraft, made up of forty Ju 87s with a heavy escort, attacked the forward airfields at Hawkinge and Lympne. At the latter a heavy dive-bombing attack cut all water and power supplies, caused a direct hit on the station sick quarters, and damaged several other buildings. Various sections had to be evacuated to nearby houses and the field was not serviceable for forty-eight hours.

At Hawkinge the damage was far less with one hangar hit and a small barrack block destroyed. One of the most serious consequences in the area was the shut-down of Rye and Dover C.H. stations and Foreness C.H.L. which suffered a power failure when the electric mains were hit.

Nos. 54 and 501 squadrons met the force, 54 attacking out of the sun on to the dive-bombers, but the devastation at Lympne could not be prevented.

Then followed an attack which was to be the most interesting of the whole day. Banking on tactical surprise and conveniently forgetting the radar chain, Luftflotte 5 launched two simultaneous thrusts in the north and north-east. They expected little opposition and their reception came as a painful surprise.

At eight minutes past twelve radar began to plot a formation of twenty+ opposite the Firth of Forth at a range of over ninety miles. As the raid drew closer the estimates went up to thirty in three sections flying south-west towards Tynemouth.

At Watnall the approach of No. 13 Group's

first daylight raids was watched on the operations table with particular interest. With an hour's warning the controller was able to put squadrons in an excellent position to attack, with 72 Squadron Spitfires in the path of the enemy off the Farne Islands and 605 Squadron Hurricanes over Tyneside. Nos. 79 and 607 were also put up, but while the latter was right in the path of the raid, No. 79 was too far north.

No. 72 Squadron from Acklington was the first to make contact and it came as a distinct shock when the thirty materialised as I and III/KG26 with sixty-five Heinkel 111s, and the entire I/ZG76 from Stavanger with thirty-four Me 110s. After a brief pause in which to survey the two massive groups flying in vic formation, Squadron-Leader E. Graham led No. 72 straight in from the flank, one section attacking the fighters and the rest the bombers.

The Me 110s formed defensive circles, while the Heinkels split up. Some of them jettisoned their bombs in the sea and headed back for Norway, leaving several of their number in the sea. The separate parts of the formation finally reached the coast, one south of Sunderland and the other south of Acklington. No. 79 intercepted the northern group over the water while a flight from No. 605 squadron caught it over land. Most of the bombs fell harmlessly in the sea.

The group off Sunderland found Nos. 607 and 41 squadrons waiting for it and they too bombed to little effect apart from wrecking houses. The raiders turned back to Norway, the Me 110s having already departed some minutes before. Of a total force of about 100, eight bombers and seven fighters were destroyed and several more damaged without British loss. The airfield targets such as Usworth, Linton-on-Ouse and Dishforth went unscathed. One Staffel of III/KG26 lost five of its nine aircraft in the course of the fighting.

Farther south, an unescorted formation of fifty Ju 88s from I, II and III/KG30, based on Aalborg, was heading in to No. 12 Group off Flamborough Head. Full radar warning was given and 73 Squadron Hurricanes, 264 Squadron Defiants and 616 Squadron Spitfires were sent to patrol the area, the force being supplemented later by Blenheims from 219 Squadron in 13 Group.

Left: Two Me 110s fell to the eight Browning machine guns of this Hurricane of 87 Sqn on August 15th. The pilot was Flt Lt Ian 'Widge' Gleed, leader of A Flight and later CO of the squadron, while his aircraft LK-A P2798 was a long-serving machine that had previously seen combat with the unit in France.

Below left: A typical Form 'F' or Combat Report from the Battle of Britain. This one was completed by Pilot Officer J. A. Phillipart, a Belgian pilot with No. 213 Squadron who, as shown, shot down no less than three Me 110s on this sortie on August 15th. P.O. Phillipart was killed later in the Battle

Both No. 616 and a flight of No. 73 engaged, but the enemy split into eight sections. Some turned north to bomb Bridlington where houses were hit and an ammunition dump blown up. The main force, however, flew to the 4 Group Bomber Station at Driffield, Yorkshire, where four hangars were damaged and ten Whitleys were destroyed on the ground. Heavy anti-aircraft fire was directed against the bombers and one was brought down. Altogether, six of KG30's Ju 88s were destroyed, representing about 10 per cent of the force sent over.

In all, the northern attacks lost sixteen bombers out of a serviceable Luftflotte 5 force of 123, and seven fighters of the thirty-four available.

In the south at noon it was the turn of Manston once again. Twelve Me 109s attacked with cannon and machine-gun fire, destroying two Spitfires and causing sixteen casualties.

This was followed at 3 p.m. by a force of Ju 87s, Me 110 fighter bombers and Me 109s attacking the fighter station at Martlesham Heath without being intercepted. The Ju 87s concentrated on an incomplete signals station to the west, while the 110s hit the airfield. The signals station escaped with broken windows and a punctured water tank, but Martlesham itself had workshops and officers' mess wrecked, a burst water main and cut telephone wires. A visiting Fairey Battle blew up, smashing two hangars, the watch office and the night-fighting equipment sheds. The station was engaged on repair work throughout the following day.

Simultaneously about 100 aircraft were approaching Deal to be followed by 150 over Folkestone at 3.30. Only four fighter

squadrons were on patrol to deal with this influx, although followed by three more (Nos. 1, 17, 32, 64, 111, 151 and 501) and they were warded off by the escorts through sheer weight of numbers. The German formations broke up to deal with separate targets, one being the Short Brothers and Pobjoy factories at Rochester. The production of four motor Stirling heavy bombers at Rochester suffered a severe set-back due to six complete aircraft and the finished parts store being destroyed. This was a real victory for the Luftwaffe but it had no effect on Fighter Command. Several German machines attacked Eastchurch and the radar stations at Dover, Rye, Bawdsey and Foreness, although without useful results.

Two further attacks were made in the early evening, the first – a feint – in the south-west and the second against Kent and Surrey. Some 250 aircraft from Luftflotte 3 moved towards the Isle of Wight in two groups at 5 p.m. and spread out over Hampshire and Wiltshire.

Ju 88s with Me 110 escort attacked Middle Wallop but did less damage than the three aircraft of the previous day. No. 609 Squadron got off just before the dive-bombing started, and harried the stragglers out to sea. This raid had been intercepted at intervals by

Production of Britain's first four-motor heavy bomber, the Stirling, suffered a serious set-back on August 15th when the Short Brothers factory at Rochester was hit. Here wrecked Stirlings stand on the final assembly line after the raid

no less than eight R.A.F. squadrons and one section of it which reached Worthy Down caused little damage, while another dropped bombs on Portland. In their combat reports the crews who raided Odiham claimed to have hit Andover instead.

Out of the whole German force twenty-five aircraft were lost against sixteen by Fighter Command. Thirteen Me 110s were brought

A classic example of the Me 109's limited radius of action. This aircraft ran out of fuel but just reached a beach in northern France.

down of which three fell to the guns of Belgian Lieutenant J. Phillipart of 213 Squadron. Altogether eleven R.A.F. squadrons were put up against these raids, being Nos. 32, 43, 111, 601, 604, 609, 87, 152, 213, 234 and 266.

At 6.15 over seventy aircraft were plotted coming in from Calais, and as most of his forward squadrons were refuelling and re-arming, Park switched four squadrons from the eastern sectors following up with four and a half more as they became available.

Intercepted over the coast by two squadrons, including No. 501, which was almost at the end of its fuel, the Germans split up and missed their primary targets of Biggin Hill and Kenley. Instead they spotted West Malling, Kent, from high altitude and damaged runways and buildings.

Other bombers wandering over Surrey decided to deliver their loads on Croydon, the home of No. 111 Squadron, which unit was officially not yet operational.

Me 110s from Gruppe 210 with Me 109 escort came in at 2,000 feet just after 6.50 p.m. to drop their bombs, which destroyed the Rollason and Redwing factories, together with many trainer aircraft, and a radio component works. Over eighty casualties were caused and it was the first recorded raid on Greater London.

Over the airfield on patrol at 10,000 feet were 111 Squadron's Hurricanes which promptly dived on the raiders and together with 32 Squadron from Biggin Hill shot down four as they went flat out for the coast. This made Gr.210's losses eight Me 110s in five days.

During the day No. 151 Squadron took delivery of the first Hurricane with four 22 mm. cannon which had been rebuilt from a crashed machine. No. 151 already possessed a two-cannon Hurricane, but like 19 Squadron with cannon Spitfires, the problems of mechanical failure and ammunition feed were not overcome before the end of the Battle.

That night there was no relaxation of German activity with some seventy bombers hitting Birmingham, Boston, Kirton, Beverley, Southampton, Crewe, Yarmouth, Harwich, Bristol and Swansea.

At the time the R.A.F. claimed to have shot down 182 German aircraft in the course of its 974 sorties, but the records show that the actual figure was 75. British losses were less than half, with 34 aircraft lost, 17 pilots killed and 16 wounded. The Luftwaffe claimed 82 Spitfires and Hurricanes, 5 non-existent Curtiss Hawks and 14 miscellaneous types.

The day's losses for the Luftwaffe covered practically every basic type in operational use – Do 17, He 111, Ju 88, Ju 87, Me 109 and Me 110. In addition an Arado 196, an He 59 and an He 115 (all floatplanes) were destroyed.

The revised figures in no way detract from the significance of August 15th, which altered the whole course of the Battle. The Luftwaffe had put up 1,786 sorties in the twenty-four-hour period of which 520 were bombers. Practically every available fighter had been used in an attempt to destroy Fighter Command in the air while the ground facilities were being wrecked by bombing. The attacks had covered all four fighter groups and yet despite some airfield damage no success was achieved.

The German Air Force could have committed its whole bomber force to the operation but instead it put in less than half, a tacit admission that all-out bomber operations could not be carried on over Britain until air superiority had been achieved. The full force was in fact never employed on any day throughout the Battle.

The German losses were far heavier than anticipated, and the 15th had three lasting effects on the outcome of the conflict:

1 First and foremost, Luftflotte 5 was to all intents and purposes finished in the daylight battle apart from reconnaissance. Towards the end of August most of its bomber strength and some of the fighters were transferred to France to swell the ranks of Luftflotte 2.

2 The spirited opposition in the north swung the battle back to the south-east of England where heavier loads could be carried over the short ranges and where the Me 109 had sufficient tankage to provide escort.

3 The Stuka and the Me 110 were confirmed as unsuitable for their tasks, and in

the latter case it meant that escorts had to be provided for the twin-engined fighters themselves.

From the 15th onwards the Me 109s were allowed less free run over the battle zone, and were brought in closer to the bomber formations. This was the complete antithesis of the purpose for which they were built and instead of bringing the R.A.F. to combat, they had to sit and wait for the attack to come to them.

During the day, while the assault was at its height, Göring was in conference at Karinhall with his senior staff and the Luftflotten commanders.

The Reichmarschall opened his address with a warning against Stuka losses:

> The fighter escort defences of our Stuka formations must be readjusted as the enemy is concentrating his fighters against our Stuka operations. It appears necessary to allocate three

fighter Gruppen to each Stuka Gruppe, one of these fighter Gruppen remains with the Stukas and dives with them to the attack; the second flies ahead of the target at medium altitude and engages fighter defences; the third protects the whole attack from above. It will also be necessary to escort Stukas returning from the attack over the Channel.

He stressed that 'Operations are to be directed exclusively against the enemy air force including the targets of the enemy aircraft industry. . . . Our night attacks are essentially dislocation raids, made so that the enemy defences and population shall be allowed no respite.'

After directing that the pathfinder unit K.Gr.100 should be thrown into the general attack. Göring proceeded to save the all-important British radar chain from destruction by saying: 'It is doubtful whether there is any point in continuing the attacks on

Left: Sergeant Jack Mann of 64 Squadron landed this Spitfire at Kenley in mid-August. The nose of a cannon shell had jammed the control column causing a landing on one wingtip and starboard wheel. During the Battle of Britain, Mann was credited with four Me 109s destroyed. He was badly burned during air combat in 1941 and became a Guinea Pig. After the war he left the R.A.F. as a Flight Lieutenant and became an airline pilot. He made his home in Beirut and, after 40 years was taken hostage by an extreme Muslim group. Tragically he was reported dead in 1989

Dornier 17Z bombers of II/KG3 (Gruppe Finsterwalde) prepare for take-off from Antwerp/ Deurne for a raid on Britain

radar sites, in view of the fact that not one of those attacked has so far been put out of action.'

Technicians toiling to repair Ventnor C.H. station on the Isle of Wight would hardly have agreed with these last words, but the R.A.F. could be thankful that its opponent's commander-in-chief understood neither science nor engineering.

Later in the day Göring issued an order prohibiting the presence of more than one officer in any single air crew. This was an attempt to reduce the officer casualties on bombers, which had seriously increased.

AUGUST 16

Day Airfields in Kent, Hampshire and West Sussex attacked. Widespread damage. Ventnor radar out of action. Other targets in Oxfordshire, Essex and Suffolk. Göring in conference.
Night Many light attacks.
Weather Mainly fair and warm. Channel haze.

This Friday was a sunny summer day with just the amount of haze that German pilots appreciated. The plotting tables were quiet until 11 a.m. when a series of raids were levelled against Norfolk, Kent and the Greater London area with airfields as the main targets, including Manston. West Malling, an 11 Group station, was again hit while clearance was still going on after the previous day's attack. Some eighteen bombers dropped high explosives and incendiaries, destroying one aircraft on the ground and putting the station out of action until the 20th. Twelve fighter squadrons were up.

Things were quiet again until midday when the radar screens showed three heavy raids coming in. The first of 50 headed for the Thames Estuary, the second of 150 appeared off Dover, while the third of 100 massed over Cherbourg and proceeded to the Portsmouth–Southampton area. In all, radar was plotting about 350 aircraft simultaneously between Yarmouth and Portland. There was some cloud about, and, despite the despatch of twelve squadrons by Nos. 10, 11 and 12 Groups, many of the bombers succeeded in getting through and causing considerable damage.

London suburbs were bombed, including

The hangars at Tangmere sector station, Sussex, smashed and burning after a Stuka attack at mid-day on August 16th. Three aircraft were destroyed and eleven damaged. Alongside the hangars can be seen a Blenheim 1 fighter and a Blenheim IV bomber

Wimbledon and Esher, where shops and houses were hit. Bombs on Malden, Surrey, railway station killed staff and passengers and put both lines out of operation. To the north, Gravesend and Tilbury were attacked, and bombs fell on Harwell and Farnborough aerodromes.

The raid off Portland split up and sections arrived over Ventnor, Tangmere, Lee-on-Solent and Gosport. Twelve Ju 88s with Me 110 escort dived out of the sun on Gosport, damaging buildings, killing four people and seriously injuring two. At Ventnor five Ju 87s in a six-minute raid added to the destruction of the 12th. The only habitable buildings left were the diesel house, the receiving block and

the protected rooms. Ventnor was thus out of action from August 12th to 23rd, and service was only resumed when a mobile station was rigged nearby at Bembridge. A number of Fleet Air Arm aircraft and hangers were destroyed by fire at Lee-on-Solent.

Tangmere, with its satellite Westhampnett, was an important sector station. The Ju 87s approached from the east and had a clear run up over the airfield dropping a pattern of bombs which destroyed all the hangars, workshops, stores, sick quarters, pumping station and the officers' mess. The Tannoy broadcasting system, all light, power, water and sanitation were temporarily out of action. Losses in aircraft were heavy, with three Blenheims destroyed and three Blenheims, seven Hurricanes and one Magister damaged. Ten service personnel and three civilians were killed, while twenty others were injured.

The Royal Aircraft Establishment at Farnborough, Hants, was attacked by 8 Ju 88s doing extensive damage to the motor trans-

port yard. The last delayed-action bomb from this raid did not explode until 49 hours afterwards.

In the evening, two Ju 88s carried out the most destructive raid of the day, on Brize Norton, Oxfordshire, a training station and Maintenance Unit in No. 23 Group. Thirty-two bombs burned out forty-six trainer aircraft in the hangars of No. 2 Service Flying Training School, wrecked other buildings and caused ten casualties.

In the twenty-four hours of the 16th, the Luftwaffe put up 1,715 sorties for the loss of forty-five aircraft. The R.A.F. had twenty-two fighters shot down in which eight pilots were killed. The large number of British aircraft destroyed on the ground altered this picture somewhat, but most of them were not fighters. Eight airfields had been hit, but only three of them belonged to Fighter Command, proving that Schmid's intelligence assessments were still wrong.

During the attack on Gosport, Flight

Lieutenant J. B. Nicolson of 249 Squadron won Fighter Command's first and only V.C. of the war. Hit by cannon shells and with the cockpit on fire, he succeeded in shooting down an Me 110 before baling out. Burned and wounded, his immediate reward on reaching the ground was to be shot in the seat by a trigger-happy Home Guard.

The English Channel had by this time become a sort of no-man's land where German seaplanes and British boats competed to pick up survivors. On this day the motor lifeboat Canadian Pacific, off Selsey, Sussex, found a German seaplane and a British naval speed boat on the water – the latter unable to move because of a rope round her propeller. The lifeboat passed two dead German airmen to the seaplane which took off, while the lifeboat towed the speedboat into harbour.

The two hectic days of effort by Luftflotten 2 and 3 called for a rest for the weary German crews, repairs to damaged aircraft and replacement of lost machines and

A very battered Ju 87B of 3.St.G.2 fascinates onlookers of all ages at Bowley Farm, South Mundham, near Chichester, on August 16. This Stuka was caught by R.A.F. fighters after the strike on Tangmere Aerodrome. Both pilot and observer were hit in the head by bullets, one being dead and the other dying as the aircraft virtually landed itself

personnel. Thus the night raids were on a much reduced scale with small attacks on Bristol, Newport, Swansea, Portland, Worcester, Chester, Tavistock, Farnborough and various aerodromes.

In a summary of operations put out by the Luftwaffe Command Staff on the 16th, it was confidently stated that 372 Spitfires, 179 Hurricanes, 9 Curtiss Hawks and 12 Defiants had been destroyed in the period July 1st to August 15th. By a series of extraordinary calculations it was computed that at 10 a.m. on August 16th Fighter Command possessed only 300 serviceable aircraft whereas in fact there were over 700.

AUGUST 17

Day Activity limited to reconnaissance. Fighter Command faces pilot shortage.
Night Light raids midlands, Merseyside, South Wales.
Weather Fine in Channel, haze and some cloud in the east.

The lull continued throughout the day. Reconnaissance flights were plotted and, although Fighter Command flew 288 sorties, Luftwaffe losses amounted to only three machines. The R.A.F. lost none.

At night, raids were scattered and light, the targets being industrial centres in the midlands, Merseyside and South Wales. One raid at 2 o'clock in the morning, first plotted at Hucknall and tracked to Newark, Lincoln and Duxford, was finally shot down off Lincolnshire by a Blenheim night fighter from 23 Squadron.

The serious drain on fighter pilot resources was recognised by the Air Ministry on the 17th. Dowding had been pressing for Fairey Battle pilots to fill the gaps, but the Air Staff felt that wholesale withdrawals from the remaining light bomber squadrons might affect striking power on invasion day.

Finally they agreed to five volunteers each from the four Battle squadrons and three each from Lysander Army co-operation squadrons in No. 22 Group. These were sent for a six-day O.T.U. course at Hawarden and some carried out their first operational patrol within a fortnight of volunteering.

If the unnecessary wastage of the Battle squadrons in France had not occurred there would have been many more first-class pilots available to Dowding without involving a serious strain on Bomber Command's forces.

Left: British soldiers remove machine guns, parachute and other equipment from a Dornier 17Z of KG2, brought down at Stodmarsh, Kent, on August 17th. Additional armament was being fitted to all Luftwaffe bombers at this time. The makeshift machine gun position in the rear window has been equipped with a metal safety rail to restrict the field of fire and stop the gunner from shooting holes in his own aircraft

Right: Roaring past the damaged hangers at RAF Hawkinge, two Hurricanes of 501 'County of Gloucester' Sqn lift off for combat with the Luftwaffe at the height of the Battle in mid-August. Both aircraft were shot down shortly after this picture was taken.

AUGUST 18

Day Massed formations return. Airfields in south and south-east attacked. Luftflotte 3 against Sussex and Hampshire.
Night Light bombing, Bristol, East Anglia and South Wales. Minelaying.
Weather Fine and fair early. Rest of day cloudy.

The Luftwaffe's all-out efforts to destroy Fighter Command in one week ended with a final flourish on this Sunday. The main objectives were once again airfields with a lesser effort against radar stations.

The first of the massed formations crossed the coast about midday in the Dover area and attacked airfields to the south and south-east of London, including Kenley, Croydon, Biggin Hill and West Malling.

At Kenley two raids of Do 17s with Me 109 escort came in simultaneously at 1.30 p.m., one of about fifty aircraft at altitude and the other low down at 100 feet with nine machines. The Kenley sector controller had detailed all his squadrons – No. 615 to a raid over Hawkinge, No. 64 to intercept the high raid over base and No. 111 to intercept the low raid.

Both raids were met, but 111 Squadron could not effectively deal with the low-flying machines as they themselves were too low and too close in over Kenley. As the approach

was masked by trees and hangars, the A.A. guns were unable to open fire until the raiders were directly over the camp. Nevertheless the combined efforts of Parachute and Cable and A.A. brought down two aircraft. Both 615 and 64 Squadrons intercepted the high fliers, causing several casualties.

One machine, piloted by Oberleutnant Lamberty, crashed in flames in a field, and the following day it was attributed to rifle-fire by the Home Guard. In fact it is doubtful whether any of the Home Guard hit the aircraft as it was already beyond hope, riddled with Bofors shells and machine-gun bullets.

Intense anti-aircraft fire and the P.A.C. barrage, with the help of the fighters, accounted for two Dorniers straight away and damaged five to such an extent that two fell in the Channel and three force-landed in France. Two aircraft returned safely out of the whole Staffel, one being flown back by the flight engineer with the pilot dead on the floor.

Altogether 100 bombs fell on Kenley aerodrome and buildings, destroying four Hurricanes, one Blenheim, two Magisters and a Proctor and damaging six other aircraft. Three hangars were total wrecks and many of the camp buildings demolished.

Most of the operations-room communications were cut, nine people were killed and ten injured, including one of the medical officers killed by a hit on a shelter trench near

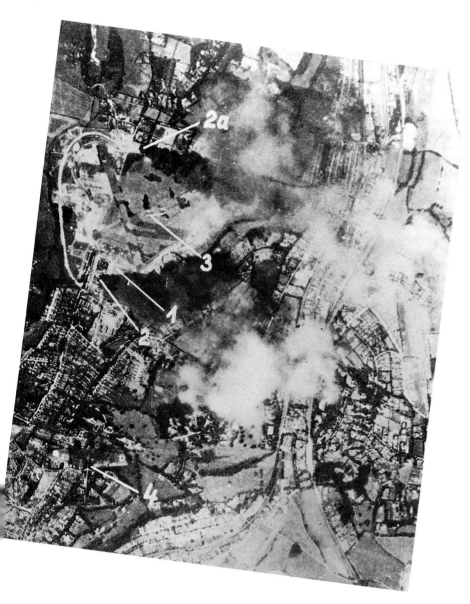

One of the most dramatic events of the Battle was the attack on RAF Kenley by Do 17s of KG76 on August 18. The low-level part of the raid was recorded by a Propaganda Ministry war photographer, Rolf von Pebal, and the picture top left shows a 64 Sqn Spitfire in its blast pen as the nine Dorniers crossed the northern edge of the sector airfield. The bomb bursts have been painted in. The fate of one of the raiders is seen on the left. Hit by a parachute and cable device, AA fire and fighters, it crashed in a field at Leaves Green, near Biggin Hill. The pilot, Oberleutnant Lamberty, was injured as were his crew. Out of nine low-level aircraft only one returned intact to base. The third picture was taken from the high flying Dorniers a few minutes after the first attack. Just below is another Dornier (4) while bomb hits are shown (1, 2 and 3). 2a is marked by the Germans as British wreckage, but is, in fact, believed to be a shot-down Dornier. The Kenley runways have been carefully painted to merge with the surrounding countryside.

the hospital. Fire broke out and so many local fire brigades answered the SOS that they blocked the roads leading into the airfield. The operations block was moved into a shop and within two and a half days 90 per cent of the lines had been restored by the G.P.O.

While the station was temporarily out of action No. 615 Squadron was ordered to land and refuel at Croydon and No. 64 to go to Redhill. Due to lack of ground staff at Redhill, No. 64 in fact returned to Kenley, landing on a strip marked out between the craters.

Croydon received nineteen bombs, which further damaged hangars and buildings, and some hits were scored at West Malling.

The attack on Biggin Hill was to be carried out in a similar way to that at Kenley with Ju 88s at high level and Do 17s lower down, both formations from KG76. The high-level strike was delayed due to rendezvous difficulties over France, and the Dorniers came in on their own. The airfield defences were fully prepared and on his own initiative the station commander, Group Captain Grice, scrambled Nos. 610 and 32 Squadrons. Group orders did not come through until after the raid, due to the mass of plots on the situation map.

As the firing died down the high-level raid came in and added its quota of bombs, although during both attacks the main damage consisted of airfield craters. KG76 flew back minus four Ju 88s and six Do 17s.

The second major assault also came in the early afternoon, when Loftflotte 3 concentrated on airfields and a radar station in the Hampshire–West Sussex area.

Gosport was still being cleared from the raid on the 16th, when at 2.30 p.m. twenty-two Ju 87s in three groups of seven dive-bombed the airfield, wrecking buildings, aircraft and transport, but causing no casualties.

Twenty-five Ju 87s and a flight of Me 109s had Thorney Island, Hampshire, a 16 Group airfield, as their objective. Two hangars were hit, one aircraft destroyed and one damaged.

Ford, a Fleet Air Arm station in Sussex, was heavily bombed, with workshops and two hangars destroyed and thick smoke rising from punctured fuel stores. Casualties were 28 killed and 75 wounded.

The only radar station hit was Poling, between Arundel and Littlehampton. Ninety bombs were dropped, including many delayed action. The station was so badly damaged that a mobile unit had to be set up to cover the gap. The Poling radar masts have long since been dismantled, but to this day there is at least one unexploded bomb annually sinking deeper into the soil on the site. In these actions two squadrons, Nos. 43 and 152, between them shot down twelve Stukas, all from St.G77. A Blenheim accounted for two Ju 87s near Thorney Island.

In the late afternoon the third and last major attack developed when aircraft from Luftflotte 2 approached via the Thames Estuary and again attacked Croydon. Twelve Me 109s sneaked into Manston at ground level, and destroyed two Spitfires on the ground, killing one airman and injuring fifteen others. There was also heavy fighting over Essex.

At night bombs were dropped on East Anglia, South Wales and Bristol, while mines were laid in the Thames Estuary and the Bristol Channel.

So ended a day which was almost as decisive in its results as August 15th. Fighter Command in 766 sorties, together with A.A., had accounted for seventy-one German aircraft, of which thirty-seven were bombers and eleven were Me 109s. K.Gr.100, the pathfinder unit operating in daylight for the first time, at Göring's behest, also suffered its first loss, a Heinkel 111 in an accident.

Twenty-seven R.A.F. fighters had been destroyed, with ten pilots killed.

The Luftwaffe had pressed home attacks on airfields using high- and low-level techniques. By far the more dangerous was the hedge-hopping raid which was difficult to plot overland and was often missed by the radar screen. Instead of correctly assessing the value of this type of approach, the German operations staffs felt the losses on the 18th were too great and thereafter formations mainly flew higher and higher with a close fighter escort.

August 18th was the virtual death-knell of the Ju 87s over Britain. Losses had been mounting at an alarming rate and, apart from a few isolated sorties, they were pulled out of the Battle.

In Fighter Command the week had shown up a number of serious problems in defence and in control layout.

Above and right: A German reconnaissance camera on August 18th recorded the naval airfield at Ford with hangars smashed and fuel stores burning. The River Arun can be seen on the right of the picture. The other photograph shows the scene on the ground at the same time; outlined against the pall of smoke are rows of Blackburn Shark biplane torpedo bombers

Left: Out of control, its crew dead, a Ju 87 dives to destruction at White House Farm on the outskirts of Chichester, Sussex, on August 18th. The observer baled out but the pilot was killed. All that remained of the aircraft is shown in the picture, below left, where the local Fire Brigade are seen putting out the flames

In a report after the Kenley raid it was recommended that more Bofors guns and mountings should be provided for the southern approaches to the airfield; the operations room should be removed from the station; new V.H.F. radio buildings and the sick quarters be sited away from the main camp; and that more personnel be made available at unoccupied satellite airfields for refuelling and rearming.

These requirements were put in by one station, but they applied to the whole of Fighter Command. Key sector operations rooms were on the airfields themselves, and while protected from blast and shrapnel at the sides, were wide open to a direct hit on top. The same applied to radio buildings. At Middle Wallop, for instance, the sector control was housed in a hut and the blast of bombs moved the whole building until finally the squadron 'tote board' and its lights collapsed from vibration.

The operations rooms and radio stations should not have been built on the airfields, but as they were, construction should have been underground and in reinforced concrete.

It was only due to German Intelligence's lack of information on the sector layout and on the sites themselves that so many vital buildings and their crews survived the battle.

AUGUST 19

Day Göring again confers. Isolated raids on Britain. Heavy reconnaissance activity.
Night Widespread harassing raids. Minelaying.
Weather Mainly cloudy. Occasional showers in the east.

From 15th to 18th, inclusive, the Luftwaffe had lost 194 aircraft, and this showed conclusively that, despite the high British casualties claimed, Fighter Command was by no means beaten.

When Göring met his fighter commanders at Karinhall on this Monday morning, he stated that: 'Until further notice the main task of Luftflotten 2 and 3 will be to inflict the utmost damage possible on the enemy fighter forces. With this are to be combined attacks on the ground organisation of the enemy bombers conducted, however, in such a manner as to avoid all unnecessary losses.'

The reference to Bomber Command targets was obviously the result of complaints by the other services and by the O.K.W. over the continued attacks by British aircraft. The demand for raids on bomber airfields was nevertheless almost beyond the Luftwaffe's capabilities as most of them were outside the operational radius of action of escorting Me 109s.

Göring concluded by saying: 'There can no longer be any restriction on the choice of targets. To myself I reserve only the right to order attacks on London and Liverpool.' This gave the Luftflotten and Fliegerkorps virtually a free hand and each followed its own particular pattern for target selection.

It was indicated that heavy raids would continue on the R.A.F. ground organisation and that British aircraft production must be disrupted, even to the extent of using single raiders in cloudy weather. Luftflotte 3 was ordered to plan for a night raid on Liverpool and Luftflotte 5 for one on Glasgow.

The Reichsmarschall felt far from happy about the performance of the fighter groups following rising bomber losses. He attributed this to a lack of aggressiveness on the part of pilots when in fact it was nothing of the sort. The Me 110 was a failure but remained in use, while the Me 109s were too few for massive escort and suffered at all times from lack of range.

As occurred throughout the Battle, Göring endeavoured to attribute failures to the operational units instead of to the manifest shortcomings of Luftwaffe Command planning.

In order, as he thought, to boost morale among fighter pilots, he promoted Mölders and Galland, two of his 'star' pilots, each to command of a fighter Gruppe. This was part of a belated policy of promoting younger operational officers to senior rank in place of those who were too old and lacked proper experience. It was a good idea, but it was to have no effect on the outcome of the Battle.

No. 11 Group, meanwhile, had been reassessing the situation in the light of a week's heavy fighting and on the 19th Park issued Instruction No. 4 to his controllers to meet changed requirements.

He began with a note that attacks had been switched from coastal shipping and ports to inland objectives, particularly airfields. His instructions were as follows:

(a) Despatch fighters to engage large enemy formations over land or within gliding distance of the coast. During the next two or three weeks we cannot afford to lose pilots through forced landings in the sea. (Protection of all convoys and shipping in the Thames Estuary are excluded from this paragraph.)

(b) Avoid sending fighters out over the sea to chase reconnaissance aircraft or small formations of enemy fighters.

(c) Despatch a pair of fighters to intercept single reconnaissance aircraft that come inland. If clouds are favourable, put a patrol of one or two fighters over an aerodrome which enemy aircraft are approaching in clouds.

(d) Against mass attacks coming inland despatch a minimum number of squadrons to engage enemy fighters. Our main object is to engage enemy bombers, particularly those approaching under the lowest cloud layer.

(e) If all our squadrons around London are off the ground engaging enemy mass attacks, ask No. 12 Group or Command Controller to provide squadrons to patrol aerodromes Debden, North Weald, Hornchurch.

(f) If heavy attacks have crossed the coast and are proceeding towards aerodromes, put a squadron, or even the sector training flight, to patrol under clouds over each sector aerodrome.

(g) No. 303 (Polish) Squadron can provide two sections for patrol of inland aerodromes, especially while the older squadrons are on the ground refuelling, when enemy formations are flying over land.

(h) No. 1 (Canadian) Squadron can be used in the same manner by day as other fighter squadrons.

For a few days cloudy weather was to lose 11 Group the opportunity of trying out the new tactics on a large scale. On the 19th large numbers of the enemy made threatening moves in the Channel and estuary areas, but only isolated raids came through. The most intense Luftwaffe activity was put up by the long-range reconnaissance Gruppen who carried out photographic sorties.

At 12.30 p.m. sixty+ aircraft were off the coast between Dungeness and North Foreland at 20,000 feet and at 12.50 a further fifty left Calais. Dover was the main target but the formations consisted largely of fighters. A few bombers penetrated to outer London.

Between 2.30 and 3 p.m. a small secondary attack came over Dover while raids approached Portsmouth and the Southampton Docks from Luftflotte 3. One raid succeeded in

setting fire to oil-tanks at Pembroke Docks. Three hours later fifty+approached the east coast between Dungeness and Harwich and bombs fell on houses and airfields, although without much effect on the latter.

Fighter Command flew 383 sorties, losing three aircraft and destroying six German machines of which two were He 111s from K.Gr.100.

During the night there were continual small raids which operated over a wide area, to the extent that at some times almost three quarters of the country was under a yellow or red air raid warning. Bombs were dropped on Liverpool, Southampton, Hull, Derby, Wolverhampton, Sheffield, Bristol, Leicester and Nottingham. Eight airfields were attacked and at Driffield a hangar was set on fire.

AUGUST 20

Day Scattered raids in morning. Kent and Essex airfields attacked in afternoon.
Night Negligible activity. One or two raids in south-west.
Weather Cloudy generally, rain spreading from north. Channel mainly fine.

The weather was autumnal, with low clouds, strong winds and intermittent rain which restricted German operations. The Luftflotten planning staffs spent the day digesting Göring's requirements outlined on the 19th. These were contained in orders put out by the Luftwaffe Command Staff IA which covered 'the weakening of enemy fighter forces, attacks on the enemy ground organisa-

Exeter airfield, Devon, in August. A Hurricane of No. 213 Squadron has crashed into the dispersal area of B Flight, No. 87 Squadron, after an air battle over Portland. In the background are Hurricanes of 87 Squadron

tion, the aircraft industry, and aluminimum and steel rolling mills'.

Activity over Britain in the morning was limited to small raids on Cheltenham, Oxford and Southwold, while reconnaissance aircraft surveyed Duxford, Debden, North Weald, Hatfield, Northolt and Hornchurch airfields. At 11.24 bombs were again dropped on the oil-tanks at Pembroke Docks, still burning from the previous day.

During the afternoon several waves of aircraft came in from Calais, starting just after

2 p.m. Objectives were the balloon barrage at Dover and the airfields of Eastchurch, Manston and West Malling. There were also isolated raids on convoy 'Agent' off the east coast and on *S.S. Orford* off Angelsey. Twelve fighter squadrons were despatched to intercept, but due to bad weather only accounted for six enemy aircraft in the course of 453 sorties, although one was a four-engined FW 200 over Ireland. Two R.A.F. aircraft were lost during the day. The Polish Air Force had its first success over Britain, No. 302 Squadron destroying a Junkers 88.

By night German activity was negligible with single bombers off the south-west

AUGUST 21

Day Small raids in the east and south. Targets airfields.
Night Slight activity, some in Scotland.
Weather Cloudy, occasional rain.

The bad weather continued throughout the day, and the Luftwaffe resorted to 'tip-and-run' raids round the east and south coasts. Instead of mass attacks, small formations or single aircraft were used in some cases, while others had groups of three divided into two at low level and one stepped up.

Fighter Command had difficulty in meeting this type of attack but 599 sorties yielded thirteen German aircraft destroyed for the loss of one British fighter.

Airfields attacked or threatened were Exeter, St. Eval, Horsham St. Faith, Bircham Newton, Ford, Coltishall, Stradishall and Watton. Bombs were also dropped on Grimsby, Norwich, Canterbury, Southampton, Newmarket, Bournemouth and Pembroke.

After dark, raiding was again slight with bombers off Harwich, the Humber Estuary and the Firth of Forth.

During the day the operators at Dover radar station would have been intrigued to know that their tall aerial masts were the subject of close scrutiny by a small group of officers on Cap Gris Nez.

It was the occasion of Göring's first visit to Luftflotte 2's forward headquarters, and with him were Milch, Kesselring, Sperrle, Lörzer and Wenniger, who had been the air attaché in London.

A pair of very high-powered naval binoculars had been set up through which the Dover masts were clearly visible. The sight does not, however, appear to have influenced the Reichsmarschall to change his orders of the 15th abandoning heavy attacks on the radar chain.

AUGUST 22

Day Shipping reconnaissance and attacks on two Channel convoys.
Night Increased activity. Industrial targets in Midlands, north and west. Minelaying.
Weather Cloudy and squally.

At nine o'clock in the morning the convoy 'Totem' was passing through the Straits of Dover and reported being under air attack. Investigation showed that it was in fact being shelled by the German heavy batteries near Cap Gris Nez. The first bombardment lasted eighty minutes and 100 shells were fired without effect.

Failure of the guns brought the Luftwaffe into action and at 12.40 some forty aircraft

Senior German officers watching the British coast through binoculars on August 21st, 1940. From left to right: Generaloberst Lörzer, Generalfeldmarschall Milch, Generalfeldmarschall Kesselring and Generalleutnant Wenniger

attacked the convoy, but were beaten off by Nos. 54 and 65 squadrons.

Apart from a few reconnaissance flights, the day remained quiet until 6.50 p.m. when a series of raids developed against Dover during the course of which Manston was again hit.

Five R.A.F. aircraft were lost for the destruction of two German – a poor repayment for 509 Fighter Command sorties, which were again hampered by bad weather.

The toll of fighter pilots killed through drowning after being shot down in the sea had been rising steadily during August. The situation became so serious that on the 22nd Air Marshal Harris called a meeting at the Air Ministry to draft some organisation for rescue craft.

It was decided to combine the skeleton rescue service of Coastal Command with the boats of the Naval Auxiliary Patrol and to place R.A.F. launches under the operational control of the local naval authorities.

The R.A.F. retained the responsibility of air search, and twelve Lysanders originally borrowed from Army Co-operation Command were placed under the direction of Fighter Command. The aircraft were stationed at various fighter airfields along the coast and special liaison officers appointed to Nos. 10 and 11 Groups to assist in general handling. It had taken nearly twelve months of war to bring about even this meagre effort.

That night German activity showed a marked increase, with inland bombing, mine-laying and shipping attacks. The convoy 'Topaz' was attacked off Wick by aircraft from Loftflotte 5 and the Bristol Aeroplane Company's works at Filton were bombed including the airfield. Other stations visited were Manston, St. Eval, Northcoates and Wick. In the early hours of the morning one raider flew over and dropped his load on Wealdstone, Greater London. The aircraft

was plotted in and the incident duly noted by 17 Group Observer Post D.3 at Harrow.

AUGUST 23

Day Single raids in the south. Reconnaissance.
Night Main targets South Wales.
Weather Showers and bright intervals. Cloud in Straits, Channel and Estuary.

Low cloud and rain continued throughout this Friday, limiting operations once again to guerrilla warfare by single, or occasionally flights of two or three machines.

Outer London, Tangmere, St. Albans, Portsmouth, Maidstone, Cromer, Harwich, Southampton, Colchester, Biggin Hill and Abingdon reported small attacks, while the east coast convoys were bombed. Of the raiders attempting to penetrate the London defences, several jettisoned their bombs in the

suburbs – houses, a bank and two cinemas being hit. Fighter Command's 483 sorties showed five German aircraft destroyed without British loss.

After nightfall twenty-two raids penetrated inland, mainly to South Wales, while the convoy 'Draga' was also bombed. Among the targets hit were Pembroke Dock and the Dunlop Rubber Company's works at Birmingham.

As daylight came, the weather had improved and the Luftwaffe was about to execute its orders of the 20th for the destruction of British fighters and bases. Unknowingly, Dowding's Command was entering upon the third and most critical phase of the Battle of Britain.

Pilots of 32 Squadron relax between sorties at Hawkinge, Kent. In the background the squadron's Hurricanes stand at readiness.

THIRD PHASE

AUGUST 24 – SEPTEMBER 6

The cloudy weather from August 19th to 23rd gave some brief respite to both combatants and time to adjust tactics. In Germany senior commanders of the Luftwaffe, and in particular the Jafus and fighter Gruppen commanders, were called to Karinhall on August 19th for discussions on escort problems.

To the Luftwaffe it appeared that Fighter Command had not been fully brought to battle and that, despite the very heavy losses to the R.A.F. shown in the German intelligence reports, a hard core still existed. At all costs this must be engaged and destroyed both in the air and on the ground. The very wide range of targets laid down had meant complete lack of concentration on any particular site, although this was certainly not apparent to Göring. In addition the haphazard use of bombers to raid singly or in threes over the length and breadth of England each night had diluted the bomb capacity in favour of overload fuel.

German bomber losses had been heavy, 127 medium bombers and forty Stukas having been lost between August 10th and 23rd.

Left: The men who kept them flying: the groundcrews who laboured day and night rearming, refuelling, maintaining and repairing. This group is from 222 Sqn equipped with Spitfires and based at RAF Hornchurch.

A major disappointment to the Reichs-marschall was the abject failure of the Ju 87 Stuka. Against modern fighters it was no longer the spearhead of the Blitzkrieg, but a slow, cumbersome and vulnerable machine which had little chance in daylight. To prevent further serious losses in the Stuka formations and to conserve them for the pending invasion, Fliegerkorps VIII (with 220 out of the 280 Ju 87s engaged) was withdrawn from the battle on the 19th, and on August 29th transferred from Cherbourg to Luftflotte 2 in the Pas de Calais. The Stuka had retired from the battle against Britain apart from some isolated sorties by the few remaining units in Luftflotte 3.

As a result of the talks on the 19th, Göring issued a new directive on the following day:

> To continue the fight against the enemy air force until further notice, with the aim of weakening the British fighter forces. The enemy is to be forced to use his fighters by means of ceaseless attacks. In addition the aircraft industry and the ground organisation of the air force are to be attacked by means of individual aircraft by night and day, if weather conditions do not permit the use of complete formations.

The Luftwaffe High Command had for some time considered that the main concentration of R.A.F. fighters was in the area around London. Heavy attacks were therefore contemplated as early as August 2nd when an ObdL order was issued to this effect. The timing and implementation were left to the Luftflotten, and in turn to the individual Fliegerkorps commanders. The order of August 2nd seemed to give the right balance between Göring's dictum of August 20th and the invasion plans for an attack on a narrow front due south of London. Moreover, the detailed planning for attacks on R.A.F. installations round London had now been completed and they could be carried out forthwith.

Fliegerkorps 2, under General Bruno Lörzer, took the initiative and decided to open the attacks as soon as the weather cleared. A new variant was also added to confuse the radar stations, formations of varying size patrolling all day up and down the Straits, and occasionally delivering a feint attack.

To provide overwhelming escorts of Me 109s, it was decided to transfer most of the single-seater fighter strength of Luftflotte 3 to the Luftflotte 2 area. In the following week the units of Jufue 3 were flown across to the Pas de Calais.

In the meantime Fighter Command took stock; in the second phase (August 8th to 18th) no less than ninety-four pilots were killed or missing, and sixty were wounded in varying degrees. Since August 8th the slight improvement in strength at that date had been whittled away and the operational training units were effectively prevented from raising the length of courses from two weeks to four weeks. Squadrons were dog-tired from long hours of fighting each day, and from the constant wear on nerves occasioned by air raids.

Of aircraft there was so far still no shortage despite the loss in the second phase of 54 Spitfires and 121 Hurricanes, 40 Spitfires and 25 Hurricanes damaged beyond unit repair, and a further 30 aircraft destroyed on the ground. Production was beyond schedule, and the repair depots were helping to ensure that any replacements required at the end of each day's fighting were delivered by noon on the following day.

In the field the ground crews performed miracles. Quick servicing had been developed to a fine art – refuelling, rearming, engine checking, including oil and glycol coolant, replacing oxygen cylinders, and testing the R/T set would go on simultaneously. On many occasions all the aircraft of a squadron formation were replenished with fuel and ammunition, and got ready for another battle, in eight to ten minutes after landing. Slit trenches had been dug alongside dispersals so that work could continue until the airfield was under direct attack.

Regular repair and maintenance were carried on day and night with all maintenance personnel pooled on each station. The indefatigable station engineer officers detailed parties from the pool to squadrons in accordance with the work required to get them serviceable again.

Most of the maintenance work on the signals equipment of the fighters had to be carried out at night by the light of torches. Trouble was caused by damp, and extreme care was necessary to keep R/T sets dry in rain or dew. Occasionally sets had to be taken to a hot air blower to dry them out.

Wherever possible maintenance was done

in the open as hangers were primary targets for German bombs, and many had already been destroyed. Dispersal of aircraft not only to satellite aerodromes, but over wide areas at each of them combined with lack of transport, increased the labour requirement for a given job. The blackout, damage to power and water mains, and to the station organisation, added to the difficulties.

Initially bomb craters and building repairs were undertaken by the station works and buildings detachments. As the damage grew, these units could no longer cope, and works repair depots were called in. Manned by between 50 and 200 workmen, these depots had lorries, bulldozers, excavators and mobile power generation and water plant.

In many cases the depots performed sterling work, but often during an air raid a gang would retire to the shelters and refuse to

budge. They claimed that they were not going to do the job if it was dangerous. There was little thought for the young fighter pilots above being killed or maimed to ensure the labourers' continued freedom of choice in the matter.

Invariably a lot of the crater filling and rubble clearing was carried out by the airmen of the station itself.

To Park at 11 Group, the lull provided by four days of bad weather was a boon, as he was already extremely worried by his rising pilot losses and the damage being caused to his delicate network of communications. The

Left: This Me 110 was brought down in one of the August battles. To stop this machine falling into British hands, a Ju 88 dropped bombs on the field but only succeeded in throwing up great lumps of turf

Below: Luck ran out for Fw. Bischoff, pilot of this Me 109E-1 of 1/JG52 during a patrol over the Thames Estuary on August 24th. Engine failure rather than combat damage forced him down to crash-land at Westgate-on-Sea, Kent, and he became a PoW. The officer in the peaked hat is the late Sqn Ldr Rex King of Technical Air Intelligence who, post-war, became Editor of the weekly magazine Flight.

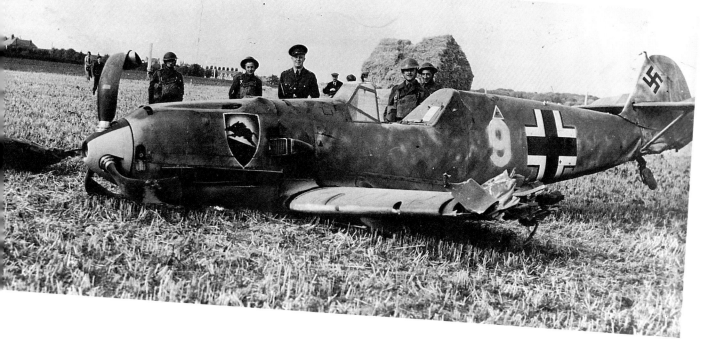

*Appointed Kommodore of JG26 in August 1940,
Adolf Galland was one of the best known fighter pilots
of the Luftwaffe. He is shown here taxiing in at
Audembert after a sortie, and (right) about to leave the
cockpit. The Mickey Mouse emblem was much
publicised*

savage attacks on fighter airfields required
new tactics if the German intention of bringing as much of Fighter Command's strength as
possible into battle and destroying it was not
to be realised.

Park's directive of the 19th was therefore
of the utmost importance and underlined
Dowding's policy of keeping the fighter force
in being by any means at his disposal.

On August 24th the weather cleared, and
both sides began to try new tactics, the
Germans achieving their greatest successes of
the Battle of Britain.

AUGUST 24

Day Crucial phase begins. Airfield attacks in southeast. Heavy raid on Portsmouth. Manston evacuated.
Night Heavier attacks, widely spaced targets.
Minelaying.
Weather Fine and clear in south. Drizzle in north.

The early part of the Saturday morning was cloudless and fine and the controllers in 11 Group watched anxiously for the inevitable signs of a build-up over France. At 9 a.m. a big raid began to boil up around Cap Gris Nez and some 100 fighters and bombers of Fliegerkorps II advanced on Dover, stepped-up from 12,000 to 24,000 feet. Two formations broke away from the mass in mid-Channel and attacked Dover itself from the north. Eleven fighter squadrons were despatched and the raid broke up at about eleven o'clock.

An hour and a half later a series of feints developed, from which one raid was detached to attack Manston, as No. 264 Squadron's defensive patrol for the airfield landed. The nine Defiants took off before the first bombs were dropped, and were then joined by a Hurricane squadron. The force was driven off with a loss of five bombers and two fighters but not before extensive damage had been done.

At 3.30 another big raid stacked up over Le Havre, and flew to Manston and Ramsgate. The Manston attack was to be the last straw for the station. The living quarters were now badly damaged, hardly any buildings remained intact, all telephone and teleprinter lines were cut and the field was littered with unexploded bombs.

Before the afternoon raid, at 2.15, all communication between Manston and 11 Group ceased. The controller at 11 Group contacted No. 1 Observer Group at Maidstone to see if the Corps could find out what was going on. A mile from Manston was Post A.1, and Observer Foad volunteered to cycle to the airfield and obtain information. Coastal airfields had been reduced to dire straits.

When the cable maintenance inspector at Manston was informed that all lines had gone he took two jointers and went to the particular crater despite the continuing explosion of delayed action bombs. Working like beavers, and with only an occasional glance at a large bomb adjacent to them, the three men got the

Low and fast; a staffel of Me 110s from ZG26 'Horst Wessel' heads inland from the British coast for a raid during late August 1940

essential circuits (out of 248 severed) restored in two hours and completed permanent restoration the following day.

As soon as word got through of the state of the station Fighter Command decided to evacuate it, except as an emergency airfield. Administrative personnel were transferred permanently to Westgate while the remainder of No. 600 Squadron's Blenheims were moved to Hornchurch.

Part of the raiding force split before reaching Manston, and one section attacked the small aerodrome at Ramsgate. The town itself was heavily hit and whole rows of seaside villas were wiped out with a number of casualties.

Concurrently with the south coast attacks, another raid flew to targets north of the Estuary, especially Hornchurch and North Weald, where high-altitude techniques were used. The No. 264 Squadron Defiants, withdrawn from Manston to Hornchurch earlier in the day, found themselves once more in the fray at 3.45, and just airborne as bombs began to rain down.

At North Weald nearly fifty Dorniers and He 111s escorted by Me 110s dropped 150

to 200 bombs. The airmen's and officers' married quarters suffered severely, and the power house was badly damaged. Nine people were killed and ten wounded.

No. 12 Group were called upon to assist over North Weald and Hornchurch, but the Duxford wing was flown in too late to have any major effect.

With the raiders approaching London, the city registered its 11th, 12th and 13th air raid warnings, but the population did not seem unduly perturbed. In Regent's Park, where *A Midsummer Night's Dream* was being performed, few of the audience moved. They seemed to find very appropriate Titania's wish 'To each word a warbling note'.

While the sector stations were under fire a formation of 100 Luftflotte 3 fighters and bombers from North of the Somme headed for Portsmouth and Southampton. They managed to get well toward the coast before their targets were deduced from radar, which at the time was cluttered with other tracks.

At Portsmouth only one fighter squadron was near enough to intercept, and that was still climbing when fifty bombers were heavily fired on by the anti-aircraft guns. The aircraft jettisoned their loads over the city, causing much damage and killing 100 civilians.

During the day Fighter Command flew 936 sorties – only slightly less than the Luftwaffe's 1,030 – and lost twenty-two fighters to the German total of thirty eight aircraft

Luftflotte 3 from this time on began to fade from the daylight picture as the full weight of the assault switched to Luftflotte 2 and the Pas de Calais. After dark on the 24th the attacks were stepped up, and some 170 German aircraft ranged over England from the borderland to Kent. Largely due to bad navigation, bombers directed to Rochester and the Thameshaven oil-tanks dropped their loads on the City of London. For the first time since the Gothas of 1918, Central London was damaged in an air raid. Fires burned at London Wall, and boroughs like Islington, Tottenham, Finsbury, Millwall, Stepney, East Ham, Leyton, Coulsdon and Bethnal Green all received their share. It was a foretaste of things to come.

Airfields had been the main focus of the attack in the south, but lack of Knickebein trained crews and general interference with direction-finding aids caused confusion. In the west only Driffield was hit, and this by a single machine. Fighter Command flew forty-five night sorties, but the only interception made was by a Hurricane pilot of No. 615 Squadron who successfully destroyed a Heinkel 111.

AUGUST 25

Day Slight activity in morning. Main raids by Luftflotte 3 in afternoon in south-west.
Night Continued widespread attacks, main concentration the midlands.
Weather Early morning fair. Remainder of day cloudy.

For most of the morning and afternoon of Wednesday the Luftwaffe rested, although the Channel was filled with small formations which kept the radar plotters busy waiting to see which would turn north and become a genuine raid.

At 5 p.m. 50+ appeared near St. Malo and proceeded to Cherbourg where escort and escorted swelled the ranks to 100. Off the Channel Islands another raid of 30+ built up, and behind it further formations of 20, 60 and 20 joined up to form a mass of 100+ aircraft which headed for Weymouth.

Two squadrons, judiciously placed by 10 Group, intercepted, but were unable to get through the fighter screen which numbered nearly 200. A third squadron fared no better and the bombers attacked Warmwell aerodrome, dropping twenty bombs. Two hangars were damaged and the station sick quarters burnt out. Nine unexploded bombs were left to be dealt with, and communications were disorganised until noon on the following day. Bombs also fell on Fareham, Pembroke and the Scilly Isles, at the last mentioned a direct hit being scored on the R.A.F. wireless station.

Within an hour a further mass raid of 100 headed from Cap Gris Nez for Dover and the Estuary, but was attacked by several of the eleven fighter squadrons sent up. This final action brought Fighter Command's losses for the day to sixteen with nine pilots dead, four missing and four wounded.

The Luftwaffe left behind twenty aircraft and their crews, but after nightfall they had it all their own way, carrying out widespread attacks without suffering any loss. Some mines were laid on the east, south and west coasts, while most of the sixty-five raids plotted in attacked industrial centres in the midlands, where bombs fell on forty places, including Birmingham, Coventry and towns in southern England, South Wales and Scotland. Montrose, a fighter airfield between Dundee and Aberdeen, was the recipient of an unexpected attack.

While German bombers droned over England, eighty-one twin-engined R.A.F. bombers were heading the other way – for Berlin. Industrial and communications targets were the orders for the night. Cloud prevented accurate identification and bombs

Sgt. C. Babbage of 602 Spitfire Squadron, Westhampnett, Sussex, who baled out into the sea after a Luftflotte 3 attack on Portsmouth on August 26th. He was picked up by a fishing boat and brought ashore at Bognor Regis. Note the pier in the background with a large piece removed to stop its use by a seaborne invading force

were dropped on several sections of the city, some damage being done to residential property. The R.A.F. raid was a reprisal for the German bombing of London the previous night. This incursion into German territory was the first of several and within a fortnight there were to be far-reaching results with changed Luftwaffe daylight tactics, and a reprieve for Fighter Command.

AUGUST 26

Day Airfields in Kent and Essex attacked. Bombs on Dover and Folkestone. Raids in the Solent.
Night Widespread raiding, targets industrial centres and airfields.
Weather Mainly cloudy, but dry. Brighter in south, but Channel cloudy.

This was another day of widespread activity in the course of which the Luftwaffe delivered three main attacks: (a) on Kenley and Biggin Hill, (b) on Hornchurch, North Weald, Debden and east London, and (c) on Portsmouth and the aerodrome at Warmwell in No. 10 Group.

Following several reconnaissance flights, Luftflotte 2 put in an appearance just after 11 a.m. when 150 aircraft were crossing the coast at Deal. Bombs dropped on Folkestone and more balloons were set on fire at Dover, but the main effort was directed at Biggin Hill and Kenley. Six squadrons and three flights from No. 11 Group intercepted well forward, and the raids were broken up.

In the early afternoon a second Luftwaffe concentration was observed by radar to be forming up over Lille. Further units joined it from St. Omer and Calais, until raids of 60+ and 20+ and 30+ were being plotted in towards Dover and Harwich.

The main objectives for the bombers from KG2 and KG3 off Harwich were North Weald and Hornchurch, with diversions in the east London area. Their efforts were disorganised by 11 Group which put up ten squadrons and one flight. One section of the raid fared better, however, and despite the attentions of two R.A.F. fighter squadrons it successfully reached the sector station at Debden. Over 100 bombs damaged the landing area, the sergeants' mess, the N.A.A.F.I., a motor transport depot and the equipment section. Electricity and water

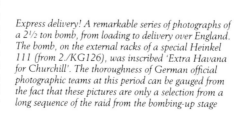

Express delivery! A remarkable series of photographs of a 2½ ton bomb, from loading to delivery over England. The bomb, on the external racks of a special Heinkel 111 (from 2./KG126), was inscribed 'Extra Havana for Churchill'. The thoroughness of German official photographic teams at this period can be gauged from the fact that these pictures are only a selection from a long sequence of the raid from the bombing-up stage

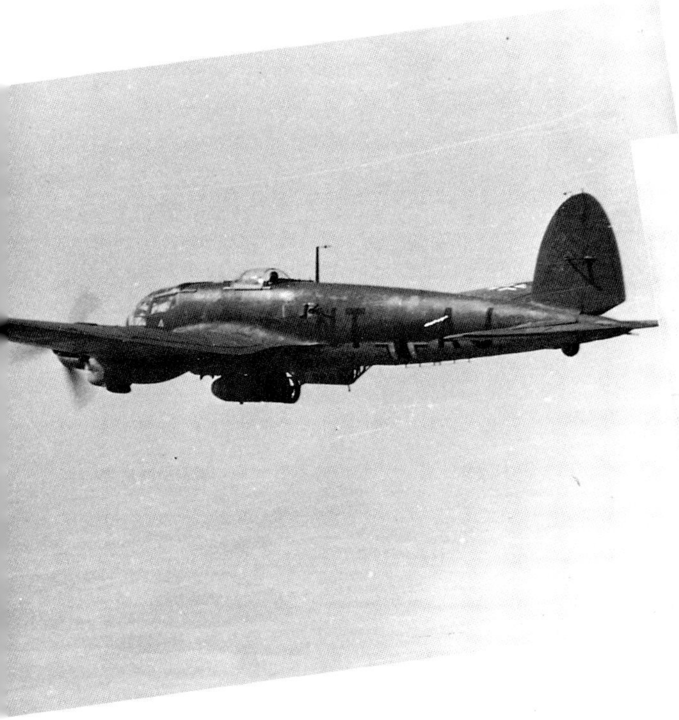

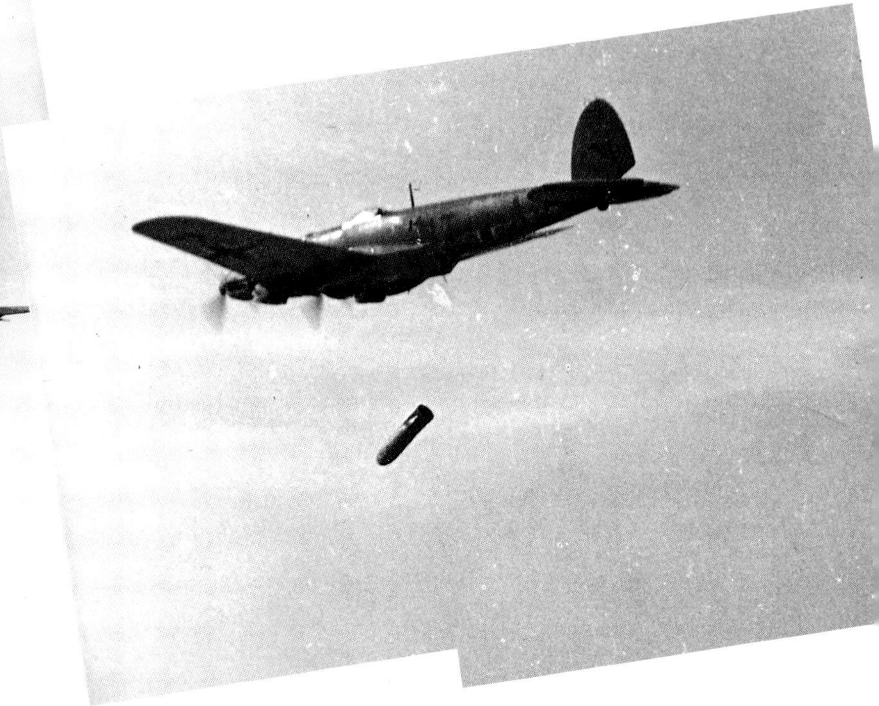

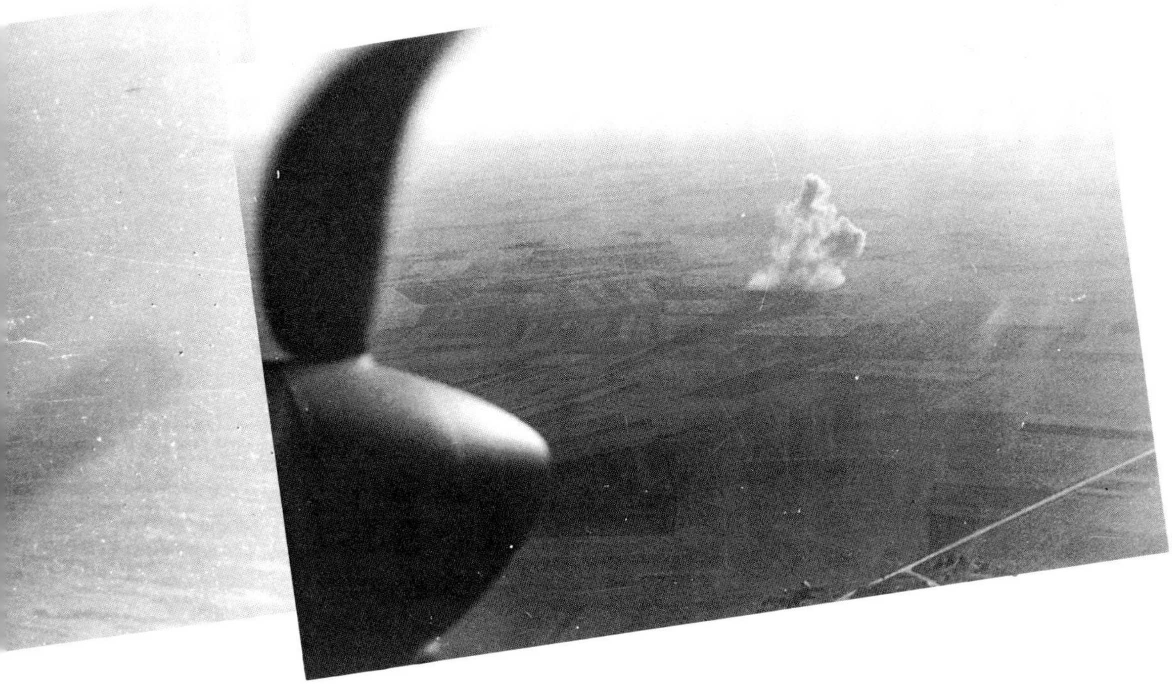

mains were hit and five personnel killed.

A squadron from Duxford had been sent up to patrol Debden, but due to late vectoring saw nothing of the enemy. Hurricanes of No. 310 (Czechoslovak) Squadron attempted to catch the raid as it left the Debden area, but most of them were unable to get proper courses to steer as they lacked the right radio-frequencies.

At 4 p.m. 150 aircraft of Luftflotte 3 approached Portsmouth at high altitude while two small diversions were laid on in an attempt to distract the fighters. No. 11 Group despatched five squadrons and No. 10 Group three. Independently three of the squadrons intercepted the formation short of the target, destroying three Heinkel 111s from KG55 and causing many of the bombers to jettison their loads in the sea. By five o'clock the raid had been repulsed. This was Luftflotte 3's last major effort in daylight for some weeks, as its units concentrated on night bombing. To Nos. 10 and 11 Groups it had been one of their most bitter fights with twenty-eight aircraft lost in one engagement, out of thirty-one for the day. Four pilots were killed near Portsmouth, and twelve were wounded. Altogether Fighter Command flew 787 sorties, over 300 more than on the 25th. The losses in pilots were rising alarmingly and replacements were few. German losses for the 26th were 41 aircraft.

On this day another link in the Observer chain was forged through the formation of No. 20 Observer Group H.Q. at Truro with a small nucleus of posts. Gradually the gaps in the warning line were being closed, although the areas in Wales and the north were still without coverage. Communications were uppermost in Fighter Command's mind, as exercises were being held to try out the 'Beetle' emergency signals system which would come into operation on invasion day.

By the 26th Fighter Command was getting a clearer picture of German lines of approach and overall target priorities in this third phase of the battle. Some authorities had suggested that the Luftwaffe was looking for gaps in the defences from the north and west by which to approach London. A full-scale study had been carried out by the operational research staff at Bentley Priory which proved conclusively that the Germans were proceeding to their targets with almost mathematical precision and that the priorities were still airfields and industrial centres.

The operations-room raid tracings and the Observer Corps tracks showed the main entry routed for their current industrial attacks on Birmingham and Coventry at night were either Abbeville-Pevensey-Birmingham, or Cherbourg-Bournemouth-Birmingham, as if drawn with a ruler and pencil.

To prove the point, the raids that night were mainly directed against Bournemouth and Coventry with about fifty bombers aiming at Plymouth. Widespread sorties by other aircraft included an attack against the 15 Group airfield at St. Eval in Cornwall, where the 'Q' site or decoy aerodrome for the station was bombed for several hours. The false flarepath was set on fire, and most of the sixty-two craters were made on open heathland. Some six airfields were on the Luftwaffe's night list to back up the day offensive, but little damage was done due to poor navigation and low clouds.

For some days Park at 11 Group had been worried about the low rate of interceptions compared with sorties flown and the fact that single squadrons had been engaging large formations. This was due to cloud and consequent errors in time and position of Observer Corps plots. To overcome the defect he sent a signal to his controllers requiring that formation leaders should report 'the approximate strength of enemy bombers and fighters, their height, and approximate position immediately on sighting the enemy. A special R/T message would be "Tally Ho! Thirty bombers, forty fighters, Angels 20, proceeding north Guildford." These reports should enable us to engage the enemy on more equal terms and are to take effect from dawn August 27th.'

AUGUST 27

Day Reconnaissance chiefly in Portsmouth-Southampton area.
Night Widespread activity industries and airfields from Lincolnshire to Portsmouth.
Weather Central and east England light rain. Some cloud in Channel and haze over Dover Straits.

The Tuesday morning dawned dull and hazy, but no Luftflotte 2 major raids developed.

The main effort was devoted to small attacks and photographic reconnaissance at very high altitude to assess the damage done to date.

No. 11 Group had little opportunity to practise its new 'Tally Ho!' procedures but interrupted the flow of aerial pictures back to northern France by destroying three of the long-range aircraft involved, two being Dornier 17s.

Park took the opportunity of the quiet spell to address another instruction to his controllers (No. 7) and this brought into the open the disagreements between himself and Air Vice-Marshal Leigh-Mallory at 12 Group over tactics. Park wanted to be assured of 12 Group squadrons over his north-eastern airfields when raids were being plotted into them, and his own forces were fully engaged elsewhere.

Within 12 Group the pilots were fretting at their lack of activity compared with their southern neighbours. Through Squadron-Leader Bader, the gallant legless C.O. of 242 Squadron, a new system of interceptions at wing strength was shortly to be evolved. Leigh-Mallory had long fostered the idea, based on a maximum strength build-up against large raids instead of squadrons intercepting singly or in pairs. At Air Ministry Air Vice-Marshal Sholto Douglas, the D.C.A.S., lent a sympathetic ear.

To Park the assembling of large formations of fighters was both time-wasting and unwieldy. In any case with the enemy on his doorstep he could not afford the expensive luxury of testing the scheme with consequent damage to sector stations. His fighters might be massed at one point against raids which could at any time split up and seek separate targets. The warning from radar was far too short to allow for anything but forward interception techniques with reserves on the back patrol lines to meet divided raids, or those not shown early on the group's operations table.

The wing theories were not really born until three days later, but Park's ire had already been aroused by the fact that on two occasions (one of which was the Debden raid of the preceding day) assistance had been requested from 12 Group for patrols over 11 Group airfields. The squadrons requested had not materialised and he suspected that they had gone elsewhere to find a fight.

A member of the crew of a Do 17Z-3 of 6./KG3 being escorted ashore. Four men were rescued by local boatmen and the Margate Lifeboat after the aircraft had been shot down in the sea in the course of a raid on Eastchurch and Rochford on August 28th

trollers were from then onwards immediately to put the requests for 12 Group assistance to the Controller, Fighter Command.

The controversy of wings versus squadron forward attack and 12 Group versus 11 Group was to become a major bone of contention for the rest of the daylight battle and ultimately it was, unjustifiably, to cost Park his command of 11 Group. It was not until 1942 that he had a further chance to prove the correctness of his techniques when he was posted as A.O.C. Malta. There he changed from wing to forward interception and produced remarkable results in two weeks.

While on the evening of the 27th the control-room staff were digesting and discussing Park's forthright instruction, raids began to come in from Cherbourg, and a widespread attack by Luftflotte 3 was made. Bombs were dropped on Gravesend, Calshot, Southampton, the Isle of Wight, Tonbridge, Tiptree and Leighton Buzzard. Some fell within a few miles of Bentley Priory.

AUGUST 28

Day Airfield attacks, Kent, Essex and Suffolk in three phases.
Night First major attack on Liverpool, 150 bombers. Harassing attacks midlands, north-east coast and London.
Weather Fine and fair. Cold. Cloud in Dover Straits.

Once more the Luftwaffe divided its main efforts into three phases. The first began at 8.30 a.m. with a heavy build-up over Cap Gris Nez which became a mass of 100+, the larger proportion being fighters escorting two groups of Dorniers.

One section of the raid, consisting of twenty Dorniers, headed for Eastchurch, while the other with twenty-seven bombers flew to Rochford. Four 11 Group squadrons made desperate attempts to get through the escort screen of the Eastchurch raiders but without success and with the loss of eight

Accordingly in his instruction of the 27th he did not mince his words. He opened with a note of thanks to 10 Group for their consistent help in covering the Portsmouth area and then went on to deal with the subject of 12 Group co-operation. Up to date, he stated, 12 Group had not shown the same desire to co-operate by despatching their squadrons to the places requested. The result of this attitude had been that on two occasions recently when 12 Group had offered assistance and were requested to patrol over aerodromes their squadrons did not in fact patrol over aerodromes. On both these occasions 11 Group aerodromes had been heavily bombed.

He had decided that rather than argue direct each time over these patrols, he would shift the onus to the shoulders of Command itself, and accordingly he ordered that Con-

Above: The wreck of a Hurricane of No. 151 Squadron, North Weald. It was crash-landed at Eastchurch by its pilot, Sergeant Davies, after being damaged in a dogfight on August 28th, 1940. The second picture shows the same aircraft completely rebuilt by No. 1 Civilian Repair Unit at Cowley, Oxfordshire

Top: A Gotha 145 trainer which landed intact on Lewes racecourse, Sussex, on August 28th, 1940. The young pilot was delivering German forces mail from the Channel Islands to Strasbourg, but lost his way and was painfully surprised to be greeted by the Home Guard on landing. The second photograph shows the same aircraft being used by the R.A.F.

aircraft and six pilots, two of which were from the ill-fated No. 264 Squadron with its two-seat Defiants.

The Coastal Command light-bomber station of Eastchurch therefore suffered yet another attack at eight minutes past nine, with two Fairey Battles destroyed on the ground and numerous craters on the airfield. Despite this the station remained serviceable for restricted day flying and there were no casualties.

At 12.30 the second raid developed, with the main objective as Rochford aerodrome near Southend. No. 264 Squadron were again forced to take off, with danger imminent, but fortunately before the bombs began to fall. Several squadrons out of thirteen on patrol intercepted, but the defensive screen was too strong, and most of the bombers reached their target. Despite thirty craters little serious damage was done to Rochford, which continued serviceable. While this was going on, Winston Churchill visited the battered station at Manston to view the damage.

The third attack consisted of large fighter formation sweeps over Kent and the Estuary at 25,000 feet. Seven R.A.F. squadrons attempted to intercept at various times but lost nine aircraft. On this occasion Park's principle of avoiding combat with German fighters was not adhered to, and the day's losses of twenty Hurricanes and Spitfires was heavy in comparison with German losses of thirty-one for the whole twenty-four hours, although these included twelve bombers. Curiously, the Fighter Command assessment of German casualties was the most accurate of the period at twenty-eight.

The official records show only thirty German aircraft lost on the 28th, but in fact there was one more. A Gotha 145 biplane trainer carrying mail from the German forces in the Channel Islands to Strasbourg was diverted and came down on Lewes racecourse in Sussex, to the surprise of the young German pilot. The contents of mailbags made interesting reading for British intelligence officers.

In Göring's order for the 19th August Liverpool had been singled out for heavy raids (i.e., over 100 tons) and the preparations entrusted to Luftflotte 3. The Germans had long considered Liverpool a major target and it ranked second only to London on their port priority list.

Thus on the 28th Liverpool received the first of four consecutive night raids and about 150 bombers reached the area Liverpool-Birkenhead, causing widespread damage. Simultaneously Luftflotte 2 and a few Luftflotte 3 aircraft attacked Birmingham, Coventry, Manchester, Sheffield, Derby and London, and dropped bombs on a wide selection of other places.

While many of these raids had little or no effect on the British war effort they did disrupt production because of the air raid warning system then in operation. There were three types of warning:
1 *Yellow*, issued by Fighter Command as a preliminary to all areas over which raiders might pass.
2 *Purple*, issued at night to areas in the course of raiders. On receipt of this all exposed lighting in docks, factories, sidings, etc., had to be extinguished.
3 *Red*, a public warning upon receipt of which the sirens were sounded.

The information for the various warning signals could only be obtained from Observer Corps plots and at this time the Corps came in for a lot of uninformed criticism by the public and the Press on warnings being in force when no air raid occurred. The responsibility rested with Fighter Command and the liaison officers at Observer Corps centres, and although great discretion was used the problem was not completely solved until after the Battle of Britain, and in the meantime night raids on the midlands or the north-west could mean the greater part of England being under Purple or Red warnings as the bomber stream flew northwards from the coast.

AUGUST 29

Day Quiet morning. Airfield attacks in south and south-east in afternoon.
Night Liverpool again attacked; diversions in the midlands.
Weather Showers and bright intervals. Channel and Straits cloudy.

After the feverish activity of the previous night, the Thursday morning was dull but peaceful. Little activity was reported until after lunch, when at three o'clock radar picked up formations at Cap Gris Nez,

Boulogne and the mouth of the Somme. Brightening weather had left Luftflotte 2 to put up massive fighter sweeps in the hope of attracting British fighters to the slaughter. Jafus 1 and 2 operated over Kent with 564 Me 109s and 159 Me 110s respectively.

No. 11 Group sent up forward patrols, expecting a renewal of bomber raids. Thirteen squadrons were despatched and some were involved in combats, but in the main the pilots adhered to Park's order of the 19th and retired when it was clear that no bombers were involved. This incident was particularly noted by the Luftwaffe operations and intelligence staffs who correctly deduced that the R.A.F. was avoiding wastage in fighter versus fighter battles. These tactics paid, as Fighter Command losses were only nine machines and German casualties were seventeen for the twenty-four-hour period, of which five were Me 109s from JG3.

After nightfall, Luftflotte 3 delivered its second attack on Liverpool and over 130 bombers reached the target, dropping both high explosives and incendiaries, navigation being assisted by a cloudless night. Diversionary raids on the midlands and outskirts of London were carried on by forty-four aircraft, usually singly.

AUGUST 30

Day Feint raids on shipping, then heavy attacks on south-eastern airfields. Raid on Luton.
Night Main target Liverpool. Single raids over wide area.
Weather Fair. Channel and Straits clear.

The day began with a renewal of shipping raids, this time in the Thames Estuary, designed to act as feints for the main assault which was picked up by radar over Cap Gris Nez at 10.30. Three waves totalling 100 aircraft came at half-hour intervals at 14,000 feet.

Almost intact, a Heinkel He 111 of KG 1 coded V4+HV lies in a Surrey field at midday on August 30th. The aircraft was one of a large formation that attempted raids on a number of forward airfields in southern England. The victor of this encounter was PO Greenwood of 253 Sqn, based at Kenley; the five German crew members were captured, but one later died from his injuries.

A cloud-layer at about 7,000 feet meant that the Observer Corps had to rely on sound plotting and it was not until an hour after the build-up over France that the 11 Group controller realised that forces were heading for Kent and Surrey sector stations. Sixteen squadrons were despatched to intercept, of which two, to guard Kenley and Biggin Hill, became involved in a dog-fight over Surrey. One formation of German bombers which had split off from the main group attacked Biggin Hill at noon and was not seen by the 12 Group Squadron flying on airfield protection patrol. From high altitude delayed-action bombs were dropped which damaged the airfield surface and the village but once again did not render the former unserviceable.

A second large attack began at 1.30 when raids of 6+, 12+ and 20+ crossed the coast between Dover and Dungeness, and then split up, sections heading for Biggin Hill, Shoreham, Kenley and Tangmere. Eight squadrons of fighters were ordered up and the raids retreated just before four o'clock. During this attack the radar stations at Dover, Pevensey, Rye, Foreness, Fairlight, Whitstable and Beachy Head were out of action due to a mains supply failure.

No sooner was this over than a third attack developed from Dover in waves, the objectives being Kenley, Biggin Hill, North Weald, Slough, Oxford and a convoy code-named 'Bacon'.

Detling airfield was hit by forty to fifty bombs which set fire to oil-tanks, cut the mains cable, cratered the roads and damaged one Blenheim. It was estimated that the station would not be serviceable until 8 a.m. on the 31st.

Far worse than this, one small raid of less than ten confused the defences by flying to the Thames Estuary and then turning south to Biggin Hill where at six o'clock, by low-level bombing with 1,000-pounders, the airfield was reduced to a shambles. Workshops, the transport yard, stores, barracks, the met. office, the armoury, W.A.A.F. quarters, and another hangar were wrecked; the power, gas and water mains were severed and all telephone lines north of the camp were cut in three places. Amid the rubble and fires casualties were very heavy, with thirty-nine dead and twenty-six injured – a number of them in a shelter trench which received a

direct hit. Somehow the mess was cleared up and the station resumed operations.

During the period another raid had come in over Sheppey, and, although intercepted, part of the force managed to reach Luton, where ten bombs were dropped and one hit the Vauxhall motor works. Casualties included over fifty dead.

At dusk Fighter Command totted up its losses. Twenty-five fighters had been shot down compared with thirty-six German aircraft destroyed. The only bright spot was the saving of fifteen pilots. Altogether this Friday had been a maximum effort for both sides with the R.A.F. flying 1,054 sorties and the Luftwaffe 1,345.

On the night of the 30th/31st there was no respite for the island, with raiders coming in from 8.30 onwards. A continuous flow of bombers streamed up towards the midlands, South Wales and London, with Liverpool again the main target. Single raiders created diversions by attempting to bomb the airfields Biggin Hill, Debden, North Weald, Hornchurch, Detling, Eastchurch, Thorney Island, Broxbourne, Rochford and Calshot, while others ranged over towns from Derby to Norwich, and Cardiff to Peterborough.

On the 30th another link in the reporting chain had been forged with the opening of No. 35 Observer Group with its Headquarters at Oban in Scotland.

AUGUST 31

Day Fighter Command's heaviest losses. South-east and eastern airfields again main targets.
Night Heavy raid on Liverpool. Light attacks from north-east coast to Portsmouth.
Weather Mainly fair. Haze in Estuary and Straits.

The odds were weighted even more heavily against Fighter Command on this Saturday and its losses were the heaviest of the whole battle – thirty-nine fighters shot down with fourteen pilots killed. The Germans almost achieved parity, as they lost forty-one aircraft in the whole twenty-four-hour period.

Raiding began at 8 a.m. with waves coming in over Kent and the Estuary. Me 109s amusing themselves shooting down all the Dover balloons both land and water based. Once again airfields such as North Weald,

Duxford and Debden were the main targets. Debden received about one hundred high-explosive and incendiary bombs from a formation of Dorniers, the sick quarters and barrack block receiving direct hits and other buildings being damaged. The operations rooms continued, however, to operate right through the attack. The raid steering for Duxford was intercepted by 111 Squadron from Croydon and did not reach its target.

Less than an hour later over 100 machines advanced from Calais and concentrated on Eastchurch where the airfield remained serviceable despite cratering and damage to buildings. Detling received a heavy quota of machine-gun bullets but no bombs.

The third attack, which began soon after noon, was to be the most serious of the day. Over 100 aircraft crossed the coast at Dungeness and flew up two clearly defined corridors.

One section attacked Croydon and Biggin Hill. At the former airfield twelve bombers came in at 2,000 feet demolishing a hangar, damaging other buildings and causing casualties. At Biggin Hill the bombing came from high altitude and to the long-suffering occupants of the airfield it seemed that they must be the A1 priority target for the whole Luftwaffe. Further extensive damage was done to hangars and buildings, the married quarters and officers' mess were bombed and the operations block received a direct hit, extinguishing the lights and filling the rooms with acrid fumes, dust and smoke from the fires which broke out. The temporary telephone lines and power cables put in after the raid on the 30th were destroyed.

At 6.35 Kenley aerodrome advised the Observer centre at Bromley that all lines to Biggin Hill were dead and that the frequency and call-signs of Biggin's 72 and 79 Squadrons were urgently required. Lines from Bromley to Biggin Hill were also found to be out of action, and finally a despatch-rider had to be sent to get the information.

The raiders approaching up the second air corridor over Dungeness headed for Hornchurch, and there they caught 54 Squadron in the act of taking off. Two sections got airborne but the last was blown into the air by explosions. One machine was hurled into a field, another was thrown across the airfield to land on its belly, while the third, piloted by

Flight Lieutenant Deere, was blown upside
down. Miraculously all three pilots emerged
shaken and injured but were back on operations the following morning. The thirty
Dorniers involved dropped about 100 bombs
which left a string of craters and cut the main
power cable. Four Do 17s were shot down.

During the course of these sorties, other
German aircraft made a sharp attack on
coastal radar stations, damaging Pevensey,
Dunkirk, Rye, Foreness, Whitstable and
Beachy Head C.H.s. The advantage was not,
however, pressed home and the stations were
left to recuperate.

The fourth and last attack of the day was
delivered at 5.30 p.m. by several groups
of Ju 88s and bomb-carrying Me 110s which

*At mid-day on August 31st, 1940 Squadron Leader
T.P. Gleave of No. 253 Squadron took off from Biggin
Hill leading a formation of seven Hurricanes to
intercept a raid approaching the airfield.*
*At 12,000 feet was a large formation of Ju 88s. Despite
inferiority in numbers the handful of fighters went into
the attack. Squadron Leader Gleave hit two bombers
of the port line and was laying his sights on a third
when a cannon shell hit his starboard fuel tank. The
aircraft, P3115, burst into flames and the starboard
wing came off. Severely burned, Squadron Leader
Gleave managed to bale out and landed at Mace Farm
just east of Biggin Hill.*
*One of the Ju 88s he fired at crashed later in France.
The 19 Group Bromley Observer Corps log book at
1300 hours recorded: 'Hurricane and hostile bomber
crashed Q8779. Hurricane pilot baled out in
approximately Q9577'. The previous day he had
claimed five Me 109s destroyed. He was only credited
with one, the others being considered probables. After
the war it became clear that Squadron Leader Gleave
had in fact shot down five in one day.*
*Squadron Leader Gleave became one of the first plastic
surgery 'guinea pigs' and subsequently returned to
R.A.F. service, rising to the rank of Group Captain. He
presumed that his aircraft had completely broken up,
but in fact the engine and other large sections lay deep
in a thicket on a lonely hillside by the farm. They were
're-discovered' after more than 20 years. In 1967 the
engine was transported to Biggin Hill by the Flairavia
Flying Club and is now a museum piece. Somewhere in
the surrounding fields lie four Browning machine guns
which will doubtless come to light one day.*
*Aircraft wreckage, bullets, bombs and pieces of uniform
and equipment from 1940 are still being found in the
south of England. The photographs show (top) the
Merlin engine of P3115 lying in a thicket at Mace
Farm and (bottom) Group Captain Gleave, in 1967,
holding up a piece of the wreckage*

GB 10 160 bc   Maßstab etwa 1:13400

500m

0

1km

(1cm : 134 m)

Northolt
Fliegerhorst

G B 10 160 bc
Geheim

Kriegsaufnahme:
0853

Nachträge:
31.8.40

Karte:
1:100 000
Blatt 29

Länge
(östl. Greenw.):
0°25'

Nördl. Breite:
51°33'

Zielhöhe
über N N 37 m

G.B. 10 160   Fliegerhorst

1) Flugzeughaller
2) Werkstätten
3) Unterkunftsgebäude
4) Splittersichere Abstellplätze für Flugzeuge

cratered runways and perimeter tracks, particularly at Hornchurch, where two more Spitfires were destroyed on the ground. Both Hornchurch and Biggin Hill were serviceable again the following morning.

On the night of August 31st/September 1st raids began coming in at 8.45 p.m. with single aircraft and groups of up to three. Bombs from twenty-five aircraft were scattered north and south, keeping many awake and in the shelters, but achieving little material effect. Liverpool and the Cammell Laird yards at Birkenhead received their fourth night raid in succession and absorbed the main force. Other targets hit by error or intention included Rotherhithe, Portsmouth, Manchester, Durham, Stockport, Bristol, Gloucester, Hereford, Worcester and the York to Leeds arterial road.

One delayed-action bomb fell on the airfield at Duxford. It was dealt with in the usual way, by being hitched with 100 yards of rope to an Armadillo vehicle and then towed to a safe part of the airfield and left to explode 'at its leisure'.

On the 31st Fighter Command issued orders that the Defiants were to be used primarily for night fighting. They could continue to be used by day where suitable, i.e. where only hostile bombers were involved. The Defiant Squadrons 141 and 264 henceforth operated in Nos. 13 and 12 Groups respectively.

SEPTEMBER 1

Day Four main attacks on Fighter Command airfields. Heavy damage.
Night Liverpool again. Diversions in midlands and South Wales.
Weather Fair with cloud patches in morning. Fine afternoons.

As September opened, a Fighter Command diarist noted that 'the month of August saw the beginning of a war of attrition'. Dowding's forces were now suffering from accumulated fatigue and the mounting losses in pilots.

Left: A German reconnaissance photograph of the fighter airfield at Northolt taken on August 31st, 1940. The runways have been skilfully painted to merge with the surrounding countryside

A Heinkel 111 of III/KG53 from Lille moves out across the channel for one of the September raids

The Luftwaffe was continuing its time-table concentration on sector airfields, many of which looked on the surface to be complete wrecks: it had become a question of just how long the organisation and the squadrons could continue to operate under continuous bombardment.

During the day, which was warm and sunny, four major attacks developed and these were aimed at Fighter Command airfields. Some 450 aircraft of Luftflotte 2 took part. The first signs of activity came at 10.15 a.m. when radar plotted raids of 20+, 30+, and 12+ forming up over the French coast. Once assembled this force became eleven formations, totalling 120 machines, which flew over Dover and split up to attack Biggin Hill, Eastchurch, Detling and Tilbury Docks. Fourteen and a half Fighter Squadrons were sent up to meet them.

For Biggin Hill it was the sixth raid in three days. No. 610 Squadron had been ordered to Acklington for a rest, but the ground crews were waiting to embus on the north side, and they smartly took cover in the woods, despite the exhortations of an over-zealous officer brandishing a revolver. One pilot of 610, who had been waiting for a final check on his machine, watched from a shelter as his Spitfire blew up.

The small formation of Dorniers in this action bombed from 12,000 feet and pitted the runways with craters, rendering the airfield unserviceable until the afternoon. No. 79 Squadron's Hurricanes, returning from the fray, were forced to land at Croydon.

At 1 p.m. the usual signs of aircraft taking-off behind Calais were recorded by the gun-laying radar at Dover, and shortly afterwards the C.H. radar reported a concentration of approximately 150+ aircraft over Cap Gris Nez. These followed the same course as the morning raid and headed for the same targets.

The third and fourth attacks in the later afternoon were launched simultaneously, one mixed formation of fifty aircraft bombing Hawkinge and Lympne and another fifty raiding Detling and firing on the Dover balloon barrage. Small formations split off and one of these, consisting of Dorniers, headed for Biggin Hill where it was now realised that 6 p.m. was the regular allotted time for the last daylight Luftwaffe visitation.

The runways were again hit, but, far more serious, the sector operations room was reduced to a shambles, all lines except one out of 13 being severed, and the Defence Teleprinter Network wrecked by a 500 lb. bomb which bounced off a steel safe. Two W.A.A.F. telephone operators, Sergeant Helen Turner and Corporal Elspeth Henderson, worked on until the last moment and

Above: High level reconnaissance during the Battle of Britain was mainly carried out by specially equipped Dornier 17Ps and He 111s. Here aircraft of 1. and 3. staffel of Aufkl.Gr.123 are shown in the hangar at its base in the Paris area

Left: Caught by a British fighter, this Dornier 17Z of KG2 was riddled with bullets from nose to tail, but managed to get back to base

then flung themselves flat in time to avoid flying steel, glass and blast. Both received the Military Medal for bravery.

When the crew crawled out of the remains of sector operations they found that four Spitfires had been destroyed, and the armoury was on fire.

First priority was to get the operations room re-established in some form, and here the Post Office engineers came to the rescue. On the night of the 30th the main London-Biggin Hill-Westerham telephone cable had been cut by bombs north of the airfield. The station Post Office maintenance officer, although blown out of a slit trench himself, had made his way through the raid and had got a message to Tunbridge Wells maintenance control. An inspector and six men volunteered to repair the cable, and despite warnings from the Sevenoaks police that an air raid was still in progress they reached the crater after darkness had fallen.

Nothing could be done until dawn due to the presence of both gas and water in the crater. On September 1st the party started work. Despite the morning attack, the effects of coal-gas fumes and lack of food and drink they got the cable restored in seven hours.

Before they had finished, however, the operations room had been smashed, and every G.P.O. engineer was needed to get an emergency set-up working in a village shop. Within an hour some measure of control was once more at the disposal of the Biggin Hill Sector, and working through the night, the engineers had by the following day rigged two new switch-boards and restored the telephone services. Meanwhile, the main cable was again severed, but the tireless engineers repaired it and reconnected several Observer posts which had lost their communications.

In daylight on the 1st, Fighter Command sent up 147 patrols involving 700 machines, and suffered fifteen aircraft casualties from which nine pilots were saved. The Luftwaffe reported the loss of fourteen aircraft including night operations which for the first time gave them an advantage on the score card.

Darkness had brought a lull until midnight, but between 9 p.m. and 4 in the morning about 100 aircraft singly attacked industrial targets and laid mines. Bombs fell at Birkenhead, Sealand, Stafford, Sheffield, Burton-on-Trent, Hull, Grimsby, Ashford and Gillingham.

The most serious damage was done between Swansea and Neath where six 10,000-ton oil-tanks were set on fire.

Liberally sprayed by the fire section, this Spitfire of 92 Squadron came to grief at Biggin Hill during the September battles

SEPTEMBER 2

Day Once again four main phases of airfield attacks.
Night Scattered raids: Liverpool, midlands and South Wales.
Weather Continuing fine and warm. Early-morning mist and fog patches.

Once again the early morning was warm and hazy, although there were occasional patches of low cloud.

The Luftwaffe stepped up the tempo, determined to eradicate the southern airfields as a source of R.A.F. defence. The day's operations were divided into four main phases intended to stretch No. 11 Group to the maximum. Over 750 aircraft were despatched and the German Air Force mounted 972 daylight sorties – 332 more than the previous day.

Instead of the early-morning reconnaissance aircraft which usually preceded attacks later in the morning, formations of 30+, 40+, etc., to the tune of 100 aircraft were building up over Calais at 7.15 a.m. These resolved into 40 bombers escorted by about 60 fighters stepped-up from 12,000 to 20,000 feet east of Dover. The formations split and separate raids attacked Eastchurch, North Weald, Rochford and Biggin Hill. 11 Group despatched eleven squadrons, but of these only five made contact.

The problems of dealing with low raids were again brought out during these sorties and special orders were issued from Sectors to the Observer Corps giving priority to low-flying aircraft. The Bromley Observer Centre diary recorded: 'Biggin Hill was caught by a low flight while everybody's attention including our Corps was absorbed by heavy work in dealing with high flights.'

The second attack began to form up over France at noon and at about 12.35 some 250 fighters and bombers converged on Dover and then split up. All the raids were accurately tracked by the Observer Corps over the Isle of Sheppey and the Thames Estuary, but one of them severely damaged Debden aerodrome.

By 3.15 yet another build-up was shown on the radar screens over Calais. Two hundred

and fifty German machines transitted Dover and then spread fanwise over Kent. One raid penetrated to Biggin Hill, Kenley and Brooklands. At Detling a hangar was hit and damage was caused at both Eastchurch and Hornchurch. At the latter, successful interceptions broke up the raid to such an extent that only six out of a hundred bombs dropped fell within the airfield boundary. Bombs fell at random on other places including Herne Bay, where one crater measured 200 feet across.

Finally at five o'clock in the afternoon a large raid and several small diversions appeared over Dungeness, their targets again being airfields.

Damage to airfields had been considerable with Detling and Eastchurch the worst hit. At Detling thirty aircraft wrecked 'C' Flight hangar and rendered the aerodrome unserviceable for several hours. Eastchurch received two attacks, the first by eighteen aircraft which exploded a dump of three hundred and fifty 250 lb. bombs, wrecked the N.A.A.F.I. and admin. buildings, smashed water mains and sewers, destroyed five aeroplanes and put most of the communications out of action, including the Defence Teleprinter Network. In the second raid another hangar was hit, and it was decided on the following day to remove G.H.Q. and the accounts section. The camp was transferred to Wymswold Warden and the sick quarters to Eastchurch village. Total casualties for the day at the station were four killed and twelve wounded.

To meet this phased effort against its stations, 11 Group had put up 751 sorties and had lost thirty-one aircraft to the Luftwaffe's thirty-five. Eight R.A.F. pilots had been killed and seven wounded. Once again, Erprobungs Gruppe 210 had suffered, with eight Me 110s destroyed. On one bomber shot down were found supplies of hand grenades intended to be thrown out at pursuing fighters. A coastal raid in the north left two steamers off Aberdeenshire hit, one of them burned out.

Night brought a few hours respite until at 1.30 a.m. raiders began to arrive in ones

Refugee pilots of many nationalities flew with the RAF during the Battle. This group of 310 (Czech) Sqn was photographed at their Duxford base on September 1st. The squadron had been formed with Hurricanes on July 10th. By the end of the month, it would claim 37½ enemy aircraft destroyed.

and twos over East Anglia, of which approximately half were engaged in minelaying. Many of the bombers out of the seventy-five despatched were from Luftflotte 3, and their landfall was Swanage in Dorsetshire. Targets were again scattered, including Leighton Buzzard, Digby, Castle Bromwich, Sealand, Birmingham, Monmouth and Cardiff.

SEPTEMBER 3

Day Heavy attacks on airfields. Losses equal.
Night Main attack Liverpool. Harassing raids on South Wales and the south-east.
Weather Fine and warm. Some cloud and drizzle in north. Haze in Channel and Straits.

At eight o'clock in the morning Luftflotte 2 began the familiar pattern of building up formations over Calais, and one by one the blips appeared on the cathode-ray tubes at the C.H. and gun-laying radar stations at Dover.

The targets were Hornchurch, North Weald and Debden, but through a series of disjointed dog-fights only one intact formation reached its target, North Weald. Here about thirty Dorniers escorted by Me 110s did severe damage. Fire broke out in Nos. 151 and 25 Squadrons hangars, the motor transport yard was badly hit and several other buildings including the main stores were damaged. The new sector operations block received a direct hit but survived, although all communications with Observer Corps were severed except for one line to Watford Centre. The airfield Tannoy system was destroyed and the vital high-frequency relay system for communication between aircraft and base was cut between the receiver and transmitter. Despite all this and a liberal sowing of delayed-action bombs, the aerodrome remained serviceable for day operations.

One of the pilots from 603 Squadron shot down in this operation was Pilot Officer Richard Hillary, later to write the best seller 'The Last Enemy'. His cockpit in flames Hillary had difficulty in getting the Spitfire's hood open. When at last he succeeded he fell, badly burned, into the sea. After over an hour of pain and misery he, like so many other pilots, was picked up by an R.N.L.I. lifeboat, the *J.B. Proudfoot*, on temporary duty at Margate.

In the afternoon a second attack developed in the same area which was beaten off, and in which action the Czech pilots of No. 310 Squadron, Duxford, played a significant part.

Due to continuing bomber losses, the Luftwaffe had been experimenting with new tactics on this day. Previously the plan had been to advance in stepped formations, but this was temporarily replaced by (a) fighters and bombers flying at the same level and (b) mixed groups of fighters and bombers. Neither of these was found to be satisfactory, and a few days later there was a general resumption of stepped formations. Freiejagd, or freelance patrols of Me 109s and Me 110s, continued to fly in and then orbit in attempts to draw R.A.F. fighters away from the main attack.

The losses of the 3rd were nevertheless an ominous portent for the R.A.F. Sixteen fighters were shot down with eight pilots saved, while the German casualties for the

German bomber crews photographed on a sortie over southern England in early September. Below: flying a Heinkel He 111. Both the pilot and the Leutnant observer/gunner wear oxygen masks, indicating a high-level raid. Right: gunners in a Do 17Z searching the sky for the ever-present danger of being bounced by Hurricanes or Spitfires.

whole twenty-four-hour period were also sixteen – the Luftwaffe had achieved parity for the second time.

The main raid of the night was against Liverpool, about ninety bombers flying in a steady stream from Cherbourg. Bombing was, however, not concentrated and damage was also done at Warrington, Chester and Sealand.

SEPTEMBER 4

Day Succession of airfield raids in two main phases. Serious damage at Vickers Works, Brooklands.
Night Further raid on Liverpool. Harassing attacks.
Weather Fine and warm. Occasional rain and strong winds in north. Haze in Estuary, Channel and Straits.

On September 1st the Luftwaffe Operations Staff 1A had issued an order to the Luftflotten covering the destruction (if possible) of thirty British factories making aircraft, aero engines, propellers and ancillary equipment. This was an attempt to halt a seemingly endless flow of fighter equipment to the R.A.F., despite Intelligence IC statements that the aircraft were either destroyed or non-existent. The order covered both fighter and bomber production, and the necessary target briefings had been completed by September 3rd.

Accordingly on the 4th the raids by Luftflotte 2 were divided, with both sector airfields and factories as their targets.

The first big attack of the day concentrated on airfields, coming in via the Estuary and over Dover. At Eastchurch bombs from eighteen aircraft demolished the ration store and produced six craters in the runway, but there were no casualties. Lympne was shot up, as were the Dover Balloons.

At lunchtime successive waves of bombers with fighter escort totalling about 300 crossed the coast at Dover, Folkestone, Hastings and Beachy Head. Fourteen squadrons rose to do battle, and nine of them intercepted. In the ensuing confusion at 1.30 p.m. fourteen Me 110s of 5/LG.1 slipped through at low level and followed the Southern Railway line over Guildford, Surrey, to the Vickers Armstrong factory at Brooklands, where two-thirds of the R.A.F.'s Wellington bombers were produced.

The adjacent sector and Observer Corps operations tables were 'saturated' with raid plots and the formation 'Bradshawing' up the railway went unnoticed until the last moment. Due to an unusually quick piece of recognition by the sergeant in charge of the airfield guns, the two leading aircraft were shot down almost immediately and several others jettisoned their bombs outside the target area when intercepted by No. 253 Squadron's Hurricanes over the village of Clandon. The bombs dropped, however, scored direct hits on the machine and erecting shops. Many workers were buried under rubble and girders while hundreds more were injured by blast and flying splinters. From the six bombs in the works area eighty-eight people were killed and 600 injured, while factory output almost ceased for four days.

Other small groups of raiders got through to Rochester, Eastchurch, Shoeburyness, Canterbury, Faversham and Reigate. At Rochester the target was again the Short Brothers factory engaged in initial production of the Stirling four-motor heavy bomber.

In these fierce engagements of the morning and afternoon, Fighter Command put up a total 678 sorties and lost seventeen fighters against German losses of twenty-five – the balance was beginning to improve slighty.

The night was extremely active with nearly 200 bombers over England, the majority going to Liverpool, Bristol and South Wales. A number of raiders approached the Thames Estuary but seemed disconcerted by the London barrage. Parachute flares were dropped over Hendon and Hatfield, while other bombs fell on Manchester, Halifax, Newcastle, Nottingham, Tilbury and Gravesend.

SEPTEMBER 5

Day Airfield attacks in two phases. Park orders special cover for fighter factories.
Night Continuous activity over most of England.
Weather Again fine and warm, cloud developing later. Channel and Straits fine.

As on previous days, the Luftwaffe effort was divided up into two major attacks, the sub-formations breaking away and heading for their targets after crossing the coast in order to confuse the defences.

About 10 a.m. raids developed over Kent

Above: German 'Ace' Franz von Werra, adjutant of II/JG3, was forced down in this Me 109E in a field near Marden, Kent, on September 5th. He was transferred to a prison camp in Canada where he eventually escaped to Germany. He warned German intelligence that Britain had broken the Luftwaffe unit and R/T codes and, as a result, the system was changed. The fin of von Werra's aircraft shows thirteen victories. He was killed in October 1944

Right: Me 109s of JG53 lined up on a Belgian airfield, reportedly in September. If so, the swastika marking across both fin and rudder is overdue for change to the fin only as shown on page 69. The May–June period seems more likely. In the foreground lie the remains of a Belgian Air Force Fairey Fox biplane.

heading for Croydon, Biggin Hill and Eastchurch, while others concentrated on North Weald and Lympne. Fourteen R.A.F. squadrons joined the fight and most of the raiders were diverted before reaching their targets as occurred at Biggin Hill where 79 Squadron successfully intercepted.

Just after lunch radar began to track several formations over France, but many came in so high that they were missed by the Observers on the ground and were not plotted on the operations tables. The oil-tanks at Thameshaven were set on fire while Biggin Hill and Detling received further attention.

The bombers dispersed at two o'clock and swarms of Me 109s patrolled the Channel to see them home, as German losses through being shot down into the sea were becoming too frequent to be ignored.

In these engagements Fighter Command lost twenty machines to the Germans, twenty-three throughout the twenty-four-hour period, although five British pilots were saved.

At night during the 5th/6th there was almost continuous activity, with bombs dropped on Liverpool, Manchester, London and over forty other towns and cities.

Following the attacks on Weybridge and Rochester, Park, on the 5th, issued instructions passed on from Dowding that maximum fighter cover should be given to the Hawker factories at Kingston, Langley and Brooklands, and to the Vickers-Supermarine works at Southampton. Dowding had correctly diagnosed that part of the enemy's effort had been switched to factories and that more such raids would be forthcoming. The only direct protection he could afford was to ask for two No. 10 Group squadrons to patrol the lines Brooklands–Croydon and Brooklands–Windsor whenever a heavy attack developed south of the Thames.

In his order Park stressed the 'vital' importance to the R.A.F. of the Southampton factories and in particular the Supermarine works at Woolston. Ever helpful, 10 Group had agreed to reinforce the Tangmere sector by up to three or four squadrons whenever a mass raid approached the Southampton – Portsmouth area.

On the 5th, No. 504 Squadron was ordered to move south from Catterick. The procedure was a typical example of unit moves during the Battle. In the early morning a message was received for the squadron to transfer complete to Hendon. Bombay transport aircraft arrived to take part of the personnel, while the remainder entrained after lunch. The pilots flew down at midday and were in action over London on the 7th.

SEPTEMBER 6

Day Three main attacks, largely broken up.
Night Less activity. Harassing raids only.
Weather Fine, but cooler. Haze in Straits and Estuary.

Park's orders on factory defence had been issued none too soon for on Friday the 6th Luftflotte 2 tried to attack the Hawker works at Brooklands where half the total output of Hurricanes was produced. The squadrons on patrol were able to prevent any serious damage being done.

In all there were three main attacks during the day, which cost Fighter Command twenty-three fighters, the pilots of twelve machines being saved. German losses were thirty-five, including sixteen Me 109s and eight He 111s from KG26.

Groups of bombers with fighter escort began to mass at 8.30 in the morning, and they fanned out over Kent trying to get at five of the sector stations around London. Their efforts were frustrated and they therefore made a second attempt at midday and a third in the early evening. No great damage was done due to successful interceptions, as was evidenced at Biggin Hill where most of the bombs overshot the target and fell on the Westerham road where the much repaired main trunk cable was once more severed. An unusual present for the R.A.F. came on this evening in the shape of an Me 109 which landed at Hawkinge when it ran out of fuel.

The night of the 6th/7th was less active than usual with single raiders wandering the counties and dropping bombs sufficient to keep the sirens howling and the shelters occupied. The Fighter Command controllers presumed that the enemy was resting after the long period of sustained activity. They did not know that the Luftwaffe was about to change its policy and that the agonising strain on 11 Group was to be eased at the expense of the citizens of London. The morrow was to provide many surprises.

King George VI and Queen Elizabeth walking in the grounds of Bentley Priory with Air Chief Marshal Dowding, the architect of Fighter Command's victory. The date was September 6th, 1940, and a series of German air attacks was in progress

FOURTH PHASE

SEPTEMBER 7 – 30

The timetable for the German invasion of England was not going to schedule due to the resistance of the R.A.F. during August, and so to the High Command it appeared that they were no nearer defeating Fighter Command and achieving the air superiority for the landing. In addition the period August 24th to September 6th had shown 107 German bombers and two Stukas lost.

Intelligence under Schmid had been totally unable to assess the actual state of R.A.F. fighter forces from week to week or that the raids on sector airfields had caused great dislocation and damage with a high rate of pilot casualties. For two months the Luftwaffe had tried every device to bring the main British fighter force into battle when numerical superiority of Me 109s and Me 110s would destroy it.

From the beginning there had been many in the Luftwaffe Command who were of the opinion that only direct and heavy daylight blows against London would achieve the desired results, with the possibility that the raids might cause morale to crack as occurred at Warsaw and Rotterdam. Hitler had consistently forbidden attacks on London as he felt certain Britain would sue for peace without such extreme measures.

Left: Desolation. A London street after Luftflotte 3 had visited it on the night of September 8th. Firemen attempt to damp down the flames

The chain which led to a reversal of his policy was actually set off by the Germans themselves. On the night of August 25th a number of bombs had accidentally fallen on central London, due to bad navigation. The R.A.F. had immediately taken up the challenge and flown several night raids over Berlin. Little damage was actually caused, but the effect on both Hitler and Göring was decisive. As the glorious victors of Europe it was embarrassing to say the least to have enemy bombers droning over the Reich night after night practically unscathed.

As early as August 31st the Command Staff of the Luftwaffe issued preliminary orders for Luftflotten 2 and 3 to prepare for a daylight reprisal raid on London. On September 2nd Luftflotten 2 and 3 drew up instructions for the general plan of the attack which covered day and night raids on London and other large centres of population.

Thus, when the Luftwaffe commanders met in The Hague on September 3rd to discuss the progress of the air war against England, an attack on the heart of the British Empire seemed the only logical step. As related in Chapter 5 there were heated arguments between Kesselring and Sperrle over current R.A.F. fighter strength with the former winning the day on a theory that Fighter Command was almost finished. The attacks on sector stations from the south coast up to and around London had cleared the way, so it was thought, for the final assault. British reserves that had apparently been pulled back north out of range of the Me 109 would certainly be thrown into the defence of the city and would incur heavy losses. To Kesselring it seemed the only sensible idea, and one that he had been suggesting ever since the Battle started, i.e. massive attack at full strength against one key objective.

With the Luftwaffe committed to the plan, and the preparations well in hand, it only remained for the Führer to give his sanction. After the first raids on Berlin, Hitler had clearly given Göring permission to put in hand arrangements for such an operation, otherwise the orders of August 31st could not have come from the O.K.L. The Luftwaffe had set the date as September 7th, and five days before that Hitler personally gave orders for 'the start of the reprisal raids against London'.

In England neither Dowding nor Park were aware of any impending change in tactics. All they knew was that the unremitting attacks on airfields and the sector organisation during August had gravely impaired strength and efficiency.

The position was grim in the extreme as from August 24th to September 6th 295 fighters had been totally destroyed and 171 badly damaged, against a total output of 269 new and repaired Spitfires and Hurricanes. Worst of all, during the fortnight 103 pilots were killed or missing and 128 were wounded, which represented a total wastage of 120 pilots per week out of a fighting strength of just under 1,000.

Experienced pilots were like gold-dust, and each one lost had to be replaced by an untried man who for some time would be vulnerable, until he acquired battle know-how. Fresh squadrons, moved in to replace tired units, very often lost more aircraft and pilots than the formations they replaced. For instance, 616 Squadron lost twelve aircraft and five pilots between August 25th and September 2nd and had to be retired to Coltishall in No. 12 Group.

No. 603 Squadron, newly arrived in 11 Group on August 28th, had by September 6th lost sixteen aircraft and twelve pilots, while 253 Squadron at Kenley lost thirteen Hurricanes and nine pilots in the seven days they were in battle, from August 30th.

In contrast, the experienced squadrons, while utterly weary and often flying over fifty hours per day, continued to show far better results. No. 54 Squadron when sent north to Hornchurch on September 3rd, had lost only nine aircraft and one pilot since August 24th. No. 501 Squadron in the Biggin Hill sector during the complete phase (August 24th–September 6th) had suffered the loss of nine aircraft and four pilots.

During the whole of August no more than 260 fighter pilots were turned out by the O.T.U.s and casualties in the same month were just over 300. A full squadron establishment was twenty-six pilots whereas the average in August was sixteen. The command was literally wasting away under Dowding's eyes and there was nothing he could do about it if southern England was to continue as a defended area.

The ground organisation had also suffered severely and in a report to Headquarters Fighter Command, dated September 12th, Park stated that contrary to general belief and official reports, the enemy's bombing attacks by day had done extensive damage to five forward aerodromes and also to six out of seven sector stations. The damage to forward aerodromes was so severe that Manston and Lympne were for several days quite unfit for fighters. Biggin Hill was so severely damaged that only one squadron could operate from the airfield and the remaining two squadrons had to be placed under the control of adjacent sectors for over a week. Park added that had the enemy continued his heavy attacks to the adjacent sectors, knocked out their operations rooms or telephone communications, the fighter defences of London would have been in a powerless state during the last critical phase, and unopposed heavy attacks would have been directed against the capital.

SEPTEMBER 7

Day Bombing switched to London. Heavy attack on the capital. Pressure on fighter airfields eased.
Night London raids continue dusk until dawn. Main objectives east London and docks.
Weather Fair in the south. Some haze.

Göring decided personally to command the assault against London, and accordingly his immaculate personal train with its cooks, telephones and stocks of wine rolled north-west to the Pas de Calais. At Cap Gris Nez the entourage of field marshals, generals and colonels took their stand while the Reichsmarschall gazed skyward through his binoculars waiting for the passing of his aerial armada.

Every available fighter was being used, and bombers in far greater force than hitherto. The targets lay in East London, on the banks of the Thames, among the docks and warehouses.

Right: A photograph taken by the Luftwaffe during the course of the first big day light raid on London on September 7. It was claimed that the altitude the picture was taken from was 29,500 ft. The Thames with its bridges is clearly visible and German annotations indicate bombers below, bomb bursts, AA fire and various targets.

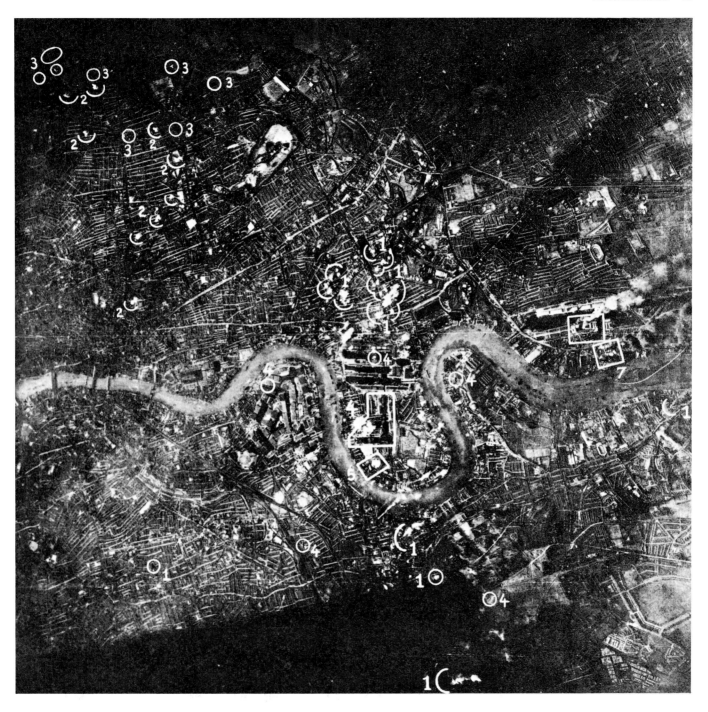

To the staff on duty in the filter and operations rooms at Bentley Priory the day began purely as a repetition of so many others. At 11.15 four raids developed with Hawkinge airfield as their main target. The fighter dispositions had been laid down with continued attacks on sector stations in view, and to this end Park in his order of September 5th had stressed the need to put fighter squadrons into battle in pairs, the Spitfires to deal with the fighter screen and the Hurricanes with the bombers. 11 Group was ready to deal with sector and factory raids, with the assistance of 10 Group on its western flank and 12 Group to the north.

Park was not, however, satisfied that fighters were being positioned correctly. In the early stages of the Battle there had been a tendency for radar plots to be shown with too low a height and many squadrons found themselves still climbing, with the enemy

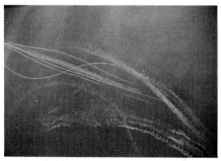

The two Air Forces meet and vapour trails criss-cross the sky. Older trails fluff out and break up as more aircraft with thin clear contrails take up the battle. These pictures were taken from the R.A.F. station at Manston, Kent

above. This had led both pilots and controllers to add a few thousand feet on to the height given in the hope of arriving above or on a level with the raid.

By early September the radar plotting and Fighter Command's filtering had improved still further with continuous practice, and the heights fed into sector operations were usually accurate. The habit of 'adding a bit' nevertheless still went on with the result that squadrons found themselves going straight into the high-altitude escort screen while the bombers got through.

On the 7th a terse instruction was issued by Park to his controllers. After pointing out that on one occasion the previous day only seven out of eighteen squadrons despatched engaged the enemy and on another only seven out of seventeen got into the right position, he commented that it was obvious that some controllers were ordering squadrons intended to engage enemy bombers to patrol too high. When Group ordered a squadron to 16,000 feet, sector controller added on one or two thousand, and the squadron added on another two thousand in the vain hope that they would not have any enemy fighters above them. The net result had been that daily some of the enemy bomber formations slipped in under 15,000 feet, frequently without any fighter escort, and bombed their objectives, doing serious damage, as at Brooklands. In fact the majority of enemy bomber formations had been intercepted only after they had dropped their bombs and were on the way out.

11 Group were also concerned about the prospects of invasion as the barge concentrations across the Channel daily grew larger. In the morning the Air Ministry informed Fighter Command 'Invasion regarded Imminent'. This was followed by standard notifications of states of readiness:

> Invasion Alert No. 3 – an attack is probable within three days.
> Invasion Alert No. 2 – an attack is probable within two days.
> Invasion Alert No. 1 – an attack is imminent.

Fighter Command had plenty on its mind when at 4 p.m. the radar stations picked up several formations of twenty+ over Calais. It was presumed they would adopt the usual tactics of crossing the coast and splitting up

straightaway. Gradually it was realised at Bentley Priory that this was no ordinary raid. Over 300 bombers with 600 Me 109s and Me 110s in attendance, stepped up in solid layers, crossed the coast in two waves. The first flew direct to the Estuary and the second, an hour later, passed over central London, then steered back over the Estuary and the East End.

It was too late to alter the carefully prepared dispositions of the fighter squadrons, and as a result many bombers were not attacked until after they had delivered their loads. The sector stations were being well covered, but the road to London was clear. The 11 Group controller got everything he could vector on to the advancing phalanx, but it was in penny numbers compared with the solid masses of the Luftwaffe.

In addition the German fighter screen had adopted new techniques. Both bombers and fighters operated at great height with the former usually at between 16,000 and 20,000 feet.

Escorts were divided into two parts, some operating in close contact with the bombers, and others a few hundred yards away and a little above. Close cover was above, behind – at a lower level – and on both sides of the bombers. If the formation was attacked from starboard the starboard section engaged the attackers, the top section moving to starboard and the port section to the top position. If the attack came from the port side the system was reversed. British fighters coming in to the rear were engaged by the rear section and the two outside sections similarly moved to the rear. If the threat came from above, the top section went into action while the side sections gained height in order to be able to follow the R.A.F. fighters down as they broke away. If attacked themselves, all sections flew in defensive circles. These tactics were skilfully evolved and carried out, and they were extremely difficult to counter.

Despite interception by four fighter squadrons and heavy anti-aircraft fire, the bombers of both waves made determined efforts to keep formation. High on the top of the Senate House, London University, the central London Observer post K.1 had a bird's-eye view of the attack and passed plots as fast as the operations room could take them.

Bombs rained down upon the London

Approaching London, a formation of Heinkel 111s during one of the September raids, with an ever-ready official cameraman in the nose of this aircraft

docks, the oil-tanks at Cliffe and Thames-haven, Beckton gasworks, and on Poplar, Woolwich, Millwall, Limehouse, Tower Bridge, Tottenham, West Ham, Barking and Croydon. Silvertown became a raging inferno and the fires raged on acting as a beacon for the night bombers, while in the little streets of the East End the inevitable pattern of death and destruction was beginning to unfold.

Rows of jerry-built terraced houses of the early Victorian era suddenly became heaps of tiles and rubble. Processions of bombed-out families – with a perambulator, a few bundles and the children clinging on for dear life – threaded their way through the glass and debris. Wardens, firemen and a host of others dug in the ruins searching for the injured. London's testing time had begun, and like the pilots, ground staff and W.A.A.F.s of

the R.A.F., the city was not found wanting. In curious irony it was a quarter of a century before, on September 8th, 1915, that Zeppelins had made their first big raid on London.

Many of the raiders did not fare so well as their companions who had a clear run over the City. The 12 Group wing at Duxford had been practising their formation techniques, and had Leigh-Mallory's blessing to operate *en masse*. No. 242 Squadron which led the wing had a bitter fight with a large formation of Dorniers and Messerschmitts and shot down several, although the remaining two squadrons – 19 and 310 – could not gain height in time to join in.

The most successful of the units operating on the 7th was No. 303, the Polish squadron from Northolt. When the Poles came into the battle they found forty Dorniers at 20,000

feet with a formation of Me 110s above and behind, and further back still, at over 25,000 feet, were the Me 109s. The engagement was a first-class piece of the kind of co-operation Park wanted. A squadron of Spitfires took on the 109s, while a Hurricane squadron attacked the rear of the bombers forcing them to turn back. At this juncture the Poles waded in, turning their whole unit broadside on to the enemy.

They dived 4,000 feet out of the sun, each pilot selecting a victim. The squadron commander, Squadron Leader R.G. Kellett, reported afterwards: 'We gave them all we'd got, opening fire at 450 yards and only breaking away when we could see the enemy completely filling the gunsight. That means we finished the attack at point-blank range. We went in practically in one straight line, all of us blazing away.' Nearly a quarter of the bombers were destroyed or badly damaged.

One of No. 10 Group's squadrons on the factory protection patrol was also involved in the general mêlée as the Luftwaffe retired just after 6 p.m. Flight Lieutenant J.H.G. McArthur, 'Blue Leader' No. 609 Squadron, reported:

> Whilst on patrol at 10,000 feet between Brooklands and Windsor, we saw about 200 enemy aircraft over London surrounded by A.A. fire. We climbed towards them and I led the squadron into a quarter attack on a large number of twin-engined and twin-tailed bombers which I think must have been Do 17s. I went for the nearest bomber and opened fire at about 400 yards, meanwhile experiencing very heavy return cross-fire from the bomber formation. After about twelve seconds smoke started to come from the port motor and it left the formation. I broke away as there were many 110s and 109s behind. The bomber with one motor still pouring out thick smoke continued to lose height, so I waited until it got down to about 3,000 feet and then dived vertically on to it and fired off the rest of my ammunition (about 3 to 4 secs.). It kept going on down seemingly still under some sort of control, until it hit the water about ten miles out from the centre of the Thames Estuary.

No. 7 O.T.U. at Hawarden gained their second victory of the Battle, having chalked up an He 111 on August 14th. Sergeant L.S. Pilkington, while instructing a pupil in formation flying, heard on the R/T that a 'bandit' was approaching Hoylake. Having sent the pupil home he intercepted a Ju 88 at 20,000 feet and was able to get in a good burst with his two 20 mm. cannon, which were a rarity at the time. The Ju 88 subsequently crashed in Wales.

While the day had been a frustrating one for Fighter Command with London heavily bombed and nineteen pilots lost out of twenty-eight fighters shot down, they could show forty-one German aircraft destroyed during the whole day – a not inconsiderable total which led the German radio to report that the attack had entailed 'heavy sacrifices'.

During the afternoon German radio

A complete Gruppe of KG3 forms up for the journey across the Channel to England. It was the assembly of these formations which gave British radar the warning necessary to put up fighters to intercept

stations had kept up a gleeful commentary on the raids. In the evening Göring, highly delighted, telephoned his wife to report, 'London is in flames'. He then broadcast that this was 'a historic hour' and that the Luftwaffe had 'for the first time delivered its stroke right into the enemy's heart'.

Many returning fighter and bomber pilots reported little or no opposition, and for one day at least the Luftwaffe operations and intelligence staff believed that their aim of destroying Fighter Command was nearly achieved.

On the night of the 7th/8th the blitz on London continued with unabated fury, a continuous stream of bombers, totalling 247 in all, stoking the fires in the East End from eight in the evening to nearly five o'clock the next morning. Some 330 tons of high explosives were dropped, and 440 incendiary canisters, the latter contributing to the nine conflagrations (huge spreading areas of flame) which lit up the night sky with a dull glow. Typical of the East End slums which suffered in these early September raids was Tulip

Street with its long rows of dingy terraced houses. It had been hit in the August night raids and again on September 7th. Within a few nights it had been reduced to twin rows of shattered roofless walls, and when the debris had finally been cleared away Tulip Street had disappeared for ever.

To add to the confusion the code-word 'Cromwell' was issued at 8 p.m. Many took it that invasion was in progress. Church bells were rung, road blocks put up and Home Guards roamed the countryside with loaded rifles.

Part of Banquet, the Flying Training Command reinforcement programme for invasion, was put into operation. For instance, the Senior Course at No. 2 School of General Reconnaissance at Squire's Gate was on invasion stand-by. Blackpool in 1940 was still a bouncing town in the pre-war mood and Wakes weeks were still celebrated. Stand-by in the Senior Course invariably meant that they spent their week-ends in gay Blackpool.

When the alert came through on the night of Saturday, September 7th, the Senior Course was immediately sent for. No one, however, could be found in his billet. Persistent efforts by the police and the station staff eventually routed all these officers out of bars, night clubs and beds other than their own. Rather the worse for wear, they were hurried into the navigator's seats of Ansons and flown to Thorney Island.

When they reached this southern base, they noticed in a somewhat hazy way that the aircraft were being bombed up. Upon enquiry they were informed that they were being readied to attack the German invasion fleet; one man is rumoured to have fainted.

When dawn came there had been no landing but 306 civilians in London were dead and 1,337 seriously injured. Clouds of smoke billowed up over the dock area and the fires burned on, filling the air with acrid fumes and soot. Londoners crawled out of their shelters and picked their ways towards their places of work through the hoses and rubble, round the fire engines and the rescue workers still toiling in the wreckage. Some found added difficulty in commuting as three main-line terminal stations were out of action, including London Bridge and Victoria.

Near Waterloo station three lines hung crazily over a large crater, the supporting arches beneath having disappeared. The station was not reopened for passenger traffic until September 19th.

One train from Ramsgate in Kent had bombs go off all round it with an oil bomb eventually falling on the tender. The fire was put out with the engine hose and the guard and fireman, black as soot, delivered the train safely at Charing Cross.

Many eyes looked skyward awaiting the resumption of the day battle, but except for harassing raids and odd attacks which penetrated to the centre, London had had its first and last mass daylight raid; henceforth the Luftwaffe would come by night.

SEPTEMBER 8

Day Only slight activity. Some small attack on airfields.
Night Heavy concentration on London, mainly east.
Weather Fair early morning and evening. Rest of day cloudy.

Göring on this day decided that the attacks on London would bear considerable fruit, and accordingly he issued orders for the area covered by bombing to be widened both by day and night. For target purposes the city had been divided into two sections, target area 'A' being east London and the docks and target 'B' west London. Particular emphasis was laid on power stations and railway termini. From the 8th onwards both 'A' and 'B' were bombed. In the morning German radio stations solemnly announced the fact that the Reichsmarschall had assumed command of operations for the first time since the outbreak of war.

For the R.A.F. the concentration on London was to ease the pressure on hard-hit sector stations, but it could do nothing to increase the flow of new fighter pilots to replace the heavy losses of August and the first week in September. Normally a fighter squadron remained in the line from a month to six weeks, but the intensity of the fighting and resultant losses had required some units to be replaced after a week or ten days. Reluctantly Dowding put into operation a new 'stabilisation' system of classification for fighter squadrons with top priority for groups in the daylight battle zone.

Squadrons were grouped into three categories, viz.:

Category A. Squadrons in No. 11 Group and on its immediate flanks, which bore the brunt of the fighting.

Category B. A small number of squadrons maintained at operational strength to be available as immediate reliefs should this be unavoidable.

Category C. Remaining squadrons, stripped of the majority of their operational pilots for the benefits of the A squadrons and with energies mainly devoted to training new pilots from the O.T.U.s or those transferred from other commands.

The A squadrons were stabilised and were not to be relieved unless circumstances were exceptional, their strength being maintained

Above: Neptune Street, Rotherhithe, close by the Commercial Docks in East London. Rescue workers clear the rubble after heavy bombing by Luftflotte 3 on the night of September 8th

Right: A street in west London on September 8th after the raiders had passed. A double-decker bus has been blown up into the first-floor windows of a terraced house

largely by intakes from the C squadrons. The C squadrons were considered unfit to meet German fighters, but were quite capable of dealing with unescorted bombers.

While the new system tided over a crucial period in the command it was not good for overall morale, as nobody particularly liked belonging to a unit which bore the designation Category C.

By this time the fighter resources were so stretched that Dowding could no longer maintain standing patrols for all the convoys, nor could he divert fighters even to defend such important sites as aircraft storage units.

Believing the danger of invasion to be growing, it was decided to install three retractable machine-gun pill-boxes at each operational airfield to give additional local defence against parachutists and airborne invaders. These elaborate items were raised above ground level to a height of three feet using compressed air.

While Fighter Command examined the records of the London attack the day before, the Luftwaffe somewhat reduced the scale of its efforts on the 8th, partly through fatigue and partly due to bad weather.

Between 11 a.m. and 12.30 Luftflotte 2 put in several raids over Kent with airfields once more the chief objectives. Some fifteen formations of varying size dropped bombs on Sevenoaks, West Malling, Detling, Hornchurch, Dover and Gravesend. Eleven fighter squadrons were sent up and many of the enemy were turned back, doing little damage. Compared with its 817 sorties of the 7th, Fighter Command flew 305 on the 8th and lost only two aircraft, the pilot of one returning safely. In contrast Luftwaffe losses for the twenty-four-hour period were fifteen.

At night Luftflotte 3 returned to the assault on London, sending 207 bombers via Rennes, Caen, Le Havre and Dieppe in steady succession from 7.30 p.m. until dawn. In these nine and a half hours high explosives and incendiaries again showered dockland, but many fell on the city proper, leaving twelve conflagrations for the indefatigable fire service to deal with. Three hospitals and two museums were hit, and more than fifty people died when a large bomb wrecked a block of flats in the East End. By Monday morning 412 more Londoners were dead and 747 badly hurt. Whole rows of houses were gutted or knocked down, factories were wrecked, and every railway line southwards out of the city was unserviceable.

SEPTEMBER 9

Day Unsuccessful sorties against London, Thames Estuary and aircraft factories.
Night Main target London, including City and West End.
Weather Scattered showers. Thundery in the east. Channel fair.

Once more the morning brought respite, and attacks did not develop until the afternoon, when formations began massing in the area Calais–Boulogne. Raids of 30+, 50+, 15+ and 12+ were plotted by the radar stations, and appeared over the coast as groups of escorted and unescorted bombers. A high-flying screen of fighters attempted to draw off British interceptors just before the raids developed.

This time 11 Group were not caught napping. At five o'clock, when the raids began to come in, nine 11 Group squadrons were in position, while units from 10 Group and 12 Group guarded factories and north Thames airfields respectively.

It was the German intention to attack targets in London, the Thames Estuary and the factories at Brooklands, but the fighter interceptions were so successful that most of the formations were broken up long before they reached them. German aircraft sent out a number of distress signals and radio control stations on the French coast ordered formation leaders to break off the attacks 'if the defences are too strong, or if fighter protection is too weak'. These messages were heard with great interest by British radio monitoring receivers in Kent.

Bombs were jettisoned over a wide area, including Canterbury, Kingston, Epsom, Surbiton, Norbiton and Purley, while in central London itself a few fell on Wandsworth, Lambeth and Chelsea.

After the enemy had retired the R.A.F. could show twenty-eight German aircraft destroyed for the loss of nineteen British fighters from which six pilots were recovered. London had been saved from a further onslaught, and the German bomber air crew complained bitterly at their de-briefing of the sudden upsurge of the defences and the apparent shortcomings of their Messerschmitt escorts.

A report of the Luftwaffe Command Staff of September 9th stated:

> The maintaining of the attack against London is intended to take place by day through Luftflotte 2 with strong fighter and destroyer units; by night Luftflotte 3 will carry out attacks with the object of destroying harbour areas, the supply and power sources of the city. The city is divided into two target areas, the eastern part of London is target area A with its widely stretched out harbour installations, target area B is the west of London, which contains the power supplies and the provision installation of the city. Along with this major attack on London the destruction raids will be carried on as much as possible against many sectors of the armament industry and harbour areas in England in their previous scope.

On the night of the 9th/10th London was for the third time the main target. Luftflotte 3 had now standardised its techniques. Aircraft came over in small waves at intervals and flew along clearly defined corridors of approach using other routes for the homeward journey. First waves usually flew in over the south coast and out via Essex; the second wave arrived from the east and returned over the Beachy Head area, passing the third incoming wave over that area.

In response to Göring's order of the 8th, that the London coverage be extended, 195 aircraft attacked all districts for eight and a half hours. Familiar landmarks began to suffer, and on this occasion it was the turn of the Royal Courts of Justice and Somerset House. Three hundred and seventy Londoners died and 1,400 were injured, and this was the third night running that total casualties were over 1,700.

SEPTEMBER 10

Day Slight activity. Single raiders over airfields in afternoon.
Night London main objective but also raids on Merseyside and South Wales.
Weather Generally cloudy. Some rain.

The day dawned cloudy, and on the whole it was peaceful over England. In Germany the Luftwaffe Command Staff issued orders that 'if the weather situation does not allow the engagement of strong force of Luftflotten 2 and 3 against England, the Luftflotten must carry out individual attacks against targets of the aircraft production industry'.

Nothing developed until five o'clock in the afternoon when single aircraft of Luftflotte 3, taking advantage of cloud cover, delivered attacks in 10 Group and the western part of 11 Group. One raider machine-gunned Tangmere, and another dropped bombs on West Malling. Poling radar station reported bombs in the vicinity and a few fell in the area of Portsmouth dockyard. In the airfield raids fighters accounted for two Dorniers.

Following these incursions came six small raids from Luftflotte 2, which passed over Dungeness–Beachy Head and flew towards Biggin Hill. One aircraft reached the airfield, but was intercepted some minutes later south of Kenley and shot down. Two small raids appeared near Eastchurch but turned for home without accomplishing anything and these were followed by similar sorties towards south and south-west London.

The rumours of invasion began to assume greater significance at 4.30 p.m. when a Coastal Command aircraft reported twelve merchant vessels plus five destroyers and thirty E-boats off Dieppe.

At night the attack was more varied, and while London received the main weight of bombs from 148 aircraft, others visited South Wales and Merseyside. Many German aircraft avoided detection in the early hours by mixing with a stream of R.A.F. machines returning from Berlin via Orfordness.

SEPTEMBER 11

Day Some bombs on London. Three large raids in south-east.
Raids on Portsmouth and Southampton. Seelöwe postponed until the 14th.
Night London attacked and Merseyside.
Weather Mainly fine. Some local showers. Channel and Estuary cloudy.

The spirited defence put up by Fighter Command on the 9th had important repercussions in Germany. Despite all the prognostications of the Luftwaffe C.-in-C., Command Staff and Intelligence, the R.A.F.

had shown itself undefeated and as resolute as ever. This single day's action led Hitler to postpone the warning order for invasion which was scheduled for the 11th. This warning would have led to the laying of a boundary minefield across the Channel for the landing fleet and a final positioning of vital units, in particular, flak.

The Führer decided to issue the warning for the 14th with a view to opening Seelöwe on September 24th – always providing that air superiority had been achieved. He set great store on the effects of the London bombing and hoped that an internal collapse in England would avoid the necessity for a hazardous landing operation. At this time the day and night attacks were regarded as a dual strategic and tactical concept, to destroy British will to fight at all and to bring the R.A.F. fighters into a final pitched battle.

In London itself, the postponement was naturally unknown. All the outward portents showed advanced preparations across the Channel. Winston Churchill broadcast:

The effort of the Germans to secure daylight mastery of the air over England is of course the crux of the whole war. So far it has failed conspicuously . . . For him [Hitler] to try and invade this country without having secured mastery in the air would be a very hazardous undertaking. Nevertheless, all his preparations for invasion on a great scale are steadily going foward. Several hundreds of self-propelled barges are moving down the coasts of Europe, from the German and Dutch harbours to the ports of northern France, from Dunkirk to Brest, and beyond Brest to the French harbours in the Bay of Biscay.

While the anti-invasion build-up on land and sea went on day and night, No. 11 Group was tackling the problems of new German tactics initiated on the 7th. After careful study of all available information, Park issued a further instruction (No. 16) to his controllers. He outlined that the enemy had changed from two to three separate attacks in one day, to mass raids of 300 to 400 aircraft in two to three waves following in quick succession, the whole engagement covering about forty-five to sixty minutes.

So as to meet the Luftwaffe in maximum strength he ordered paired squdrons to be used wherever possible. The 'Readiness'

squadrons were to engage the first wave, Spitfires against fighter screen, Hurricanes against bombers and close escort. The squadrons 'Available fifteen minutes' were to be brought to 'Readiness' in pairs and despatched to deal with the second wave, while the 'Available thirty minutes' squadrons were to be sent singly as reinforcements or to protect factories and sector airfields.

Should there be a third wave the last squadrons were to be paired, those from Debden and North Weald together, Hornchurch with Biggin Hill, and Kenley with Northolt.

The squadrons from Tangmere were to be employed within Kenley or the back Tangmere sector to cover factories and to intercept German formations approaching London from the south.

It was left to the group controller to name the base over which paired squadrons would rendezvous. Once sector had linked them up, group detailed the raid, etc., and sector carried the operation through.

These dispositions were timely as the Luftwaffe renewed the attack on London on the same day that they were ordered. In the morning activity was limited to patrolling, with a Henschel 126 tactical reconnaissance aircraft cruising off Dover, and one machine dropping a bomb near Poling radar station.

After the initial heavy raids on radar stations the Germans had concentrated on setting up jamming transmitters on the coast. The work of these became particularly noticeable in September. On this Wednesday morning at eleven o'clock Great Bromley C.H. station reported that it had suffered interference for nearly an hour. Under these conditions the airmen and W.A.A.F.s watching the blips on the cathode-ray tube had to insert coloured slides and strain their eyes to make out the true afterglow trace through the dancing white lights shown up from the jammers. Plotting, however, continued as before and full-scale 'blotting out' of stations was never achieved due to the distance involved and to the German lack of high-power valves.

After reconnaissance flights at lunchtime, Luftflotte 2 put up three big raids and Luftflotte 3 attacked Southampton. At 2.45 p.m. formations began building up over Calais and Ostend and aimed for London.

At 3.45 another wave came in over Folkestone, and was shortly followed by a third. Bombs fell on the City, the docks, Islington and Paddington, and others on Biggin Hill, Kenley, Brooklands and Hornchurch.

Simultaneously two raids from Seine Bay and Cherbourg had linked up over Selsey Bill and despite harrying fighters dropped bombs on Southampton and Portsmouth.

An hour later waves of Me 109s appeared over Kent, some attacking the Dover balloons. Another force attacked a convoy and single aircraft headed for Colerne, Kenley, Detling and Eastchurch. The convoy 'Peewit' was dive-bombed, its escort 'Atherstone' being disabled.

In all this widespread activity, Fighter Command flew 678 sorties. The scoreboard at the end of the day was in reality depressing, R.A.F. losses being 29 aircraft, 17 pilots killed and 6 wounded, compared with German casualties for the 24 hours of 25 aircraft. KG26 was the worst hit, with eight He 111s shot down. At the time it was estimated German losses were far higher, but the red in the British balance sheet on the final reckoning is accounted for by the fact that many squadrons became entangled with the escorting formations who attacked from above.

As the evening drew on jamming of British radar became more general, and four stations reported interference before darkness fell. Throughout the night harassing raids moved up and down the country, while London was receiving a heavy attack from 180 bombers. Merseyside was the secondary target, while single aircraft were over Scotland, the Bristol Channel, Lincolnshire and Norfolk with Fliegerdivision IX minelaying on the south and east coasts in preparation for invasion.

To Londoners there had been one comfort

By the second week in September the Luftwaffe air assault on Britain covered a 24-hour cycle. As the last of the daylight raids faded out, the bombers were preparing to deliver their deadly loads by night. Here Do 17s of KG3 are seen on take-off, and heading out towards the Channel. For night operations the white outline of the wing crosses had been blacked over but the white bar denoting first Gruppe on the starboard wing had been retained. In early September KG3 had been transferred from Luftflotte 3 to Luftflotte 2 in the Pas de Calais

Victor and vanquished. A crashed He 111 of 1/KG26 burns among anti-invasion poles as a Spitfire orbits the pyre. The location is Burmarsh, Kent on September 11th. Right: the pilot (left) and a crewman are escorted away from the crash by troops which were billeted in the area.

The two-seat Me 110 long-range fighters of the Luftwaffe lived a dangerous life during the Battle, with heavy casualties causing eventual unit amalgamation. Top: a staffel of ZG26 'Horst Wessel' aircraft flies in over southern England. Above: one that didn't make it back to France, ending up in a field at Charing, Kent on September 11th. To prevent possible destruction by other German aircraft, the fuselage cross between the code U8+HL and the tail swastika have been covered.

on this Wednesday night; the anti-aircraft defences had been doubled since the 7th and a tremendous barrage was kept going. The Inner Artillery Zone fired no less than 13,500 rounds and although they inflicted little damage on the bombers, they did cause many to drop their loads outside the central area, and others to fly higher than usual.

Once again the bomber stream bound for London mixed with returning aircraft, confusing the plots. On several occasions 11 Group reported that raiders coming in from the south were giving the correct R.A.F. recognition signals and then unloading their bombs.

SEPTEMBER 12

Day Only small raids in south. Reconnaissance.
Night Reduced effort. Main force London. Single aircraft over wide area.
Weather Unsettled, rain in most districts. Channel cloudy.

Thursday proved mainly quiet thanks to cloud and poor weather over the south and east coasts. The morning was marked by continuous German reconnaissance. At lunch three small raids appeared on the operations table, and dropped bombs on the radar station at Fairlight – although without doing any real damage. Fighters chased one raider as far as Cap Gris Nez and there shot it down.

Incursions by single raiders went on during the afternoon and early evening but the 247 R.A.F. sorties flown were hampered by the weather. No Fighter Command machine was lost, and the Luftwaffe for the whole period suffered only four casualties.

Even the Luftwaffe's night efforts were heavily reduced, with fifty-four bombers over London and singles over the midlands, Merseyside, Essex, Suffolk, Cambridge, Kent and Surrey. One bomber was brought down by 966 Balloon Barrage Squadron at Newport, Monmouthshire.

Of the bombs on London, one of the delayed-action variety, fell within a few yards of the north wall of St. Paul's Cathedral. It took three days to remove it from a depth of twenty-seven feet. The bomb disposal officer, Lieutenant R. Davies, and his chief assistant, Sapper Wylie, became the first recipients of the George Cross.

The various stages in the preparations for a Luftwaffe raid. First, target maps and photographs are studied, then the meteorological staff assess the weather situation; a detailed pictorial lecture on the harbour is given before a final briefing to the crews

Subject of a head-on attack by British fighters, this Ju 88 of KG30 crashed on the beach at Pagham, Sussex, in September

SEPTEMBER 13

Day Small raids mainly directed at London, Hitler in conference, discussing air offensive and invasion.
Night Renewed effort against London.
Weather Unsettled. Bright intervals and showers. Rain in Channel. Straits cloudy.

Hitler was far from dissatisfied with the results of the bombing so far, and the reports he received on the operations of the 11th indicated that British opposition was weak and the German casualty rate low. At a luncheon in Berlin attended by a group of naval, army and air force officers (notable among them being Brauchitsch, Göring, Jodl and Milch) Hitler delivered a speech on the current situation. He commented particularly on the need for air superiority and the audience gathered that he was dropping the idea of invasion in view of the success of air bombardment. Nevertheless he indulged in considerable detailed discussion with the army chiefs on their dispositions and strength.

At seven o'clock in the morning the Luftwaffe began its weather reconnaissance for the day's work, aircraft covering the Biggin Hill, North Weald and Hornchurch sectors and another Kenley and Northolt. The weather reports radioed back to France were picked up by the British radio monitoring service although the actual targets could not be deciphered.

Three quarters of an hour later a Focke-Wulf 200 of I/KG40, on maritime patrol, bombed the S.S. *Longfort* off Copeland Light near Belfast and fired on a motor vessel in the same area. This was followed from 9.30 to 11.30 a.m. by single aircraft from Dieppe, passing over Hastings and heading for south London, while simultaneously the Canewdon, Dover and Rye radars suffered jamming.

Near midday, radio monitoring reported that an enemy bomber over Kent was sending messages to the effect that 'cloud is 7/10th at 1,500 metres, and that attack is possible

In the morning raids single aircraft had penetrated to central London, where bombs hit Downing Street, Whitehall, Trafalgar Square and the Chelsea Hospital. Buckingham Palace had its third bombing, with the Royal Chapel wrecked, and four near-misses.

Due to the intermittent rain and low clouds and the high altitude of the raiders, fighter squadrons had difficulty in finding their prey and only four bombers were destroyed for the loss of one fighter.

During the day the expectation of invasion was sharpened by a report from a coastal post in No. 1 (Maidstone) Observer Group, which had sighted ten enemy transports each towing two barges from Calais to Cap Gris Nez.

Main target of the night raiders was again London, with 105 bombers over the capital. Harassing raids covered the Home Counties and East Anglia.

SEPTEMBER 14

Day Hitler postpones Seelöwe until September 17th. Succession of afternoon raids aimed at London, but mainly composed of fighters.
Night Reduced activity. Main force over London.
Weather Showers and local thunder. Cloud in Straits, Channel and Estuary.

In Berlin, Adolf Hitler gathered the Cs.-in-C. of his army, navy, and air force and addressed them on the progress of the war. He pointed out that naval preparations for the invasion were complete and that the 'operations of the Luftwaffe are above all praise'. He felt that four to five days of good weather were required to achieve decisive results, conveniently forgetting that was exactly what Göring had stated before Adler Tag in August.

Hitler blamed the weather for the lack of complete air superiority so far but stressed once again that a 'successful landing means victory, but complete air superiority is required to carry it out'.

Despite contrary opinion expressed by the navy (who had lost eighty barges through R.A.F. action the previous night), Hitler decided to postpone Sealion only until September 17th, and the build-up went on with top priority. It is clear that while Hitler hoped for decisive results from the Luftwaffe,

he still put his confidence in a landing if all else failed.

The main German target for the 14th was again London and throughout the morning reconnaissance aircraft probed the weather and the defences, while between Poling and Great Bromley radar stations there was continual electronic interference. One raider was destroyed over Selsey Bill at lunchtime and bombs were dropped at Eastbourne.

Just after 3 p.m. three raids in quick succession crossed the coast at Deal and Dungeness, and headed for London up two corridors, one via Kent and the other up the Thames. No. 11 Group were involved in a series of combats, and requested two 12 Group squadrons to patrol Hornchurch and North Weald, while other 12 Group aircraft shot down a Ju 88 off Lowestoft. In all, 11 Group sent up twenty-two squadrons against these raids, and 12 Group five squadrons.

At 5.15 a feint came in over Bournemouth from Cherbourg, but turned back before being intercepted, and shortly afterwards a flurry of raids appeared on the Bentley Priory tables with 12+, 20+, 30+, 15+ and 10+ between 17,000 and 20,000 feet. From then until nine o'clock a succession of individual attacks were made covering the south-eastern area, and aimed towards London.

The final score of fourteen to each side was poor from the R.A.F.'s point of view, particularly as 860 sorties were flown. Six R.A.F. pilots were, however, saved. Most of the German aircraft sent over were fighters and these lured the squadrons into combat.

To the Luftwaffe the opposition appeared scrappy and un-co-ordinated, and they felt that during the last few days Fighter Command had begun to collapse. This news was, of course, conveyed to the Reichsmarschall, and via the situation reports to Hitler. Both felt that the hour of destiny was approaching.

That night Luftwaffe activity was at a much lower level, while they prepared for a major blow on the following morning. Fifty-five German bombers attacked London whilst others went to Cardiff, Gloucester, Maidstone, Ipswich and Farnham. One naval patrol vessel was attacked by aircraft from Luftflotte 5 off the Firth of Forth.

The unusually low level of attack was noted by Fighter Command, particularly as the

between 1,500 and 2,500 metres'. No. 11 Group were alerted, and sure enough just over an hour and a half later several raids attempted to attack Biggin Hill and the mid-Kent area, while three more, including a few Ju 87s from Luftflotte 3, crossed the coast at Selsey heading for Tangmere. One Heinkel which arrived over Maidstone was promptly shot down by 501 Squadron from Kenley.

At this time a curious report came in from the naval liaison officer to the effect that a long-nosed Blenheim 4, positively identified, had dropped two bombs in Dover harbour. Several Blenheims had been captured on the Continent but there has never been documentary evidence to confirm their use in the Battle of Britain.

weather was fine, and it could only betoken a great effort on the following day.

SEPTEMBER 15

Day Heavy attacks on London, broken up by Fighter Command. Highest German losses since August 18th. Serious rethinking by German High Command.
Night Main target London. Heavy damage.
Weather Fair but cloud patches. Fine evening.

Now celebrated annually as Battle of Britain Day, Sunday the 15th was remarkable for its ultimate change of German policy and not for its heavy losses, as the 185 German aircraft claimed would lead many to believe.

The weather was misty but promised to be fine and the chance had come for a heavy blow against London which would show once and for all the desperate state of Fighter Command, and perhaps have a decisive effect on British morale. It was to be a repeat of Septmber 7th in German eyes, and a lead-in to invasion.

The usual reconnaissance aircraft patrolled the east and south coasts during the morning, one of which, an He 111, was shot down off Start Point.

At eleven o'clock radar showed mass formations building up over Calais and Boulogne. No. 11 Group put up eleven squadrons, 10 Group one, while No. 12 Group sent five squadrons as a wing to patrol Debden–Hornchurch. No real feints developed and complete attention was devoted to the advancing armadas. The stupidity of large formations sorting themselves out in full view of British radar was not yet realised by the Luftwaffe.

All the way up from the coast, the raids stepped up from 15,000–26,000 feet were constantly under attack, first by two Spitfire squadrons over mid-Kent, next by three more over the Medway towns, then by four Hurricane squadrons over the suburbs of London, and finally by the Duxford wing from 12 Group over London itself. The wing on Leigh-Mallory's instructions was now five squadrons strong. In all, twenty-four fighter squadrons operated and twenty-two engaged the enemy.

Accurate bombing was out of the question, and as formations broke so they scattered

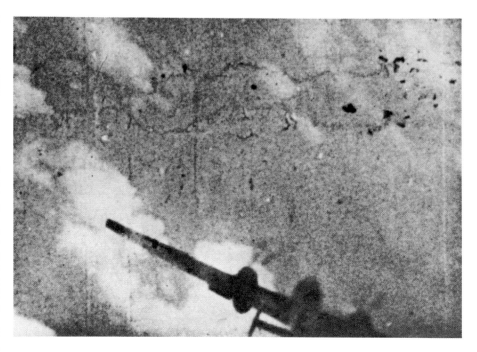

An Me 110 on the point of being shot down over Hastings, Sussex, on the afternoon of September 15th. The camera gun which took the film was mounted on Spitfire R6691 of No. 609 Squadron, piloted by Flt. Lt. F.J. Howell

their loads on Beckenham, Westminster, Lambeth, Lewisham, Battersea, Camberwell, Crystal Palace, Clapham, Tooting, Wandsworth and Kensington. A heavy bomb damaged the Queen's private apartments in Buckingham Palace, while a second fell on the lawn.

The 609 Squadron diarist recorded that one portion of a Dornier they destroyed during the engagement 'is reported to have reached the ground just outside a Pimlico public house to the great comfort and joy of the patrons'.

No. 504 Squadron had a busy morning. At 11 a.m. Generals Strong and Emmons of the U.S. Army Air Corps and Rear-Admiral Gormley of the U.S. Navy paid a visit to see 'the life of a fighter squadron'. No sooner had introductions been completed than an attack developed with the squadron to patrol North Weald at 15,000 feet. Using a stop-watch, the Americans recorded that twelve Hurricanes

got away in 4 min. 50 sec. from the word 'Go'. No. 504 met a formation of Dorniers between Fulham and Gravesend and shot down several. One pilot, Sergeant R.T. Holmes, attacked and damaged a Dornier, and then found another, which he fired at four times. On the fourth occasion the bomber exploded, sending the Hurricane into an uncontrollable spin.

The Dornier crashed in the station yard at Victoria, with the crew landing by parachute on Kennington Oval cricket ground. Sergeant Holmes baled out and finally came to rest in a dustbin in Chelsea.

Before they could eat lunch the squadron was again engaged with German formations between London and Hornchurch.

After a two-hour break the second attack was seen by radar just after 1 p.m. and began to come in in three waves an hour later. Squadrons were ready to receive them and a running fight took place all the way to the capital. Twenty-three squadrons from 11 Group were airborne, five from No. 12 Group and three from No. 10. Two formations were broken up before reaching London, one turning back in the face of a head-on attack by a lone Hurricane flown by Group Captain Vincent, commander of the Northolt sector.

The remaining bombers were engaged over the city itself by five pairs of squadrons from No. 11 Group and the full five-squadron wing of No. 12 Group. Two squadrons each from 10 and 11 Groups harried the enemy as they retired. Scattering of formations and frequent jettisoning of bombs caused hits over a very wide area in contrast to the concentration achieved on September 7th. West Ham and Erith were the main recipients but other targets were Woolwich, Stepney, Hackney, Stratford, Penge and East Ham – at the last mentioned a telephone exchange and a gasholder being smashed.

While every effort was being made to deal with the attack on London, a force of Heinkel 111s of KG55 from the Villacoublay area set out to bomb Portland. Although seen by radar at three o'clock, the count was only given as six+. The raid detoured and approached Portland from an unusual angle which confused the A.A. gunners. The bombing was inaccurate and only slight damage was done in the dockyard. The one squadron left in the Middle Wallop sector succeeded in inter-

cepting, but after the bombs had dropped.

The final daylight sortie came about six o'clock when some twenty bomb-carrying Me 110s from Epr. Gr.210 at Denain attempted to hit the Supermarine works at Woolston. They were heavily engaged by the Southampton guns as they dived in and this undoubtedly upset their aim as no bombs fell on the factory. Five R.A.F. squadrons were put up, but most of them were unable to find their quarry, and those that did only encountered the 110s as they were streaking for the safety of the French coast using any available cloud cover.

During the morning Winston Churchill had been on one of his periodic visits to the 11 Group underground operations room at Uxbridge. From the balcony with Park at his side he watched the raids pouring in. The operations table became saturated with plots, and two by two the squadrons of 11 Group were committed, followed by the 12 Group wing. Finally the tote board showed all squadrons engaged and that nothing was left in reserve. No new raids developed, however, and slowly the bulbs began to glow again as fighters were re-fuelled and re-armed.

Churchill was greatly impressed with the gravity of such a situation and with the calm methodical way in which 11 Group's nerve centre worked. He recorded the incident at length in Volume II of *The Second World War*, although there had been many similar occasions during the Battle which passed unnoticed.

Families throughout the country listened in to the evening news bulletin and heard '185 shot down'. The figures became the sole topic of conversation and the nation glowed with pride. It was a tremendous and much-needed tonic for civilians and R.A.F. alike.

In the cold light of history the actual German losses of sixty machines make poor reading to the layman. In fact, for a force which had suffered a heavy loss rate for over two months they were extremely serious, not to mention the numerous aircraft which limped back to France with dead gunners, burned engines and broken undercarriages.

The bomb aimer of this He 111 can be clearly seen getting ready for the run-up to the target. The aircraft is from KG55, V Fliegerkorps, Luftflotte 3

The 12 Group wing under Bader was not so pleased. It felt that it should have earlier warning in order to get at the enemy with the advantages of height and time. Unfortunately most raids kept climbing after the initial radar plots and split up over the coast making interception more difficult. In addition the links between 11 Group and 12 Group were not properly streamlined and 11 Group sectors dealing with raids could not control 12 Group squadrons.

Hitler and Göring and the whole of the Luftwaffe Command had expected great things of the 15th. After the apparently successful efforts of the 12th it seemed that at long last the R.A.F. was ready for the *coup de grace*. Instead the losses were higher than on any day since August 18th. At de-briefing bomber pilots complained of the incessant R.A.F. attacks by squadrons that had long since ceased to exist – if the German radio and intelligence reports were to be believed.

Naturally, but unfairly, they vented their wrath upon the Jafus and the long-suffering fighter pilots. Instead of being allowed full rein, the fighters were ordered to stick even closer to the bomber formations which further nullified their essential space to manoeuvre and attack.

When the tally book was closed at nightfall on the 15th, Fighter Command had lost twenty-six aircraft and saved thirteen pilots; the balance was swinging sharply in favour of the weary defence.

Before the next day's fighting losses in pilots and aircraft had to be made good. One Polish squadron had only four aircraft serviceable by the evening. The remainder had suffered all sorts of damage; control surfaces shot away, radiators smashed, cables cut and wings riddled with bullets. The mechanics worked until dawn patching and repairing so that on the 16th twelve aircraft were ready for operations.

After dark the Luftwaffe returned to the attack, knowing that it was safer than operating in daylight. Some 180 bombers formed long processions from Le Havre and Dieppe–Cherbourg, all heading for London. Once again the barrage opened up, and more scars were added to the city's face. Shell-Mex House and the Embankment were hit, bombs fell on Woolwich Arsenal, and large fires were started in Camberwell, Battersea and Brixton.

Other smaller raids dropped their loads on Bristol, Cardiff, Liverpool and Manchester.

SEPTEMBER 16

Day Göring confers on losses on the 15th. Policy changes. Park changes tactics. Only slight air activity.
Night Continuous attacks on London. Smaller raids Merseyside and midlands.
Weather General rain and cloud.

Göring called a conference of his Luftflotten and Fliegerkorps commanders in France and decided to return to a policy of attack against Fighter Command itself. It appeared to the Reichsmarschall that the R.A.F. had produced many fresh pilots and aircraft when in reality it was the same force using the new tactics devised by Park.

Bomber formations, Göring outlined, were to be reduced in size, and Gruppen would bomb targets in the London area with maximum fighter escort. 'As many fighters as possible' would be destroyed and he estimated that the R.A.F. fighter force should be finished off in four to five days. Göring was mesmerised by 'four to five days' as this was the time taken in the Polish and French campaigns. He had uttered the self-same words before Adler Tag and nearly five weeks had passed.

His lecture included orders for mass formations only to be used in perfect weather conditions, and for raids to be stepped-up on aircraft production centres. Göring clung to his theory that the Luftwaffe would render Seelöwe unnecessary and went so far as to note that air force operations must not be disturbed by any plans for a landing. For the first time he admitted that air crews were tiring and that for the fighter arm the incessant attacks were 'very exhausting'. Fighter Command pilots were not the only ones weary at this stage.

In England Park took advantage of the lull due to bad weather (rain and cloud-base 300 feet) to issue another instruction, No. 18, to his controllers. Despite the successes of the 15th and the improved loss ratio, he felt that still more interceptions could be made. He listed the faults as he saw them:

Individual squadrons failing to rendezvous.
Single units being detailed to large raids.

Paired squadrons being rendezvoused too far forward, and too low.
High-flying massed formations of German fighters attracting most of the Group while the bombers got through.
Delays in vectoring of paired squadrons on to raids by Group controllers.
Errors in sector reports on pilot and aircraft effective strengths.

To improve the situation he ordered that in clear weather the Hornchurch and Biggin Hill squadrons should attack the high fighter screen in pairs. Rendezvous of pairs was to be made below cloud base in the event of overcast, and at height in clear weather or well in advance of any raids.

Whenever raid information was scanty, fighter squadrons were detailed to short patrol lines, if necessary with two squadrons very high and two squadrons between 15,000 and 20,000 feet.

To deal with high-flying German fighter diversions, Park required several pairs of Spitfire squadrons to be put up while ample Hurricane squadrons were assembled in pairs near sector airfields. The Northolt and Tangmere squadrons were to be despatched as three squadron wings to intercept the second and third waves of attack which experience had shown normally contained bombers.

From this it is quite clear that Park was not averse to using wing formations, where the warning time was sufficient and the type of mass raids required it.

During the 16th the weather precluded any heavy attacks and from the few small raids which penetrated to east London, nine German aircraft were shot down for the loss of one R.A.F. pilot. The dull weather was lightened for both sides by the solemn announcement in the German war communiqué that Göring himself had flown over London in a Ju 88. Apart from lacking the courage for such an enterprise, it was a physical impossibility, as the Reichsmarschall's girth precluded him getting through the door of a Ju 88, and even in the four-motor Condor he had to have a special wide seat with thigh supports.

At night heavy attacks were renewed on London, commencing at 7.40 and going on until 4.30 a.m. Over 200 tons of bombs were dropped by 170 aircraft, while other towns

Bombing up for a raid against the invasion fleet assembled in the Channel ports. This Blenheim IV of No. 110 Squadron is seen here at Wattisham in September 1940. This Squadron carried out the first R.A.F. raid of the war, on September 4th, 1939

hit by harassing raids included Liverpool and Bristol. Some bombs fell on Stanmore, but did no damage to Fighter Command headquarters. One enemy aircraft was claimed by the balloon barrage, but during the night balloons at ten major centres broke away.

SEPTEMBER 17

Day Slight activity. One large fighter sweep in afternoon. Seelöwe postponed until further notice.
Night Heavy attacks on London. Lighter raids on Merseyside and Glasgow.
Weather Squally showers, local thunder, bright intervals. Channel, Straits and Estuary drizzle.

The continued strength of both Fighter and Bomber Commands of the R.A.F. and an adverse weather report for the coming week led Hitler on this day to postpone Operation Seelöwe until further notice and he issued a directive to this effect. A high state of preparedness was, however, to be maintained.

The naval staff war diary recorded that an order from the Führer to carry out Sealion was still to be expected at any time, and that if the air and weather situations permitted, the invasion might be got under way as late as October.

The weather was unsuitable for mass raids on London, and in accordance with Göring's directive of the 16th, Luftflotte 2 sent waves of fighters across, with a few bombers as bait, in the hope of luring 11 Group into an unprofitable battle.

Seven to eight main raids totalling some 250 aircraft built up over France and crossed the coast at Lympne, Dover and Deal at 15,000 feet. Intercepting R.A.F. fighters found that the majority of the formations were Me 109s and the twenty-eight squadrons put up succeeded in turning them back over Maidstone. A few bombs were dropped, and British losses were only five aircraft (one pilot killed and two wounded) out of the 544 sorties flown. Luftwaffe casualties totalled eight aircraft for whole twenty-four hours.

By night the German Air Force returned at full strength with 268 bombers over London arriving in a stream via Dungeness and Selsey Bill. Much residential damage was done. It was the turn of the big department stores with John Lewis's in Oxford Street almost completely burnt out, and both Bourne and Hollingsworth and D.H. Evans hit. By this time 30,000 Londoners had lost their homes.

By way of diversion, a few raiders undertook the long flights to Mersey and to Glasgow. Fighter Command put up thirty-eight single-engined fighter sorties, but they groped in vain, except for a Defiant of 141 Squadron which shot down a Ju 88 near Barking at 11.30.

While the Germans concentrated on London with the A.A. barrage the only opposition, Bomber Command was out in force attacking the barges, transport and munitions being mustered for the invasion. Throughout the Battle and afterwards, in its historical surveys, the Luftwaffe always spoke disparagingly of the R.A.F's offensive efforts from July to October 1940. The German naval staff, however, were under no illusions, as they were at the receiving end.

On this night Bomber and Coastal commands, also taking advantage of the full moon, despatched aircraft to Dunkirk, Calais, Boulogne, Cherbourg and den Helder. The following morning the German naval staff described losses as 'very considerable'. At Dunkirk twenty-six barges were sunk or badly damaged and fifty-eight slightly damaged. A tremendous explosion heralded the detonation of 500 tons of stored ammunition, while a ration depot and dock-handling equipment were destroyed. At the other ports buildings were smashed and a steamer and a torpedo-boat sunk.

A Spitfire of 92 Squadron taxies across a southern airfield during the Battle.

SEPTEMBER 18

Day Oil targets in Thames Estuary attacked.
Night London and Merseyside raided.
Weather Bright and squally.

At 9 a.m. the first blips appeared on Fighter Command radar screens. They showed a heavy build-up over Calais. The raiders, mainly fighters, penetrated between North Foreland and Folkestone at 20,000 feet. They were split up over Maidstone and the Estuary and turned for home after running engagements with seventeen R.A.F. squadrons. One was shot down by anti-aircraft fire.

Two hours later radar betrayed four raids totalling 190 planes. They crossed the coast at Deal and attacked Chatham. At least sixty reached the centre of London. The rest roamed over Kent.

At 2 p.m. Luftflotte 2 began to assemble 150 aircraft over Calais. As they climbed to 20,000 feet the Germans sorted themselves into neat formations and set course for Gravesend.

Breaking cloud over Kent the Germans were met in force, and although some of them penetrated the defences, the majority of formations were broken up and repelled.

Flying up the Thames, later, two groups of between twenty and thirty bombers were heading for London when Spitfires and Hurricanes of the Duxford wing attacked them. The wing had taken off at 4.20 p.m. and was patrolling Hornchurch when A.A. fire betrayed the presence of the enemy groups.

Leaving No. 611 Squadron on patrol and No. 19 Squadron to look after the escorts, Bader led his three Hurricane squadrons into an almost vertical diving attack on the first formation. The Germans scattered, leaving only four vics of five aircraft. These were soon broken up and the bombers turned for home.

Sergeant Plzak, a Czech pilot with No. 19 Squadron, fired a couple of bursts at an He 111 and stopped both its engines. The crew baled out and the bomber crashed near Gillingham, Kent.

The Duxford Wing claimed thirty destroyed, six probables and two damaged in the engagement. They lost none. But when the score came to be verified against the German Quartermaster General's records, it was found that only nineteen Luftwaffe machines

had actually been shot down during the whole day.

Twelve British fighters went down in the fighting of the 18th, but only three of the pilots were killed, during 1,165 sorties.

No. 7 O.T.U. scored a third victory that day. Squadron Leader McLean, Flying Officer Brotchie and Sergeant Armitage took off from Hawarden, Chesire, and intercepted a raid flying towards Liverpool. They damaged one Do 17 and shot down another which dived into the sea off the Welsh coast.

Dowding's efforts to remedy the chronic shortage of fighter pilots bore further fruit on the 18th when the Air Ministry agreed to another combing of the Fairey Battle squadrons for Fighter Command's benefit. They also agreed to allot to the Command more than two-thirds of the entire output of the flying training schools in the four-week period during the middle of October.

On September 7th 984 Hurricane and Spitfire pilots were flying with the squadrons – a deficiency of nearly twenty-two pilots per squadron, and of these 150 were only semi-trained.

On the other side of the Channel German preparations for the invasion were reaching their peak. On the 15th 102 barges were photographed by reconnaissance aircraft in Boulogne. On the 17th there were 150. Calais harbour contained 266. By the 18th the Channel ports held 1,004 invasion craft and a further 600 waited up-river at Antwerp.

From September 7th Blenheims pressed home their attacks by day whenever the weather permitted and Wellingtons, Whitleys, Hampdens and Battles operated at night. Operating under Coastal Command, Fleet Air Arm Swordfish and Albacores also took part.

During September 60 per cent of the bombing was directed at the invasion ports on which 1,400 tons of bombs were dropped. The remaining effort was concentrated against rail communications, shipyards and oil targets in Germany and occupied Europe.

Night bombing on Britain started on September 18th at 7.30 p.m. and the flow of raids lasted until 5.30 a.m. the following morning. London and Liverpool were the principal targets. Bombs were also scattered over Kent and Surrey and in Middlesex 120 parachute mines fell near Stanmore.

SEPTEMBER 19

Day Reduced activity, attacks chiefly over Thames Estuary and east London.
Night London and Merseyside.
Weather Showery.

Piccadilly, Regent Street, Bond Street, North Audley Street, Park Lane and many less famous thoroughfares in the centre of London were blocked after the night's raids. Big cranes surrounded Marble Arch and men of the Civil Defence Corps, Pioneers and Police worked to clear the rubble and rescue the victims trapped in the wreckage.

A lull was expected after the intensity of the previous day's operations. Only seventy hostile planes, flying singly, crossed the coast via Dungeness. A few reached Liverpool and London where a lone roof-top raider machine-gunned Hackney.

Near Bury St. Edmunds, Suffolk, a Ju 88 fell to the guns of No. 302 Squadron. Engine failure compelled another to land intact at Oakington airfield near Cambridge. Losses for the day were eight German and no British.

Rain in the night interfered with German plans, but they managed to despatch 200 aircraft to mine coastal waters. A few went for the Home Counties and London. At Heston aerodrome a parachute mine wrecked or damaged thirteen planes, including five Photographic Reconnaissance Unit Spitfires, a Lockheed 12A and a visiting Wellington bomber. Liverpool sirens sounded for six raids plotted approaching from the Irish Sea.

In Germany, Hitler formally ordered the assembly of the invasion fleet to be stopped, and shipping in the Channel ports to be dispersed 'so that the loss of shipping space caused by enemy air attacks may be reduced to a minimum'.

SEPTEMBER 20

Day One large fighter sweep towards London: otherwise reconnaissance only.
Night London.
Weather Fair with bright periods. Showery.

There were few early-morning raids but at 10.30 a.m. the Luftwaffe started massing at Calais. Then twenty planes crossed the coast at Dungeness at 13,000 feet, thirty overflew

Dover, at 12,000 feet, and a dozen or more passed over Lympne. The R.A.F. lost seven planes near Kenley, Biggin Hill and the Estuary, and the Germans lost eight.

At night the waning moon was still bright enough to help the Germans but they chose to curtail their activities which were mainly directed against London.

Reporting on his trip to Britain, in New York, Brigadier Strong, Assistant Chief of the U.S. Military Mission sent to London to observe the results of the Luftwaffe's attacks, did much to influence American opinion. The German Air Force, he said, had made no serious inroad on the strength of the R.A.F. and the damage inflicted on military targets was comparatively small. Strong concluded by stating that the British were conservative in claiming German aircraft casualties.

SEPTEMBER 21

Day Slight activity; some fighter sweeps in east Kent.
Night London and Merseyside attacked.
Weather Mainly fine.

London, cloaked in haze, enjoyed a relatively quiet day, as did the rest of the country except for isolated attacks and extensive reconnaissance in coastal areas.

Among the lone raiders was a Ju 88 which bombed the Hawker works at Brooklands in a low-level attack. Production was not affected.

When an unidentified aircraft was plotted at 4.30 p.m. 25,000 feet over Liverpool, Pilot Officer D.A. Adams of No. 611 Squadron was ordered to investigate. He found a German bomber and sent it crashing into a field near Dolgelly, North Wales.

The bulk of Fighter Command's 563 sorties were flown in the evening when five raids crossed the coast at Dover, Lympne and Dungeness to assail Kenley, Biggin Hill, Hornchurch and central London. Twenty No. 11 Group squadrons, the Duxford Wing and one No. 10 Group squadron scrambled to intercept but only one of them engaged. The German casualties numbered nine while the R.A.F. suffered no loss.

Scattered cloud and moonlight made the night perfect for the raiding, but the Germans chose to exert no more than moderate pressure on London, Liverpool, Warrington, Nottingham, Bolton and Colchester.

Ein Angriff und seine Wirkung

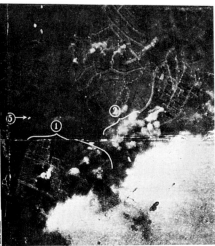

Unsere Aufnahmen haben das große Flugzeugwerk von Filton zum Gegenstand. Das Bild links ist wenige Tage vor dem Angriff aufgenommen, der das Werk vernichtet hat. Deutlich erkennbar sind neben der Bahnlinie die riesigen Werkhallen, deren Tarnbemalung gegen Fliegersicht schützen soll. Das Luftbild beweist aber, daß der Anstrich der Dächer allein nicht genügt. Die Hallen sind vollkommen klar zu erkennen. Das Bild oben ist während des ersten Bombenangriffs aufgenommen. Das Hauptwerk ist in der linken unteren Ecke zu erkennen. Mitten im Werk schlagen Bomben ein. Das etwas kleinere Zweigwerk oberhalb der quer durch das Bild laufenden Bahn ist von Bombensalven vollkommen eingedeckt. Die weißen Stellen in der rechten unteren Ecke des oberen Bildes sind Wolken, die sich zwischen die Erde und die Kampfflugzeuge geschoben haben. Das obere Bild läßt mit aller nur wünschenswerten Deutlichkeit erkennen, daß da unten, im Flugzeugwerk von Filton, die Hölle ist. Einschlag neben Einschlag prasselt in die großen Hallen. Dieses Werk wird nicht mehr viel Flugzeuge herstellen. Die Zahlen bedeuten (1) das Hauptwerk, (2) das Nebenwerk, (3) sieben aufgestellte Flugzeuge, (4) drei Flugzeuge am Boden, (5) Sperrballone am Boden, (6) die Startbahn, die mitten durch den Flugplatz führt
Aufnahmen Luftwaffe

SEPTEMBER 22

Day Slight activity.
Night London bombed.
Weather Dull with fog in morning. Cloudy in afternoon, fair to fine late. Some rain.

Twelve single raiders flying high over London and the noise of No. 234 Squadron's Browning guns shooting down a lone Ju 88 scarcely disturbed this Sunday's congregations. Even the sound of Merlin engines was strangely absent, for the squadrons flew only 158 sorties – the smallest number since the Battle began. German loses were five machines while the R.A.F. lost none.

By midnight the situation had changed; London in the words of Lord Alanbrooke, was like Dante's Inferno. Twelve night fighters – Blenheims and Defiants – tried to intercept, but though the Luftwaffe gave them a selection of 123 bombers to shoot at no victories were recorded.

Nazi bombers were still over the capital in

'An Air Raid and its Results' – the German caption to photographs showing the raid on the Bristol Aeroplane Company, Filton, when production was severely curtailed.

'Our photographs show the large aircraft factories at Filton. The picture on the left was taken a few days before the raid which destroyed the factory.

Easily recognised, close to the railway, are the huge workshops, whose camouflage was intended as protection against aerial observation.

The aerial photograph, however, proves that the paint on the roofs alone is not enough. The workshops are clearly recognisable.

The upper picture was taken during the first bombing attack. The main works can be recognised in the left-hand lower corner. Bombs are seen exploding in the middle of the works. The somewhat smaller branch factory above the railway which crosses the picture is completely covered by salvoes of bombs.

The white patches in the right-hand lower corner of the upper picture are clouds which have drifted between the ground and the bombing planes. The upper picture enables one to recognise with all desirable clarity that hell has been let loose on the Filton works below. Blow after blow rains on the great shops. This factory will not produce many more aircraft.

The numbers indicate: 1. The main works. 2. Adjoining works. 3. Seven aircraft parked in line. 4. Three aircraft on the ground. 5. Barrage balloons on the ground. 6. The main runway crossing the middle of the aerodrome'

the early hours. Others mixed with Bomber Command streams returning from Germany and sneaked through the defences to attack airfields in Lincolnshire, including Digby, where they set fire to a hangar.

SEPTEMBER 23

Day Fighter sweeps towards London.
Night London and Merseyside.
Weather Fine.

At 9 a.m. a build-up of nearly 200 planes was detected over Calais. Chiefly Me 109s, they came over in four large and two small waves fanned out beyond Dover. Twenty-four squadrons were up to cut them off and ten intercepted. A further force of 109s came in at 7 p.m.

Between 5 and 6 p.m. Uxbridge despatched twelve squadrons in four wings to counter five waves of Messerschmitts intruding through South Foreland, Dover and Hythe. The sweep lasted forty-five minutes but the attackers were elusive.

Eleven British aircraft and three pilots were lost in the day's engagements. Eight of the pilots were wounded. German losses were sixteen.

With London under heavy bombardment

the Cabinet were determined to retaliate and they ordered the indiscriminate bombing of Berlin with parachute mines. Nothing could have been less in keeping with Air Staff thinking, which contrasted the effect of four bombs on Fulham power station with several thousand bombs which fell elsewhere.

The dispute ended in compromise. The Air Staff agreed to include Berlin in their forthcoming directives on the understanding that only targets of specific military value were to be bombed. The directive was issued on September 21st and on the night of 23rd 119 Whitleys, Wellingtons and Hampdens took off for the German capital.

In contrast 261 German planes turned London into another inferno and damage was widespread.

SEPTEMBER 24

Day Tilbury and Southampton raided.
Night London and Merseyside attacked.
Weather Early-morning fog in northern France. Channel cloudy, haze in the Straits and Thames Estuary.

British service chiefs, unaware that Seelöwe had been postponed on September 17th, continued to await the invasion. Equinoctial gales which had swept the Channel earlier in

Two Focke Wulf FW 200C-1s of KG40.

the week had now died down and the sea was quieter. By 8.30 a.m. the only sign of enemy activity was in the air where some 200 aircraft, mainly bombers, crossed the coast on a ten-mile front in five formations ranging from three to fifty planes in size.

Flying between 10,000 and 25,000 feet the Germans tried to get through to London, but were repulsed. Three hours later another 200 assembled into five formations over Cap Gris Nez and headed north. Of the eighteen British squadrons sent up to intercept them only two engaged.

Soon after lunch between fifteen and twenty Me 109 fighter-bombers came up the Solent in two waves. Diving singly, they attacked the Supermarine works at Woolston near Southampton. They did little damage to the factory itself but hit a shelter and killed nearly 100 of the staff.

The Messerschmitts then turned over Portsmouth and for twenty minutes trailed their coats. Not a British fighter was to be seen but the A.A. guns blazed away and shot down one German aircraft, making eleven for the day. This brought German losses since September 19th to fifty-nine. In the same period twenty-two British fighters were destroyed of which four were lost on the 24th.

From early evening until 5.30 the following morning there was widespread bombing over the whole country.

SEPTEMBER 25

Day Bristol and Plymouth bombed.
Night London, North Wales and Lancashire attacked.
Weather Fair to fine in most districts. Cool. Channel cloudy with bright intervals; hazy.

Apart from the usual reconnaissance flights and the detection of intense activity over France at 8.20 a.m., the morning was quiet. At 11.20 a large raid crossed the coast.

Fighter-bombers made diversionary attacks on Portland while some sixty Heinkel 111s comprising the three Gruppen of KG55 slipped through the defences with Me 110s of ZG26 and reached Bristol at 11.45. They attacked the Bristol Aeroplane Company's works at Filton with ninety tons of high-explosive and twenty-four oil-bombs.

Production was curtailed for many weeks. The bombing killed or injured more than 250, blocked railways near the factory and cut communications between Filton airfield and No. 10 Group Headquarters. Eight out of fifty completed bombers were badly damaged.

Three No. 10 Group squadrons and a flight of Hurricanes were scrambled in time to meet the attackers. But they were vectored to Yeovil where the Westland aircraft works seemed the more likely target. When the actual objective became known the three squadrons swung into pursuit but only a few of the aircraft caught up with the Germans before they reached Filton. Five of the enemy were shot down, one of them by AA fire.

Although Filton was acting as a temporary sector station, Nos. 87 and 213 Squadrons allocated to it were operating from Exeter and Bibury. To guard against further attacks Dowding immediately ordered No. 504 (County of Nottingham) Squadron to move to Filton from Hendon.

No. 601 Squadron engaged twelve bombers and twelve Me 110s at Start Point near Plymouth at 4.30 p.m. At the same time No. 74 Squadron, operating from Duxford, joined Nos. 611 and 19 squadrons to intercept a raid coming in over London at 20,000 feet.

By dusk Fighter Command had flown 668 sorties. The score was four British to thirteen German planes destroyed.

On the night of the 25th the highest number of people sheltering in tube stations was recorded. A Home Security operations room weekly report on this day records:

> The German attack upon London has had no fundamental ill effect either upon the capital or on the nation. Its first impact caused bewilderment and there was some ill-temper . . .
> This loss of temper . . . has almost completely vanished and a general equanimity prevails . . . Nothing has affected the unconquerable optimism of the Cockney nor has anything restricted his ready if graveyard humour . . . Without over emphasis people take the obvious precautions to ensure sufficient sleep. Having done so they regard the event philosophically. During the day they continue their ordinary business . . . It is still necessary to canvas some classes of the people to leave London.

SEPTEMBER 26

Day Supermarine works at Southampton attacked and wrecked.
Night London and Merseyside.
Weather Mainly fair to cloudy in the south.

It was obvious to the Germans as they studied reconnaissance photographs of Southampton that Supermarine's Woolston factory remained intact.

In the afternoon seventy-six planes – He 111's, Ju 88s and Me 109s – assembled over Brittany and set course for the Solent. By 5.45 they had delivered a 'pattern bombing' attack on the home of the Spitfire. It was all over in a few minutes with seventy tons of bombs dropped to such good purpose that for a short time production was completely stopped. In addition more than thirty people were killed and a nearby warehouse filled with grain was destroyed.

Engaged on the way in by anti-aircraft fire only, the attackers were intercepted after the bombing by four No. 10 and No. 11 Group squadrons. One of these was No. 303 (Polish)

Right: A sad task, pulling furniture and belongings from wrecked houses after night raids on north London on September 26th/27th

The Spitfire factory at Woolston, Southampton, after the raid on September 26th. The factory was wrecked but, by dispersal to thirty-five sites and expansion at the Castle Bromwich factory, the flow of aircraft to the R.A.F. was maintained. The Luftwaffe would have done better to concentrate on this vital production centre earlier in the battle

Squadron which had left Northolt in the middle of an inspection by the King. Three German aircraft were shot down. The R.A.F. lost six. The day's engagements cost both air forces nine planes each, the R.A.F. flying 417 sorties.

Only three Spitfires on the Woolston production line were destroyed. Many others were damaged by the blast and debris but they were soon repaired and delivered to the squadrons.

In August 149 Spitfires had been produced, mostly at Woolston, as the shadow factory at Castle Bromwich was only just coming into production. In October 139 Spitfires were built. The Southampton facilities were dispersed to thirty-five sites and by the end of the year production was back to normal.

SEPTEMBER 27

Day Heavy attacks on London and one on Bristol.
Night London, Merseyside and the midlands.
Weather Fair in extreme south and south-west. Cloudy in the Channel with haze. Slight rain in southern England.

The first sign of German activity appeared on the operations table at No. 11 Group as the 8 a.m. watch took over.

The planes were bomb-carrying Me 110s escorted by Me 109s. Harried by fighters from Dungeness to the outskirts of London they scattered their bombs indiscriminately.

Some Me 109s stuck tenaciously to the London area. They had orders to protect two succeeding formations of Do 17s and Ju 88s, but the bombers did not make the rendezvous. 11 Group was ready for them and they were intercepted over the coast by a powerful assembly of Spitfires and Hurricanes which broke up the tidy German formations and compelled them to jettison their bombs.

Badly mauled, the Messerschmitt pilots over London were obliged to split up and dive for the safety of a ground-level retreat.

Having failed to clear the skies by sending fighters ahead of the bombers in the first assault, the Germans reverted at 11.30 to a split raid, sending eighty aircraft to Bristol and 300 to London.

No. 10 Group squadrons fought the Bristol raiders across the West Country and only ten Me 110s and some 109s managed to get through. These were intercepted on the outskirts of Bristol by the Nottingham squadron, which compelled them to release their bombs unprofitably on the suburbs. The survivors were harried all the way back to the coast and out to sea.

The majority of the London raiders got no further than the middle of Kent where they were so severely mauled that they retreated in confusion. Some reached the outskirts of the city and twenty slipped through to the centre.

With fifty-five German aircraft missing (including twenty-one bombers) the Channel was alive with air-sea rescue planes and boats in the evening. Most of the twenty-eight British planes lost came down on land.

SEPTEMBER 28

Day London and the Solent area attacked.
Night The target London.
Weather Fair to fine generally. Channel, Straits of Dover and Thames Estuary cloudy. Wind moderate.

Delighted by the results of the 27th, Churchill was moved to send the Secretary of State this message: 'Pray congratulate the Fighter Command on the results of yesterday. The scale and intensity of the fighting and the heavy losses of the enemy ... make 27th September rank with 15th September and 15th August, as the third great and victorious day of the Fighter Command during the course of the Battle of Britain.'

By that evening, however, sixteen fighters and nine pilots had been lost resisting two major raids on London and one on Portsmouth.

This, coupled with the fact that only three German planes were shot down, was an indication that the British pilots were exhausted by the intensity of the demands made on them.

The Luftwaffe's losses for the day in fact totalled ten machines. Seven of them were destroyed accidentally.

Another important factor to be found in these results lay in the composition of the German formations. As a result of their losses – accentuated on the 27th – the Germans were forced to admit their large bomber formations were not paying big enough dividends to justify the heavy losses they

had incurred. New tactics were accordingly ordered, involving smaller bomber formations consisting of thirty of the faster Ju 88s, escorted by 200 to 300 fighters.

Evidence of this change in tactics did not become apparent until midday when several large formations of Me 109s appeared between Deal and Dungeness escorting some thirty bombers. The raiders were driven off before they reached central London, but not without difficulty for the British, who were placed at a disadvantage by the heights at which the German escorts were flying.

All No. 11 Group squadrons were involved, as well as five squadrons from No. 12 Group.

At 2.45 p.m. fifty Me 110s were intercepted en route for Portsmouth and driven back by squadrons of No. 10 Group assisted by five No. 11 Group units diverted to help.

From 5 p.m. until nightfall the Germans concentrated on reconnaissance. At 9 p.m. they began night operations which were centred on London.

SEPTEMBER 29

Day Reduced activity in south-east and East Anglia.
Night London and Merseyside attacked.
Weather Fine and fair early. Fair late. Cloudy for rest of the day.

The Germans, after a morning harassing convoys, struck out with several high-flying formations. Nine of their aircraft failed to return home and that night Weybridge A.A. gunners added a bomber to the score. Five British fighters were destroyed.

SEPTEMBER 30

Day Fighter sweeps towards London but few bombs dropped.
Night London attacked.
Weather Generally fair but cloudy. Winds light.

An hour separated the first two major raids which began at 9 a.m. In the first there were thirty bombers and 100 fighters; in the second sixty planes.

Crossing the coast at Dungeness the two raids were met in force. Split and harried, neither reached London.

At 10.50 a.m. radar warned of another attack – this time approaching Dorset from Cherbourg. The planes were Me 110 fighter-bombers escorted by 109s. They were so severely handled by the R.A.F. that they turned back before reaching the coast.

Midday came and with it a fierce battle over Kent. Then at 3.10 p.m. a series of minor sorties was followed by a major raid of more than 100 planes. Thirty reached London. Within fifty minutes 180 more bombers and fighters were plotted approaching Weybridge and Slough on a front of eight miles.

One hundred miles west, forty escorted Heinkel bombers crossed the coast heading for the Westland works at Yeovil. Cloud obscured the target and the Germans were obliged to bomb blind. Sherborne, some miles from Yeovil, took the full impact of the attack.

The Germans had to fight their way in against four British squadrons and they were beset by another four on the way out. Four Hurricanes fell to their gunners and an Me 110 shot down another.

Two of the British pilots baled out and the third, Wing Commander Constable-Maxwell, shot down by a single bullet puncturing the oil system of his aircraft, force-landed his Hurricane on a beach.

By dusk the last great daylight battle was over and the score was forty-seven German aircraft destroyed for a loss of twenty R.A.F. fighters and eight pilots killed or wounded.

Just as the Stuka had been withdrawn from the battle so now were the twin-engined bombers to be relegated to the night offensive – except for those rare occasions when they could use the clouds to cover their sorties over Britain.

And as if to mark the occasion the King appointed Dowding Knight Grand Commander of the Bath.

At night there were heavy raids on London, East Anglia, Liverpool and Bristol. The attack was mounted mainly by Luftflotte 2 whose 250 aircraft penetrated between Beachy Head and the Isle of Wight.

Attempting to reach London 175 of the raiders met with heavy anti-aircraft fire and stalking night fighters. A few broke through to bomb Acton and Westminster, but most of them were content to release their loads on the suburbs.

FIFTH PHASE

OCTOBER 1 – 31

Three months less ten days had now elapsed since the start of the Battle of Britain, but for all the German effort there was little to set against the loss of 1,653 aircraft. Germany had not established the superiority she needed in the air. To avoid further bomber losses, Göring resorted to the use of fighter-bombers operating at high altitude.

These tactics were difficult to counter because of the height at which the German fighters flew. Above 25,000 feet the Me 109 with a two-stage supercharger had a better performance than even the Mk. II Hurricanes and Spitfires then coming into service. Moreover, raids approaching 20,000 feet or more had a good chance of minimising the effect of radar observations and were difficult for the Observer Corps to track, especially when there were clouds about. Thirdly, the speed at which the formations, unencumbered by long-range bombers, flew was so great that at best the radar chain could not give much more than twenty minutes warning before they released their bombs. Fourthly, Park and his controllers had no way of telling which of the several approaching formations contained bomb-carrying aircraft and should therefore be given preference.

Left: By day and night the attack went on with Luftflotte 3 being concentrated on British cities during the hours of darkness. Here a Heinkel 111 on a French airfield prepared for take-off for a British target

A step towards the solution of the second and third problems was taken at the end of September when No. 421 Flight (later No. 91 Squadron) was formed to spot approaching formations and report their height and strength to Uxbridge by R/T. Although told to fly high and avoid combat, pilots so employed were sometimes at a disadvantage. After four had been shot down in the first ten days of October they began to work in pairs, a practice generally adopted later. But in any case their efforts were not sufficient to answer the problem of intercepting raiders which flew too high for detection by the radar chain.

Compared with its efficiency as an instrument of defence in daylight Fighter Command was woefully weak at night. The R.D.F. chain still only covered the coastal areas and inland there were only a handful of gun-laying radars, sound locators and the Observer Corps. In the darkness of this cloudy autumn the Observer Corps' binoculars were, so to speak, *hors de combat*.

Six Blenheim and two Defiant squadrons strengthened by a flight of Hurricanes were available for night fighting in October 1940, but none of the aircraft was designed or equipped for the purpose. The planes were gradually being fitted with Air Interception radar which at that time was no more than promising.

Between September and November, therefore, the number of interceptions was disappointingly few. Improved equipment, including the Bristol Beaufighter specially suited to night operations, was coming into service, but local ground-control radar was needed to put the planes within operating limits of A.I. It was to be some time before these local ground-control radar stations were installed.

It was not until 1941 that the night-fighter squadrons began to have telling effects on the Luftwaffe.

In the meantime some of the more experienced Hurricane and Spitfire pilots attempted to convert themselves to night fighting without being trained for the job or even having the basic essentials for approach and landing at their airfields. It is doubtful whether the risks they took in bad weather justified their courageous efforts, for they had little success, even on bright moonlit nights.

The Germans therefore had little opposition to contend with. What there was of it came from the anti-aircraft defences. But even this was ineffective owing to the inadequacy of the sound locators and the lack of gun-laying radar sets.

There is evidence to show, however, that

A crippled Me 109E, one undercarriage leg hanging down, descending into the sea off Folkestone Harbour in October. The Spitfire that shot it down circles above. An army officer jumped off the jetty and rescued the German pilot

the anti-aircraft guns did force the Germans to fly higher and some of the half-hearted crews to turn back. For the Londoners at least the guns were comforting.

Searchlights were even more limited than guns. They could not penetrate cloud or hold a bomber in their beams long enough to help the artillery or the night fighters, and by flying above 12,000 feet the bombers escaped their pointing fingers altogether.

OCTOBER 1

Day London raids, Southampton and Portsmouth also targets.
Night London, Liverpool, Manchester main targets.
Weather Mainly fair but generally cloudy.

German patrols began to appear between Beachy Head and Southwold from about seven in the morning. They gave no trouble but at 10.45 a force of 100 aircraft operating from Caen attempted to bomb Southampton and Portsmouth. They met stiff opposition.

There was a marked difference in the composition of this raid. The machines were mostly Me 109s and Me 110s, some of them carrying bombs. The Germans were beginning to reserve their bombers for night operations and place the whole burden for the daylight offensive on the fighter arm which had converted one staffel of each gruppe or one gruppe of each geschwader to fighter-bomber duties.

A third of the German fighters – 250 aircraft – were so converted, Me 109s to carry a 250 kg. bomb and Me 110s a total bomb-load of 700 kg.

Flying at great height and taking every advantage of the cloudy weather, these aircraft set Fighter Command new and difficult problems and imposed many fruitless hours of climb and chase upon the British pilots. But they did little else and Fighter Command continued the recovery which had started on September 7th.

From 1 to 3 p.m. a steady stream of aircraft

Pilots of No. 303 (Polish) Squadron at Northolt in October 1940. Second from the left is Flight Lieutenant (later Group Captain) J.A. Kent commanding A flight. In the background is his Hurricane which bears the 'Kosciuszko' crest just below the aerial on the fuselage. A flight carried on the traditions of the Polish 111 Kosciuszko squadron while B flight did the same for 112 Salamander squadron.

The crest includes a Polish hat and thirteen stars and stripes for the original States of the U.S.A. Kosciuszko had been Washington's adjutant in the War of Independence and subsequently became Dictator of Poland. Thus it was that the Stars and Stripes flew to war in the skies over Britain long before December 7th, 1941

crossed the coast between Deal and Selsey Bill. The first three waves, consisting of fifty Me 109s, reached Maidstone before 2 p.m.

Forty minutes later about seventy-five planes flew in from Calais and split some thirty miles inland. The raiders were intercepted and retired towards Maidstone but bombs landed at Brixton, Wandsworth, Camberwell and Lambeth.

The third attack was a half-hearted effort to penetrate over Dungeness; the Germans turned back before the R.A.F. could reach them.

Hit by British anti-aircraft fire, this Heinkel 111 of KG55 force-landed in Holland in October

In the north three raids were plotted over Aberdeenshire and three in the Moray Firth. One of these, a single aircraft, was seen returning to Brittany across Wales and Devon.

At 5 p.m. more than fifty aircraft assembled over Cap Griz Nez at 20,000 feet. No sooner had they crossed the coast than Luftflotte 2 massed for a follow-through with another thirty to fifty Me 109s and Me 110s. For each attack the R.A.F. were up in force.

Night raiders started coming in just after 7.30 p.m. mainly over the Isle of Wight, Beachy Head and Dungeness, 175 of them weaving and turning in the general direction of London. Liverpool and Manchester were

visited by a further twenty-five, while Glasgow and Swansea had two raiders each. Bombs dropped on the Mersey side of Manchester and on Grantham. In the course of 723 sorties during the day the R.A.F. lost four aircraft. Luftwaffe casualties were six machines.

A variety of weapons was tried out at this period against enemy bombers. One device was an airborne adaptation of the rocket-fired parachute and cable which was supposed to form a barrier to German bombers. Known as 'Mutton', this weapon consisted of a parachute with a bomb dangling at the end of 2,000 feet of piano wire.

On the morning of October 3rd a Junkers 88 of Stab 1./KG77 took off from Laon to attack Reading. Bad visibility led the aircraft astray and, by accident, Hatfield appeared. At about 60 feet the Ju 88 made two runs hitting the sheet metal shop and the technical school building, killing 21 and wounding 70. Hit by A.A. guns and small arms fire the aircraft crashed, on fire, at Hertingfordbury. The top photograph shows the damage at Hatfield while the bottom one is of the burned-out Ju 88

The idea was to launch these in the path of an approaching enemy formation. The bomb would be brought up to explode near the aircraft – at least in theory.

No. 420 Flight was formed to use the equipment and on October 1st Flight Lieutenant Burke, the commanding officer, collected the first Harrow bomber equipped to use it from the Royal Aircraft Establishment, Farnborough.

Although several 'Mutton' sorties were flown it was difficult in practice to make effective use of the weapon.

OCTOBER 2

Day High-flying and fighter sweeps on south-east London and Biggin Hill.
Night London main target. Manchester, Usworth and Aberdeen also attacked.
Weather Brilliant blue skies during the day, turning to cloudy later.

The first warning came through at 8.30 a.m. when aircraft of Luftflotte 2 began to mass over Cap Gris Nez. Climbing to between 20,000 and 30,000 feet the German machines attacked Biggin Hill and south-east London from 9 a.m. until lunch-time. Seventeen formations, ranging from one aircraft to more than fifty, penetrated inland in a continuous

stream. They were back in smaller numbers during the afternoon, a few of them penetrating as far as the centre of London. Eight of the day's raiders fell in combat to some of the 154 patrols sent up by Fighter Command. Altogether seventeen German aircraft were lost against only one British fighter.

Between 7.15 p.m. and 6.15 the next morning 180 bombers came over. More than 100 attacked London, dropping bombs on Willesden, Woolwich, Fenchurch Street, Rotherhithe, Stanmore and the districts near airfields like Northolt, Kenley, Walton, Hendon, Brooklands, Redhill, Eastchurch, Hornchurch and Duxford. Manchester, Usworth and Aberdeen were also hit. Thirty-three night fighters were scrambled during the night but they were unable to intercept.

OCTOBER 3

Day Scattered raids on East Anglian and southern England targets.
Night London and suburbs attacked.
Weather Rain and drizzle in the Channel. Visibility in England reduced to 500 yards.

Routine patrols and reconnaissance flights off the east coast opened the action for the day. Later raiders coming singly or in pairs, mostly from Belgian and Dutch bases, attacked

targets over a widespread area. These included Thameshaven, Cosford, Cambridge, Cardington, Bedford, Leamington, Worcester, Reading, Harrow and Tangmere. The weather was too bad to intercept successfully, or to protect a convoy in the Channel at 5.20 p.m.

One raider, however, reached the de Havilland works at Hatfield. At 50 feet altitude a Ju 88 of KG77 machine-gunned workers as they ran for the trenches and bounced four bombs into a sheet metal shop and the Technical School – killing 21 people and wounding 70. The 88 was hit by 40 mm. Bofors shells, .303 machine-gun bullets from an R.A.F. detachment and even rounds from a Hotchkiss manned by the Home Guard. The burning aircraft crashed at Hertingfordbury.

Low cloud during the night hampered the Luftwaffe but not enough to prevent sixty bombers getting through, for the most part singly, at 10,000 feet and penetrating the inner artillery zone. Bombs were dropped mainly in the suburbs, and at Feltham, Middlesex, the General Aircraft Company was hit. No R.A.F. aircraft were lost during 173 sorties but the Luftwaffe lost nine.

A Heinkel 111 of 1./KG53 taxies out through a wheatfield in northern France. The dorsal gunner was obviously expecting the worst as he was wearing a steel helmet!

Leader of the 'Big wing' protagonists, Sqn Ldr Douglas Bader is shown fourth from the right with some of his pilots from 242 Sqn on October 4th. Under the cockpit is his rank pennant while just visible on the nose is his personal motif, showing a boot kicking a figure of Hitler. The top picture shows Bader leading the squadron from their base at Coltishall, Norfolk.

OCTOBER 4

Day Single raiders in stream on London and south-east.
Night London again main target, with Liverpool as subsidiary target.
Weather Mist, rain and poor visibility throughout the day. Fog at night.

Seelöwe was still very much in Hitler's mind, but he was reluctant to come to a decision despite Army and Navy recommendations to call it off altogether. Holding troops on the Channel coast 'under constant British air attack', they pointed out, 'led to continual casualties'.

Remarked the Italian Foreign Minister, Count Galeazzi Ciano, in his diary, after the Hitler–Mussolini meeting at the Brenner Pass on October 4th, 'there is no longer any talk about a landing in the British Isles'.

After two attacks on convoys at 9 a.m. German fighters and fighter-bombers flying singly for the most part headed for London in an almost continuous stream. Altogether sixty to seventy crossed the coast, and at 1 p.m. twelve penetrated the inner artillery zone to drop bombs on London. Canterbury, Folkestone, Hythe and Reigate were also hit. Later in the afternoon R.A.F. fighters made interceptions and brought down two Ju 88s, making a total of twelve for the day against three British machines lost.

To counteract the Luftwaffe's latest tactics Park issued new instructions:

HEIGHT OF FIGHTER PATROLS

1.   With the prevailing cloudy skies and inaccurate heights given by the R.D.F. the group controllers' most difficult problem is to know the height of incoming enemy raids. Occasionally reconnaissance Spitfires from Hornchurch or Biggin Hill are able to sight and report the height and other particulars of enemy formations. Moreover the special fighter reconnaissance flight is now being formed at Gravesend (attached 66 Squadron) for the purpose of getting information about approaching enemy raids.

2.   Because of the above-mentioned lack of height reports and the delay in the receipt of R.D.F. and Observer Corps reports at group plus longer time recently taken by squadrons to take off, pairs and wings of squadrons are meeting enemy formations above, before they get to height ordered by group.

3.   Tip-and-run raids across Kent by Me 110s carrying bombs or small formations of long-range bombers escorted by fighters give such short notice that the group controller is sometimes compelled to detail even single fighter squadrons that happen to be in the air to intercept enemy bombers before they attack aircraft factories, sector aerodromes, or other vital points such as the docks, Woolwich, etc. Normally, however, group controller has sufficient time to detail from one to three pairs (two to six squadrons) to intercept raids heading for bombing targets in the vicinity of London.

4.   Whenever time permits I wish group controllers to get the readiness squadrons in company over sector aerodromes, Spitfires 25,000 feet, Hurricanes 20,000 feet, and wait until they report they are in good position before sending them to patrol lines or to intercept raids having a good track in fairly clear weather.

5.   This does not mean that the controller is to allow raids reported as bombers to approach our sector aerodromes or other bombing targets unengaged because pairs or wings of squadrons have not reported they have reached the height ordered in the vicinity of sector aerodromes or other rendezvous.

6.   I am sending a copy of this instruction to all sector commanders and controllers also squadron commanders in order that they may understand why their squadrons have sometimes to be sent off to intercept approaching bombers before they have reached the height originally ordered or perhaps have joined up with the other squadron or pair of squadrons of a wing. Our constant aim is to detail one or more pairs of squadrons against incoming bomb raids, but the warning received at group is sometimes not sufficient and our first and primary task is to intercept and break up bombers before they can deliver a bombing attack against aircraft factories, sector aerodromes, docks, etc.

7.   Circumstances beyond the control of group or sector controllers sometimes demand that the squadrons engage enemy bombers before they have gained height advantage and got comfortably set with the other squadrons detailed by group.

8.   I wish the squadron commanders and sector controllers to know everything humanly possible is being done by group to increase the warning received of incoming enemy raids. Meanwhile squadrons can help by shortening the time of take-off, assembly and rendezvous with other squadrons to which they are detailed as pairs or wings.

It was Luftflotte 2's turn to mount the night raids on the 4th and between 8 and 9 p.m. over 100 raiders passed over Dieppe and Le Havre steering for London. The weather made night interception impossible and so the anti-aircraft guns were given permission to fire at unseen targets.

Despite fog and intermittent rain a further 200 machines crossed the coast heading for London later that night. One-third of the formation split from the main assembly and steered for Liverpool. Parachute mines were dropped on Woolwich and Enfield.

OCTOBER 5

Day Targets in Kent and Southampton attacked.
Night London and East Anglian aerodromes raided.
Weather Local showers in most districts. Bright periods. Winds light and variable.

Thirty raiders flying singly at 10,000–15,000 feet were plotted off the coast before 9 a.m. Half an hour later another raid began to boil up at Calais and by 10 a.m. two raids of twenty and fifteen bombers and fighters were tracked inland by the Observer Corps to West Malling and Detling airfields.

At 11 a.m. a forceful attack developed on Kent. Raids of 40, 30, 50, and 12 machines crossed the coast near Lympne and fanned out over southern England to attack Detling and Folkestone. The third attack came at 1 p.m. with a fighter sweep of twenty-five Me 109s which were followed by a wave of a further 100 machines, thirty of which carried bombs. Fifty aircraft reached the centre of London. Simultaneously two formations of fifty and thirty aircraft set course from Cherbourg to attack Southampton.

With no further need to go for bombers at all costs the Spitfires and Hurricanes were now free to fight directly with the Messerschmitts. The fighter-bombers, almost helpless with their awkward loads, usually let their bombs go the moment they were engaged. The fighters on the other hand took on the British machines in spirited fashion. There were bitter dog-fights, and in clear weather the people of London and the Home Counties watched the great swirls and streaks of vapour trailing across the pale blue of the autumn sky.

In the fourth attack at 3.30 p.m. on Kent and East Sussex a mixed force of fifty

bombers and fighters from Luftflotte 3 flew in over Ashford and Tonbridge. They were met by Spitfires and Hurricanes which split them up and drove them off. Hostile operations ended with an attack in the Selsey/Southampton area at 5 p.m. by two formations of thirty aircraft each, mainly Me 110s. By sunset Fighter Command had flown 1,175 sorties and lost nine aircraft. Nine German planes were also destroyed.

Flying under cover of darkness, cloud and rain, over 200 bombers went for south London and East Anglian aerodromes during the night. Fires flared up in the London docks and the East End districts.

OCTOBER 6

Day Single raiders or small formations attacked London and East Anglia.
Night Very quiet.
Weather Dull with continuous rain all day.

Early in the morning a large raid formed up across the Straits, but whatever the Luftwaffe's original intention the weather did not lend itself to serious business. Only single raiders and small formations dashed to the London airfields in the morning.

An entry in Biggin Hill's operations book

October 5th, 1940; children settle down to sleep on the platform of a London Underground station. Every night thousands of people sought shelter in this way and in the mornings climbed, blinking, into the daylight to resume their normal lives; many found their homes destroyed

recorded 'a low-flying attack by single enemy bomber. Three barrack blocks destroyed. No. 1 parachute and cable post came into action, and hit an enemy aircraft, but failed to bring it down. One aircraft was damaged, slight damage to the aerodrome surface'.

By midday there were again signs of a big concentration at Cap Gris Nez. This resolved

Ju 88A-4 dive bombers of KG51. The aircraft in the foreground and in the distance have had swastika, cross and code markings painted out in black for night operations. It is curious that wing crosses have been retained

into smaller units, some of which attacked Middle Wallop with high-explosive and oil-bombs. Northolt and Uxbridge were also targets for small formations.

An intercepted German wireless message made it clear, however, that Luftwaffe operations were more or less cancelled for the day owing to the continuous rain and low cloud. In spite of German tactics and the weather the R.A.F. lost one plane only. German losses were six aircraft.

Considering the weather German bombing was remarkably accurate that night. A powder factory was hit at Waltham Abbey, Hertford-shire, and de Havilland's aircraft works had a

narrow escape. Disturbed by no more than seven bombers, however, Londoners slept well.

OCTOBER 7

Day Mixed force of bombers and fighters attacked Yeovil.
Night Main targets London and Merseyside, otherwise raids scattered from Harwich to Newcastle and the Firth of Forth.
Weather Occasional showers. Visibility fair. Variable cloud.

In the morning 127 German planes were engaged by eighteen No. 11 Group squadrons over Kent and Sussex.

The attack resumed at 12.30 when Luft-flotte 2 again sent over a series of small waves from Calais to Dover. More than 150 Me 109s flew in and No. 11 Group had to call upon No. 12 Group to stand by. For the third

attack at 3.30 p.m. the Luftwaffe again used Me 109s and sent in fifty via Dymchurch.

These machines made for Biggin Hill and London. At the same time a mixed force of Ju 88s, Me 109s and Me 110s from Cherbourg in formations stepped up to 26,000 feet delivered an attack with eighty high-explosive and six oil-bombs on the Westland aircraft works at Yeovil.

Between 5 and 9 p.m. seven raids were plotted from Cherbourg to Swansea, eleven from Le Havre to Selsey Bill, twenty-seven from Dieppe to Beachy Head, two from Cap Gris Nez to Dungeness, twenty-six from Holland to Harwich, Newcastle and Spurn Head, and seven from Denmark to the Firth of Forth. Hostile efforts were mainly concentrated on London and Merseyside although bombs on Hatfield damaged three Lysanders belonging to No. 239 Squadron, an aircraft was destroyed at Ford and other bombs fell on Westhampnett, Tangmere, Eastleigh and Lee-on-Solent. Bomber Command countered the flow of traffic with a raid of 147 bombers on the German capital and the invasion ports.

In Berlin, meanwhile, Göring put a new five-point plan for the war against Britain. In it he frankly admitted that the demoralisation of London and the provinces was one aim and he described the air operations against the islands as 'merely an initial phase'.

The plan he outlined demanded:
1 Absolute control of the Channel and the English coastal areas.
2 Progressive and complete annihilation of London, with all its military objectives and industrial production.
3 A steady paralysing of Britain's technical, commercial, industrial and civil life.
4 Demoralisation of the civil population of London and its provinces.
5 Progressive weakening of Britain's forces.

Far from being progressively weakened, the R.A.F. was fighting back with increased strength. On the 7th Fighter Command flew 825 sorties and lost 17 planes to the Luftwaffe's 21, one of which was an He 115 seaplane.

Examination of eight Me 109s shot down on the 7th revealed that they were from LG2 and each carried a 250 kg. bomb. They were operating in small formations of 6–18 aircraft and flying 2–3 sorties per day.

OCTOBER 8

Day London.
Night Widespread raids on London and the suburbs.
Weather Cloudy in the south-east but fair. Wings high.

After the usual morning patrols and reconnaissance flights, two formations of fifty and 100 aircraft penetrated inland from Dymchurch and approached London via Kenley and Biggin Hill at 8.30 a.m. Bombs fell on Charing Cross Underground Station, Horse Guards Parade, the War Office and the Air Ministry's Adastral House. Tower Bridge was also hit and so was the B.B.C.'s Bush House. Two hours later a second attack with thirty aircraft developed on London. An hour later another twenty attacked and at 12.30 two formations of twelve took up where the others left off. Fighter Command scrambled 639 sorties and lost four machines. Fourteen German aircraft were destroyed.

Because of bomber losses the Luftwaffe turned to fighter bombers for the assault. Initially standard Me 109s were converted to carry bombs as 109E-4/B, but later aircraft were delivered from the factory fully equipped as fighter bombers. On this 109E-4/B the bomb is just being attached to the belly rack

From Uxbridge came another order from Park:

When a Spitfire squadron is ordered to readiness patrol on the Maidstone line its function is to cover the area Biggin Hill–Maidstone–Gravesend, while the other squadrons are gaining their height, and protect them from the enemy fighter screen. The form of attack which should be adopted on the high enemy fighters is to dive repeatedly on them and climb up again each time to regain height.

The squadron is not to be ordered to intercept a raid during the early stages of the engagement, but the sector controller must keep the squadron commander informed as to the height and direction of approaching raids.

The object of ordering the squadron to patrol at 15,000 feet while waiting on the patrol line for raids to come inland is to conserve oxygen and to keep the pilots at a comfortable height. Pilots must watch this point most carefully so that they have ample in hand when they are subsequently ordered to 30,000 feet which is to be done immediately enemy raids appear to be about to cross our coast.

When other squadrons have gained their height and the course of the engagement is clear, the group controller will take a suitable opportunity to put this Spitfire squadron on to enemy raids where its height can be used to advantage.

It was a rough and windy night but aircraft from Cherbourg, Le Havre, Calais and Holland converged on Britain. Over 100 raids were entered in the Fighter Command controller's log which shows that the stream did not cease until four o'clock the next morning. The main objectives were again London and the suburbs, and as on previous nights anti-aircraft batteries were given permission to fire at unseen targets. A formidable barrage was put up.

OCTOBER 9

Day London and airfields attacked.
Night Heavy raid on London.
Weather Cloudy in Channel with rain in northern France and the Straits. Winds high. Squalls.

Targets in Kent and London were again on the Luftwaffe's agenda and from 11 a.m. until

A Heinkel 111 H brought down over Britain and put back into flying condition by the R.A.F. The aircraft was from KG26 'Löwen-geschwader'

1.15 p.m. 120 Me 109s flew in. By 2.20 p.m. they had returned in greater numbers.

Between 160 and 180 aircraft were involved and the damage they did to some of the airfields was as serious as that inflicted during August and September.

Over 400 Hurricane and Spitfire sorties were flown. Nine German planes were destroyed for the loss of one British fighter.

In Berlin, meanwhile, Göring had consulted the calendar. As his Luftflotten were preparing for their night raids on Britain he issued directives for heavy attacks on London during the next full moon. The moon was then in its first quarter, which meant London could expect some exceptionally noisy nights from about October 15th.

OCTOBER 10

Day Hostile operations over east Kent, London surburbs and Weymouth.
Night London, Liverpool, Manchester and fifteen airfields also attacked.
Weather Showery with bright intervals. Haze in the Thames Estuary and East Anglia.

Having failed to get through *en masse* the Luftwaffe was now infiltrating in continuous streams. These tactics were difficult to combat and the decrease in the rate of German loss was worrying Fighter Command.

In the course of 754 sorties the R.A.F. lost five machines, against the Luftwaffe's four.

Manchester, London and Liverpool were again assailed, and following up on Göring's directive, fifteen R.A.F. airfields were bombed.

OCTOBER 11

Day Targets in Kent, Sussex and Weymouth attacked.
Night Main objectives London, Liverpool, Manchester and Tyne and Tees.
Weather Mainly fair apart from showers chiefly in coastal areas. Mist in Straits and Estuary early, clearing later. Fog developed in the night.

Four fighter sweeps over Kent and Sussex and two over Weymouth by Me 109s flying at heights of up to 33,000 feet occupied the southern sector fighters throughout the day.

At 10 a.m. 100 Me 109s assembled at Cap Gris Nez and crossed the coast at Hastings.

They attacked Folkestone, Deal, Canterbury and Ashford. An hour later another stream went for Biggin Hill and Kenley. At 2.15 p.m. about 100 aircraft reached Southend and by 4 p.m. a similar number penetrated as far as Maidstone and Tonbridge.

No. 611 West Lancashire Squadron, based at Ternhill, Shropshire, had a lively evening. Their terse combat report tells the story.

'A' Flight took off from Ternhill at 17.30 hrs. to patrol Anglesey. At about 18.20 hrs. at 17,000 feet, three enemy aircraft, Do 17s, were sighted about twelve miles away approaching from the south-west. Yellow section attacked out of sun, meeting fire from enemy leaders, E/A broke formation and were attacked by both sections. Yellow leader opened fire at 15 degrees deflection and hit E/A's starboard engine and return fire ceased. Yellow 3 followed with No. 3 and then No. 1 attack, and Yellow 1 from above attacked causing E/A to lose height but return fire had recommenced.

Yellow 1 saw E/A jettison five bombs into the sea and then crash into the water. Yellow 3 received an explosive bullet or shell in the bottom of his cockpit, making his airspeed indicator unserviceable.

Red section carried out two No. 1 attacks on another E/A whose starboard engine stopped, and he finally crashed in the hills south of Caernarvon. They then attacked E/A leader and on the third attack saw two crew bale out and both engines on fire. Aircraft glided down and crashed in flames near Capel Curig.

Altogether seven German aircraft were destroyed. Fighter Command squadrons, which flew 949 sorties, lost nine machines, but only three pilots. Six pilots were wounded.

OCTOBER 12

Day London and suburbs again main target.
Night Fairly quiet but National Gallery damaged.
Weather Widespread mist and fog during the day, clearing with light winds off the North Sea.

The point had now been reached where Hitler had to decide on his next course of action. It was evident towards the end of September that Seelöwe could not be accomplished before the end of the year. Bomber Command had sunk 214 barges and twenty-one transports of the invasion fleet which in any case had been forced to disperse. He was thus compelled in October to choose between stopping this dispersal or postponing the whole project indefinitely.

As the bombs fell on Biggin Hill, Chatham and Piccadilly, Keitel circulated Hitler's decision:

The Führer [he wrote] has decided that from now until the spring, preparations for Sealion shall be continued solely for the purpose of maintaining political and military pressure on England.

Should the Invasion be reconsidered in the spring or early summer of 1941, orders for a renewal of operational readiness will be issued later. In the meantime military conditions for a later invasion are to be improved.

The significance of this memorandum was not to be realised at the War Office, damaged at nine o'clock that evening by a direct hit, nor at Bentley Priory, until very much later. Hitler had admitted defeat nineteen days before the Battle of Britain officially came to a close.

Despite mist and fog, October 12th was a day of almost uninterrupted German activity the R.A.F. did not find easy to counter. Raids on London and the south-east started at 8.45 a.m. and went on until late afternoon.

Met in force by the British, who flew 797 sorties, the Germans had difficulty reaching their objectives. They lost eleven planes. British aircraft destroyed numbered ten.

OCTOBER 13

Day Targets in London and Kent attacked.
Night London, Bristol, Wales, Liverpool, Birmingham and Birkenhead raided.
Weather Almost cloudless but foggy early. Fine in the morning. Fair at midday, clouding over later.

Although Hitler had unofficially conceded victory to Fighter Command, Park, still striving to work out effective counter-measures to the Germans' high-flying tactics, would certainly not have agreed that the Luftwaffe

A 19 Sqn Spitfire is refuelled from a petrol bowser at Duxford on October 9th. These triple-hose Zwicky bowsers could refuel three aircraft at the same time, allowing a quick turn-round when literally, seconds counted. A really polished performance by the groundcrew could see an aircraft refuelled and rearmed in just four minutes.

Pilots of 19 Sqn relax between sorties at the Duxford satellite airfield on Fowlmere, Cambridgeshire, in September. The pilot sitting on the left by the window is the CO Sqn Ldr Brian Lane.

was defeated. The Germans had simply been prevented from achieving their objectives but they were still taking every opportunity to harass the R.A.F.

The first threats on this day were small and they developed off the east coast where a convoy was attacked. London was then selected for the next three raids which began at 12.30 a.m. when a force of fifty Me 109s reached Woolwich. An hour later a slightly larger force fanned out over Kent and made its way to the capital. The third formation of twenty-five Me 109s got to the centre of London at 4 p.m. despite spirited opposition.

The all-clear had not long sounded when 100 night raiders flew in. Assisted by a waxing moon they were better placed to find their targets, including Stanmore, where a bomb undoubtedly intended for the heart of

Britain's air defence organisation landed plumb in the middle of the railway station.

About thirty bombers were tracked by the Observer Corps to Bristol, Wales, Liverpool, Birmingham and Birkenhead; also to Dundee.

The moon did not prove to be much of an asset to the twenty-two night fighters scrambled to intercept the raiders. They were singularly unsuccessful, but they brought the number of sorties for the day to 591. German planes destroyed totalled five. The British lost two.

OCTOBER 14

Day Widespread small attacks.
Night Widespread and serious damage in London. Coventry also damaged.
Weather Occasional rain or drizzle spreading to the south-east. Rain in the Channel, misty in the Straits and the Estuary. Cloudy in the North Sea.

It was 10.15 a.m. before the Germans showed signs of serious business. Fifty small raids were

then picked up heading for the south-east and the south midlands. Some passed over north London aerodromes, including North Weald, which was by now showing the effects of nearly 400 accurately aimed bombs. Hardly a building had escaped so that dispersal and improvisation were necessary to keep the four squadrons going.

More than 100 patrols involving 272 fighters were flown. They neither scored nor lost. Three German aircraft were destroyed, nevertheless, in accidents.

Although the East End of London bore the main burden of the early German attacks, it was not long before the West End was sharing its bombing experiences with the poorer sections of the capital.

From the clear moonlight skies of October 14th there rained a load of high explosives and incendiaries which caused widespread and serious damage to many parts of the city. More than 220 members of the Conservative Carlton Club were in the building when it was destroyed by a direct hit. By some miracle they all crawled out from beneath the rubble unhurt. A Labour M.P. remarked rather cynically: 'The devil looks after his own'.

Other Londoners were not so lucky. Five hundred were killed and 2,000 seriously injured. This was a foretaste of even worse things to come and marked the beginning of the blitz which is outside the scope of this book.

OCTOBER 15

Day Hostile elements penetrate to London targets and targets in Kent and the Estuary.
Night Unusually heavy attack on London and Birmingham.
Weather Fair but cloudy in the Straits. Wind southerly and variable. Moonlit night.

Sector controllers on the early shift had hardly had time to read Park's latest instructions when the first signs of trouble showed up on the radar screens as a build-up over Cap Gris Nez. It soon faded and for an hour they were able to assimilate and discuss the orders their group commander had penned the previous day.

Said Park:

Owing to the very short warning given nowadays by the R.D.F. stations, enemy fighter formations (some carrying bombs) can be over London within twenty minutes of the first R.D.F. plot, and have on occasion dropped bombs on south-east London seventeen minutes after the first R.D.F. plots.

Under these circumstances, the only squadrons that can intercept the enemy fighters before they reach London or sector aerodromes are the squadrons in the air on readiness patrol, or remaining in the air after an attack, plus one or two squadrons at stand-by at sectors on the east and south-east of London.

In these circumstances it is vitally important for the group controllers, also sector controllers, to keep clearly in mind the time taken for squadrons and other formations to climb from ground level to operating height. The following times are those for a good average squadron of the types stated:

(a) Spitfire (Mark 1)
13 minutes to 20,000 feet.
18 minutes to 25,000 feet.
27 minutes to 30,000 feet.
(b) Hurricane (Mark 1)
16 minutes to 20,000 feet.
21 minutes to 25,000 feet.

Pairs:
The rate of climb for a pair of squadrons in company will be 10 per cent to 12 per cent greater than the time given above.
Wings:
The rate of climb of wings of three squadrons is between 15 per cent and 18 per cent greater than the times given above.
Rendezvous:
In view of the above, controllers will see the importance of ordering pairs or wings to rendezvous over a point at operating height in order that they climb quickly, singly, and not hold one another back by trying to climb in an unwieldy mass. Bitter experience has proved time and again that it is better to intercept the enemy with one squadron above him than by a whole wing crawling up below, probably after the enemy has dropped his bombs.

At 9 p.m. thirty Messerschmitts were heading for Hornchurch and central London. They hit Waterloo Station and blocked all but two of the lines. At 9.45 another fifty went for the city and at 11.20 more came in to attack points in Kent and the Estuary. By 12.20 a.m. 110 were plotted in the Straits but these did not mature into a full-scale attack.

At 6.30 p.m. Göring's plans to use the full moon were developing. The attack on London was heavy and the destruction of two bombers by night fighters did little to compensate for the serious and widespread damage inflicted on the city. Train services were stopped at the five main stations. Traffic from others was cut by more than two-thirds. The city's Underground railway system was severed at five places. Roads were blocked throughout the city and a reservoir, three gasworks, two power stations and three important docks were hit. There were 900 fires in London that night. Over 400 people were killed and more than 800 badly wounded.

In the day and night operations of Fighter Command 643 sorties were flown against the Luftwaffe, whose units lost fourteen machines – one less than the number lost by the R.A.F.

Luftwaffe personnel show members of the Regia Aeronautica over a German airfield in Belgium. The subject of interest is a collection of bullet holes made by the R.A.F. in a Heinkel 111. The Italian Air Force's participation in the Battle of Britain was extremely brief and unfortunately not very effective

The amazing trio of American pilots who fought with No. 609 Squadron. From left to right: Gene Tobin, Vernon Keough and Andrew Mamedoff. All were killed later flying from Britain with the American Eagle Squadron

OCTOBER 16

Day Quiet.
Night Limited attacks on London by single raiders.
Weather Fog widespread in Germany and France. Warm front lying the length of French coast. Wet and misty night.

Fog kept all but the more confident and competent Luftwaffe pilots on the ground. Those who flew struck out for Kent and the west of England. Seven caught by the R.A.F., who flew 275 sorties, failed to return. Six were destroyed in accidents. British losses numbered one plane.

It was not much better during the evening but at least 200 bomber crews chanced the mist and drizzle to raid the British Isles.

R.A.F. bombers returning from Italy met with difficulties. Eight Whitleys crashed and a Czech-crewed Wellington came down on the Fighter Command headquarter's tennis court.

OCTOBER 17

Day Fighter-bomber attacks on Kent and London.
Night Targets in No. 11 Group area, Liverpool and Birmingham.
Weather Bright intervals. Local showers.

Limited visibility did much to mask the Luftwaffe whose raids started soon after breakfast. Ninety Me 109s and Me 110s raided Margate, Broadstairs and Stanmore.

They were back after lunch and throughout the afternoon appeared in large and small concentrations or in streams, feinting, weaving, splitting up and then rejoining, using cloud to maximum effect, employing every ruse to elude and confuse the defences.

At one of London's key arteries, Waterloo Station, a bomb smashed all automatic signalling and signal telephones. Fourteen inexperienced station staff and a handful of soldiers somehow kept trains moving using flags.

British fighters enjoyed a moderate success. They destroyed five enemy aircraft and lost three of their own in combat. Luftwaffe losses for the day totalled fifteen.

The speed and height at which the Messerschmitts flew continued to trouble Park, and in yet another attempt to counter their activities he issued these instructions:

ENGAGEMENT OF HIGH FIGHTER RAIDS

The general plan is to get one or two Spitfire squadrons to engage enemy fighters from above about mid-Kent, in order to cover other Spitfire and Hurricane squadrons whilst climbing to operating height at back patrol lines east and south of London.

Preparation
Whenever the cloud conditions are favourable for high raids by fighters the following preparations will be made:

(1) *Reconnaissance Aircraft*: One or two reconnaissance aircraft to be kept on patrol near the Kentish coast, height depending on cloud layers.

(2) *Readiness Patrol*: A patrol by one or two squadrons to be maintained on Maidstone line at 15,000 feet, between 0800 hours and 1800 hours.

(3) *Stand-by Squadron*: One squadron at sector providing patrol at (2) to be standing-by during the peak periods — breakfast, noon and early tea-time.

(4) *London and Debden Squadrons*: State of readiness of Hurricane squadrons to be *advanced state* whenever cloud conditions are suitable for very high fighter raids.

Attack
Immediately enemy formations are plotted over the French coast or Dover Straits, the following action will be initiated:

(1) *Reconnaissance Aircraft*: Despatched to the area enemy raids are plotted, to locate, shadow and report.

(2) *Readiness Patrol*: Ordered to climb to 30,000 feet on the Maidstone patrol line to cover other squadrons whilst climbing over base patrol lines.

(3) *Stand-by Squadrons*: Despatched to operating height over base, and then to join the readiness squadrons at 30,000 feet.

(4) *Readiness Squadrons*: Despatched to rendezvous over base at 20,000 to 27,000 feet, and when assembled, detailed to raids or forward patrol lines.

(5) *Squadrons at Available, Spitfires*: To be brought to readiness, and if necessary despatched to assemble in pairs on back patrol lines at 25,000 to 30,000 feet, and then detailed to raids.

(6) *Squadrons at Available, Hurricanes*: Brought to readiness, and if there is a second or third wave, assembled in pairs over back patrol lines so as to protect sector aerodromes and London area whilst climbing.

(7) *Hurricane Squadrons from Tangmere and Debden*: Despatch in wings or pairs at 20,000 to 27,000 feet according to time and weather conditions, of one of the following purposes:

(a)   To reinforce London sectors if there is a second or third wave of enemy raids;

(b)   To protect sector aerodromes and London area whilst the earlier squadrons are refuelling.

(8) *Close Defence of Important Bombing Objectives*: If enemy raids are approaching aircraft factories, London area, sector aerodromes, etc., single Hurricane squadrons that have not been included in pairs or wings should be detailed to protective patrols between 15,000 and 18,000 feet depending on clouds.

With recollections of the Luftwaffe's August tactics, Park felt the Germans might renew their massed bomber raids. Accordingly he ordered the engagement of the enemy's

high fighter screen with Spitfire squadrons from Hornchurch and Biggin Hill half-way between London and the coast, and so enable Hurricane squadrons from North Weald, Kenley and Northolt to attack bomber formations plus close escort before they reach the line of fighter aerodromes east and south of London.

The squadrons from Debden and Tangmere (if disengaged) to be despatched and employed in wings or pairs so as to form a screen east and south-east of London to intercept third or fourth wave coming inland, also the retreating earlier waves.

Spitfire Squadrons:
Assembled at height in pairs on the back patrol lines, then detailed to engage high fighter screen at 30,000 feet.

Role: To protect pairs or wings of Hurricane squadrons whilst climbing up, also while attacking bombers plus escort. If the high fighter screen withdraws to the coast a proportion of the Spitfires may be detailed to attack the escorts to incoming bomb raids.

Hurricane Squadrons:
Squadrons at readiness to be despatched in pairs to back patrol lines covering line of aerodromes.

Immediately pairs have reached operating height, detail to bomb raids or to forward patrol lines under Spitfires. Squadrons as available to be brought to readiness and assembled in pairs at operating height on back patrol lines covering sector aerodromes, and detailed to second wave of bomb raids.

Whilst gaining height the latter squadrons may have to be detailed to split raids by bombers that attempt to attack vital points on the flank of the mass of bombers plus escort.

Hurricane Squadrons from Flank Sectors (Debden, Tangmere, and possibly Northolt):
Despatch in pairs or wings, according to clouds, to patrol mid-Kent patrol lines at 20,000 to 25,000 feet to engage:

(i)   Third or fourth wave attacks of bombers plus escort;

(ii)   Retreating bomb raids of first and second waves;

(iii)   To protect fighter aerodromes whilst the earlier Hurricane and Spitfire squadrons are refuelling.

Reinforcements from other Groups:
Immediately the enemy numbers appear to be more than 150, request two to three squadrons to cover the northern approaches to London, or the south-western group of vital points near London, as directed in Controllers' Instructions No. 7, dated August 27th, 1940.

In these orders can be seen the flexibility of mind displayed by Park. He was sometimes surprised by German tactics, but they never caught him off balance. He was equal to every challenge.

OCTOBER 18

Day Relatively quiet.
Night Raids on a reduced scale.
Weather Fog in Straits of Dover and Estuary; also in North Sea. Visibility poor.

After a fairly busy night the morning was unusually quiet. Between lunch and tea thirty-five raids were counted flying high over East Anglia. Forty-five R.A.F. fighter patrols were flown. Some intercepted and shot down four Luftwaffe machines. Total German losses were fifteen. The British lost four.

Night raids were on a reduced scale also, and by 1.45 a.m. the 160 bombers counted had returned home.

It was clear from an address to his aircrews that Göring did not realise how little

impression his night bombers were making on British morale.

In the past few days and nights [he said] you have caused the British world enemy disastrous losses by your uninterrupted destructive blows. Your indefatigable, courageous attacks on the heart of the British Empire, the City of London, with its eight and a half million inhabitants, have reduced British plutocracy to fear and terror. The losses which you have inflicted on the much-vaunted Royal Air Force in determined fighter engagements are irreplaceable.

OCTOBER 19

Day Isolated patrols and reconnaissance.
Night London, Liverpool, midlands and Bristol main targets.
Weather Cloudy in Channel, mist in northern France clearing later.

Swirling mists gave the Germans an easy morning but where possible they mounted some patrols. One bomber sent out was brought down over Kent.

At lunchtime it began to clear and by 2 p.m. fourteen Me 109s had assembled over the Pas de Calais for a sweep on England. They steered for London unopposed but dropped no bombs. Later, a dog-fight over Beachy Head developed and two British fighters were shot down, bringing Fighter Command's losses to five for the day. Two Germans failed to return home.

OCTOBER 20

Day Fighter-bomber raids on south-east and London.
Night Heavy attacks on London and industrial centres in the midlands.
Weather Mainly cloudy in most districts. Channel and Straits cloudy. Hazy.

All was quiet until 9.35 a.m. when the first of five Messerschmitt waves were plotted on R.D.F. In the afternoon high-flying raiders again penetrated inland.

Squadrons of Fighter Command flew 475 sorties and lost four of their machines. German losses were fourteen aircraft.

Nearly 300 bombers gave London a bad night. Traffic was dislocated by severe damage to the railways.

In Coventry the Armstrong-Siddeley and Singer Motor Works were hit.

Eleven night-fighter sorties were flown, but they were not successful. Dowding reported that the Beaufighter squadrons were having trouble with their airborne interception radar equipment and their aircraft.

Quoting the case of 219 Squadron, Dowding said that at 4 p.m. on October 19th the unit had four Beaufighters ready for night operations. By dusk they were all unserviceable.

Although there was not a single item for which a cure would not be found, it was the aggregation of defects which hindered rapid progress.

What depressed Dowding was that the Germans could fly and bomb with considerable accuracy in weather which prevented British fighters leaving the ground.

Fighter Command's task, he said, would not be finished until 'we can locate, pursue and shoot down the enemy in cloud by day and night'. The A.I. had to become a gunsight. They had a long way to go before approaching this ideal, but nothing less would suffice for the defence of the country.

Every night Dowding spent watching attempts at interception strengthened his conviction that haphazard methods would never succeed in producing more than an occasional fortunate encounter and that night interception depended on the laborious development of a system, the defects of which would have to be eliminated by means of practical trials and thoughtful analysis of the results.

OCTOBER 21

Day Sporadic raids on capital, Liverpool and West Country.
Night London, Wolverhampton, Coventry, Birmingham and Liverpool main targets.
Weather Mainly cloudy with fog and intermittent rain. Visibility poor.

Taking advantage of the overcast, single aircraft and small formations of bombers des-

Left: The view from one of Winston Churchill's windows at No. 10 Downing Street, on the morning of October 18th after single night raiders had penetrated to the heart of London. The wrecked building was part of the Treasury offices

patched by Luftflotten 2 and 3 reached widely separated targets in England.

Between 11 a.m. and 1 p.m. the number of raids increased. About sixty machines flying singly flew in from the Continent and dropped bombs on London and the suburbs. About fifteen were detected going to the West Country.

The weather clearly put the British at a disadvantage and in the course of the day Fighter Command squadrons flew only 275 sorties. They lost no aircraft whereas six German planes were destroyed. One of these, a Ju 88 which had been posing as a Blenheim and machine-gunning the airfield at Old Sarum, Hampshire, from a height of about fifty feet, was shot down by Flight Lieutenant F.J. Howell and Pilot Officer S.J. Hill.

> Howell dived to decide what it was [says the No. 609 Squadron record book] and even after making sure that it was a Ju 88 with a big cross, was surprised to see the rear gunner signalling with smoke cartridges. Both pilots attacked in turn and after an unusual chase above and below the tree-tops, the enemy aircraft hit the ground and blew up near Lymington.

Fog and intermittent rain did not hinder the Luftwaffe during the night. London, the midlands and Liverpool were raided. Bombs on the south-east coast temporarily affected several radar stations.

OCTOBER 22

Day Quiet morning and afternoon.
Night London, Coventry and Liverpool main targets.
Weather Widespread fog in the south, clearing to rain later. Visibility poor.

With No. 12 Group now receiving the same indications of hostile activity as No. 11 Group, it must have been galling for the Duxford Wing to be grounded by a thick fog which closed all but Tangmere, Kenley and Biggin Hill and the airfields of No. 10 Group.

The morning was therefore quiet with the Luftwaffe content to despatch a few small fighter-bomber raids. At 2 p.m., however, a big formation began to form up over north-east France and three raids totalling thirty-six aircraft were plotted. The expected raid on London did not materialise, but convoys off Dover and the Estuary were unsuccessfully attacked.

At 4 p.m. four small raids of about thirty-three machines were plotted flying high. Convoy 'Fruit' off Dover called for help and Uxbridge diverted two squadrons to cover it. Six other squadrons intercepted the main German formation and a dog-fight developed over Dungeness.

The Luftwaffe lost eleven aircraft – four in combat, the rest in operational accidents. Fighter Command lost six planes.

Poor weather limited night operations, but Coventry, Liverpool and London were raided.

OCTOBER 23

Day Mainly reconnaissance.
Night London and Glasgow raided. Minelaying off Yorkshire coast.
Weather Low cloud and drizzle. Visibility poor.

For Fighter Command this was the quietest day of the Battle of Britain. Hampered by the weather, the squadrons flew ninety sorties. They lost six planes, however. The Germans, who made some minor raids on London, the midlands and the Thames estuary, lost four machines.

London Bridge, St. Pancras Station, Victoria Docks, East Ham and Watford were hit by night raiders. In the north Glasgow was bombed by Stavanger-based aircraft. One fouled a balloon cable and crashed into the sea.

OCTOBER 24

Day Very quiet.
Night London and Birmingham main targets.
Weather Overcast and hazy in Channel, clearing to starlit sky at night.

Apart from a few reconnaissance patrols, the morning was quiet. A single raider crossed the coast at Southwold, Suffolk, and penetrated as far as the midlands. It was shot down at St. Neots, Huntingdonshire, on its return flight.

During the afternoon nuisance raids over the south-east and East Anglia kept British pilots on the alert. They flew 476 sorties without loss and shot down two hostile aircraft. The Germans, nevertheless, lost eight operational machines.

Nearly a month had now elapsed since Park and Leigh-Mallory had clashed over their respective tactics. But Dowding had been so preoccupied that he had been able to do little about the controversy. The lull on the 24th gave him an opportunity to pen a memorandum.

In it he asked Park to give Leigh-Mallory as much notice as possible of a 'probable intention to call for assistance', and warned Leigh-Mallory that Park would seldom be able to tell whether he needed help until preliminary symptoms indicated the manner in which an attack would develop. 'It may often happen,' said Dowding to his group commanders, 'that the first raid had been met in strength by No. 11 Group and that the assistance of No. 12 Group is required when it is seen that further raids are building up over the Straits of Dover.'

Park, he continued, had to remember Leigh-Mallory's requirements with regard to warning; even if there were doubts about the need for help, Dowding asked that warning should be given to enable No. 12 Group to bring units to readiness at stand-by.

Leigh-Mallory, he continued, should not send less reinforcements than asked for if he was in a position to meet the requirements, but he might send more at his discretion.

'It may be imperatively necessary,' Dowding went on, 'that No. 12 Group shall keep No. 11 Group informed of the position of his formations which should not normally penetrate beyond the range of R/T control.'

To save time communications between groups were to be direct. Only in cases of inability to comply with a request for reinforcements, or a difference of opinion, was the channel of communications to be through Fighter Command's operations room, concluded the commander-in-chief.

Right: A full squadron turn-out by Hurricane Is of 85 Sqn on October 23rd, led by the CO Sqn Ldr Peter Townsend. During August, Townsend had shot down five Me 109s and one Me 110.

Inset: A typical anti-aircraft gun site during the Battle. These mobile 3.7 inch guns are shown on October 23rd 1940. In the background flies a barrage balloon. As air attack over Britain intensified in the summer months, the accuracy of AA increased and the Luftwaffe developed considerable respect for British guns

London was attacked again during the night. About fifty machines were over the capital. Seventy other bombers were detected heading for widely separated targets, including Birmingham.

Only one successful interception was made – by an A.I. equipped Beaufighter of No. 219 Squadron off Beachy Head. The pilot reported damaging the enemy plane.

OCTOBER 25

Day Fighter-bomber raids on Kent and London.
Night Italian Air Force raids Harwich.
Weather Fair but overcast.

How far the Luftwaffe succeeded in reducing business and industrial output cannot be calculated. Suffice it to say that the Germans certainly succeeded in disrupting the normal industrial life of the country more often than most Britons would care to reckon.

One thing they did not succeed in doing, however, was to undermine morale. After each raid, whatever the district hit and whatever the suffering, the inhabitants cheered the Civil Defence forces, went on planting flowers around their Anderson air raid shelters and shouting defiance at Hitler and the German Air Force in the fruitiest of Cockney terms. And so they continued as on this day a sprinkling of Do 17s surrounded by fighters renewed the Luftwaffe's assault on the capital.

Signs of activity showed on the radar screens as the first business commuters were disgorging from London's deepest shelters – the Underground railway stations. High over Kent they flew, only to be dispersed by Hurricanes and Spitfires, several of them newer and more powerful than those which had borne the brunt of the earlier battles.

Kent took the full force of the bombs released indiscriminately as the R.A.F. dived on the German bombers and fighters, although London came in for a share.

Raids continued throughout the day, during which 809 Fighter Command sorties were flown. Twenty German machines were destroyed. Ten R.A.F. machines were lost.

In Belgium, meanwhile, an excited band of Italians of the Reggia Aeronautica's Corpo Aereo Italiano prepared for their first direct action against Britain. They were there more as a political gesture than as a serious military effort, and had been despatched by Mussolini as a reply to the embarrassing raids Bomber Command were flying against industrial targets in Northern Italy.

The two Fiat BR.20 bomber units, Nos. 13 and 43 Stormos, were allocated the bases of Moelsbroek and Chièvres. No. 18 Gruppo with Fiat CR.42 biplane fighters went to Moldegchen and No. 20 Gruppo with Fiat G.50 fighters was sent to Usel. A fifth unit, No. 172 Squadrillia, equipped with CZ.1007 Bis aircraft was allocated Chièvres.

On this October Friday 16 BR.20s were despatched to bomb Harwich. One of them crashed on take-off and two were abandoned over the sea after running out of fuel.

According to Milch, Mussolini's contingent was more of a liability than an asset. The men themselves were not to blame. They were excellent pilots, but they had not been trained to fight.

That their presence was unheralded is understandable. They were indistinguishable from the streams of German night bombers that crossed into Britain from bases in France, the Low Countries and Scandinavia.

OCTOBER 26

Day Fighter-bomber raids on London and Kent.
Night Targets in London, the midlands, Manchester and Liverpool.
Weather Cloudy with local showers chiefly in the north and east. Bright intervals in the west. Channel hazy. Cool.

The whole of London was now under the lash of Göring's night blitz and as the German News Agency put it inadvertently at the time: 'Bombs fell all over the place.' The *New York Herald Tribune* summed up the situation more accurately, 'What appears to be happening,' it said, 'is that the Germans have found the defences too strong for their daylight attack, permitting accurate fire, and so are putting their effort into night attack . . .

The railway bridge at Blackfriars with wrecked trams and other vehicles. The picture was taken on the morning of October 25th and the cameraman himself narrowly missed injury as the bomb burst

But against a people with courage it is unlikely to prove fruitful . . . and there is no doubt of British courage.'

The Luftwaffe was keeping up the pressure in daylight, but now it had to reckon with a greater measure of co-ordination between Park and Leigh-Mallory.

Park outlined the arrangements made for the Duxford wing operating in the No. 11 Group area.

The No. 12 Group Controller [he instructed] will advise the A.O.C. or the Duty Controller of the hours between which the Duxford wing will be at readiness. This information will if possible be given by 0900 hours daily in order to fit the Duxford wing into the programme for the day.

As soon as the Group Controller gets a clear indication of raids building up over the French coast he is to request No. 12 Group Controller to despatch the Duxford wing to patrol east of London on approximate line north and south through Hornchurch. The arrival of the wing patrol will be communicated to No. 11 Group Controller who will indicate to the No. 12 Group Controller the best position in the Estuary or northern Kent to which the wing should be directed to effect an interception.

The No. 12 Group Controller will inform No. 11 Group immediately the Duxford wing has left the ground.

No. 11 Group Controller is then to inform Senior Controller at Hornchurch who is to fix the position of the Duxford wing. This will be possible as two aircraft of the VHF squadron in the Duxford wing are fitted with Hornchurch fixer crystals (one working, one in reserve).

On arrival on the patrol line Hornchurch will give zero to the Duxford wing on its operational frequency. Hornchurch will hold a crystal of the leading squadron's frequency in the Duxford wing and set up a channel on air frequency with R/T facilities as indicated. Hornchurch Controller will be able to fix the Duxford wing and inform the Observer Corps liaison officer, flank sector and group operations of the position of the Duxford wing at frequent intervals.

On the 26th the Luftwaffe kept the whole of south-east England on the alert. Raids started early in the morning and began to intensify after 10 a.m. when high-flying fighter sweeps started to penetrate from the Channel. Maidstone, London and convoys in the Thames estuary were bombed. Off the coast of Ireland a FW 200 bombed and set fire to the 42,000 ton liner *Empress of Britain*.

Fighter Command mounted 723 sorties.

Ten German and two British planes were destroyed.

Although airborne in reasonable numbers British night-fighter pilots again had the galling experience of failing to intercept the raids which disturbed thousands all over Britain.

OCTOBER 27

Day Mainly fighter and fighter-bomber sweeps.
Night Widespread raids with London the principal target.
Weather Cloudy all day except for fair period in late morning.

The two Luftflotten made an early start and by 7.45 a.m. were raiding London and convoys in the estuary with a series of formations of as many as fifty aircraft.

By 9 a.m. the London suburbs had been hit and the docks damaged. Further sweeps were flown later in the morning and early in the afternoon. At 4.30 p.m. the Germans raided Southampton, London and Martlesham Heath simultaneously.

To repulse the attackers Fighter Command pilots flew 1,007 sorties. Ten British aircraft were shot down, but only five pilots were killed. The Germans lost fifteen machines.

Unknown to Fighter Command, however, they had driven off the penultimate major assault in the Battle of Britain.

The night was marked by the usual attacks on London, the south-eastern counties, Liverpool and Bristol, but they differed in detail. In addition to bombing, the Germans made a point of machine-gunning aerodromes in eastern England, including Leconfield, Driffield, Coltishall, Hawkinge, Kirton-in-Lindsey, Feltwell and Honington.

OCTOBER 28

Day Convoy off Dover and shipping in the Estuary attacked. London the main afternoon target.
Night Widespread attacks throughout the country.
Weather Misty in northern France. Fog over Estuary and Straits, clearing later. Cloudy.

Mist in northern France restricted the Germans to nuisance raids by single aircraft which also attacked some ships in the Channel.

They were more active in the afternoon when two raids of twenty and one of forty aircraft flew in over Kent. At 4.30 p.m. fifty more planes crossed the coast at Folkestone and headed for London. They were followed by more than 100 German machines which flew in four waves.

British fighters, which flew 639 sorties, fought off the Messerschmitts and lost two planes in the fighting. Eleven German aircraft were destroyed.

That night Nos. 85 and 247 squadrons intercepted and fired on two bombers caught by searchlights. The daylight battle was dying out but Fighter Command was only just beginning to get the measure of the task it had to undertake at night.

OCTOBER 29

Day London and Southampton main targets.
Night Heavy raids on the capital and midlands.
Weather Channel overcast. Haze in northern France and Dover Straits. Winds southerly.

In what seems in retrospect like a last convulsive spasm, the Luftwaffe pilots gave of their best. By 11 a.m. thirty of them were fighting it out with British fighters over Kent, although some managed to escape the net to attack Charing Cross bridge.

In the second phase of the day's assault ninety minutes later, No. 602 City of Glasgow Squadron distinguished themselves by shooting down at least six Messerschmitts in ten minutes. With three other squadrons No. 602 were given a tactical advantage by their positioning and height. Moreover, they were able to achieve greater success by working in pairs.

The encounter developed thus: No. 222 Squadron climbed to deliver an attack on the enemy from the rear. No. 602 attacked simultaneously from above, just as Nos. 615 and 229 Squadrons were climbing for height. Outmanoeuvred, the invaders turned for home, whereupon No. 602 gave chase.

While Luftflotte 3 were raiding Portsmouth with two groups of fifty and twelve machines, fifteen Italian BR.20 bombers and seventy-three Fiat fighters attacked Ramsgate.

It was not until November that the first Italians were shot down on British soil. They

included three Fiat CR.42 biplane fighters and three Fiat BR20 bombers, all of which came down in East Anglia. One of the bombers carried the surprisingly large crew of six. They wore tin hats and were armed with bayonets.

By the end of the day Fighter Command had recovered its old ratio of victories and destroyed nineteen of the enemy for a loss of seven of its own machines.

OCTOBER 30

Day Nuisance raids on reduced scale.
Night Activity reduced.
Weather Low cloud and continuous drizzle in all areas.

It was not until 11.30 a.m. that the first plots began to appear on operations room tables. They were comparatively small. At midday eighty raiders flew into the Estuary and at 12.15 two waves of fifty and sixty machines penetrated via Dymchurch. Ten R.A.F. squadrons were on patrol at the time, and of these six sighted the raiders. No. 41 Squadron shot down two of them.

Luftflotte 3 fighters were responsible for the next flurry of activity when they despatched a succession of raids totalling 130 machines. These started to cross the coast at 4.15 p.m. and some reached London.

Eight German planes were destroyed. The British lost five.

The first night raiders appeared soon after dark, but the weather was closing in and by midnight none was left over Britain.

OCTOBER 31

Day Fighter bomber and fighter sweeps.
Night Activity greatly reduced.
Weather Drizzle in the Channel. Haze in the Estuary and Dover Straits.

The rains came, as it were, to douse the last remaining embers of a bonfire. A few of them spat, however, into sixty half-hearted incur-

While the Battle of Britain dragged on, the weapons of reprisal were being forged. The first squadron of four-engined Stirling bombers was in formation by September and trials were advanced with the Manchester and Halifax long-range bombers. One of the most potent weapons of the air war, the Mosquito, was nearing the flight test stage in an imitation barn at Salisbury Hall, five miles west of Hatfield. The picture shows the prototype de Havilland Mosquito under construction in October 1940. This prototype first flew on November 25th, 1940

sions across the Channel. By nightfall the Battle of Britain was over.

For all the effort put into this phase the Germans achieved singularly little of strategic value. They were no nearer invasion and the sky was no less fraught with danger for the long-range daylight bombers than it had been in earlier phases.

It would be inaccurate to suggest the Germans relaxed the pressure on Fighter Command or indeed that October was an anticlimax. On the contrary, in many ways

October gave British fighter pilots one of the most severe tests of the whole Battle.

The physical strain of fighting at great heights was exacting. The continuous German fighter sweeps and rapid fighter-bomber attacks called for far greater vigilance and operational activity.

When the weather was clear and the Luftwaffe was able to multiply its attacks, British fighter squadrons of twelve aircraft averaged forty-five hours flying a day and occasionally as much as sixty hours. The volume of operational flying was also increased by the need to maintain standing patrols over Kent.

These counter-measures were an effective reply to the high-flying tactics of the Luftwaffe, but they shattered one of the basic principles of Fighter Command organisation, namely economy of effort by keeping planes grounded until they were needed.

The casualties and damage inflicted on the fighter squadrons by the night raiders were insignificant, but the bombing kept many awake and this had an effect on efficiency. Fatigue began to tell not only on the pilots but on staff in the operations rooms.

German losses in October were comparatively large – 325 planes. Fighter Command's losses in terms of pilots were 100 killed and eighty-five wounded – more than half of them in No. 11 Group.

During the war the Air Ministry claimed that between July 10th and October 31st a total of 2,698 German aircraft had been destroyed. Actually the Germans lost 1,733. Luftwaffe's claims were even more exaggerated. The German High Command's figures for the period were 3,058 British planes destroyed. In fact the R.A.F. lost 915.

Both air forces were bereaved of irreplaceable men, most of them in the flower of their youth. Counting pilots alone, Britain lost 415. In contrast it is interesting to note that 451 pilots went through the whole of the Battle and that 217 had been operational since the outbreak of war. The record for service goes to Flight Lieutenant J.C. Freeborn. He was posted to No. 74 Squadron on October 29th, 1938, and was still with the squadron at the end of November 1940.

It was estimated in the summer of the Battle that every pilot kept in action for more than six months would be shot down because he was exhausted or stale, or even because he had lost the will to fight. In terms of flying hours the fighter pilot's life expectancy could be measured at eighty-seven.

During that crucial summer the average pilot rarely got more than twenty-four hours off in seven days, or seven days a quarter – if he could be spared from constant availability, readiness and actual fighting.

Among public figures Churchill was the first to grasp the significance of the job they had done. He summed it up in what was perhaps his most famous speech of all. 'Never in the field of human conflict was so much owed by so many to so few.'

A postman searches in vain for the residents of a smashed house in London in October. Even postmen had been issued with steel helmets and of course carried the inevitable gas mask. On the railing outside the ruin hangs a Union Jack

AIRCRAFT OF THE BATTLE OF BRITAIN

BRITISH AIRCRAFT

Of the many types of aircraft operational at the time of the Battle in 1940, the main combat participants totalled only three British and six German. All were front-line aircraft and at the time were the very best the respective industries could produce.

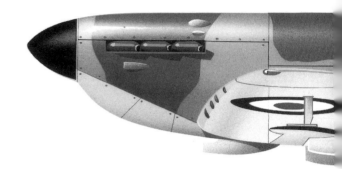

HAWKER HURRICANE Mk I
above Single-seat fighter powered by one Rolls-Royce Merlin V-12 liquid-cooled engine. Armament was eight ·303in Browning machine guns mounted in the wings, each gun having 333 rounds. Maximum speed 511 km/hr (318mph); service ceiling 10,973m (36,000ft); range 740 km (460 miles). Wing span 12.2m (40ft), length 9.75m (32ft).

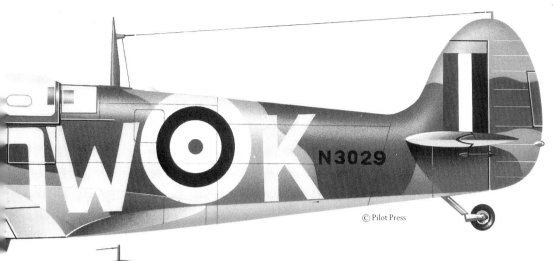

© Pilot Press

SUPERMARINE SPITFIRE MK IA

above Single-seat fighter powered by one Rolls-Royce Merlin V-12 liquid-cooled engine. Armament was eight ·303in Browning machine guns mounted in the wings, each gun having 300 rounds. Maximum speed 580 km/hr (360mph); initial rate of climb 770m (2530ft)/min; range 637 km (395 miles). Wing span 11.23m (36ft 10in), length 9.12m (29ft 11in).

BOULTON PAUL DEFIANT MK I

below Two-seat fighter powered by one Rolls-Royce Merlin V-12 liquid-cooled engine. Armament was four ·303 Browning machine guns, each with 600 rounds mounted in a hydraulically-operated gun turret. Maximum speed 488 km/hr (303mph); initial rate of climb 579m (1900ft)/min; service ceiling 9300m (30,500ft). Wing span 12m (39ft 4in), length 10.75m (35ft 4in).

© Pilot Press

© Pilot Press

GERMAN AIRCRAFT

MESSERSCHMITT Bf 110

right Two-seat day fighter powered by two Daimler-Benz DB601 V-12 liquid-cooled engines. Armament was two 20mm MG FF cannon and four 7.9mm MG 17 machine guns fixed forward firing in the nose and one 7.9mm MG 15 machine gun manually operated in the rear cockpit. Maximum speed 562 km/hr (349mph); service ceiling 10,000m (32,800ft); range 850 km (528 miles) at 490 km/hr (304mph). Wing span 16.25m (53ft 5in), length 12.1m (39ft 8½in).

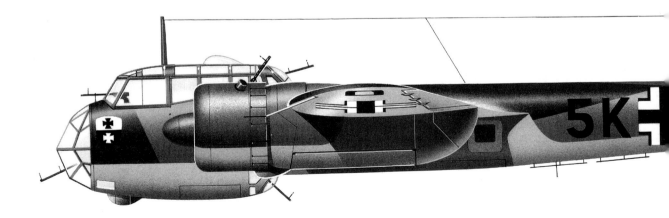

© Pilot Press

MESSERSCHMITT Bf 109E

left Single-seat fighter powered by one Daimler-Benz DB601 V-12 liquid-cooled engine. Armament was two 20mm MG FF cannon with 60 rounds per gun in the wings and two 7.9mm MG 17 machine guns, each with 1000 rounds per gun, above the engine (some aircraft carried two 7.9mm MG 17 machine guns with 500 rounds per gun and one 20mm MG FF/M cannon with 180 rounds mounted on the engine crankcase and firing through the centre of the propeller spinner). Maximum speed 560–570 km/hr (348–354mph); service ceiling up to 11,000m (36,090ft); range 700km (435 miles). Wing span 9.87m (32ft 4½in), length 8.64m (28ft 4in).

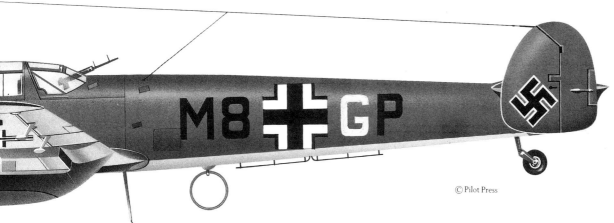

© Pilot Press

© Pilot Press

DORNIER Do 17Z

left Four-seat medium bomber powered by two Bramo Fafnir 323 nine-cylinder radial engines. Armament was normally six 7.9mm MG 15 machine guns in the nose, rear cockpit and ventral positions. Bomb load included up to 20 50kg (110lb) or four 250kg (551lb). Maximum speed 425 km/hr (263mph); service ceiling 8150m (26,740ft); range about 1160km (721 miles). Wing span 18m (59ft), length 15.79m (51ft 9½in).

JUNKERS Ju 88A

right Four-seat medium and dive bomber powered by two Junkers Jumo 211 12-cylinder liquid-cooled engines. Armament was one fixed or free-mounted 7.9mm MG 15 machine gun firing forward from the cockpit and two further MG 15s on flexible mountings firing aft above and below the fuselage (augmented by two lateral-firing MG 15s in the rear cockpit). Bomb load comprised a maximum of 28 50kg (110lb) internally and four 100kg (220lb) on external racks. Maximum speed 433 km/hr (269mph); service ceiling 8200m (26,900ft); range 1790 km (1112 miles). Wing span 20.13m (65ft 10in), length 14.4m (47ft 2in).

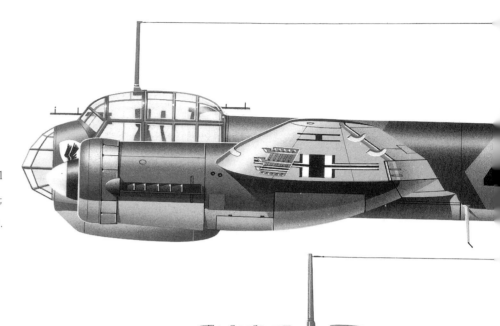

JUNKERS Ju 87B

centre Two-seat dive bomber powered by one Junkers Jumo 211 12-cylinder liquid-cooled engine. Armament was two 7.9mm MG 17 machine guns in the wings, one 7.9mm MG 15 machine gun manually operated in the rear cockpit and provision for a single 500kg (1102lb) bomb under the fuselage and four 50kg (1101lb) bombs under the wings. Maximum speed 390 km/hr (242mph); service ceiling 8000m (26,250ft); range with bomb load 600 km (373 miles). Wing span 13.8m (45ft 3in), length 11.1m (36ft 5in).

© Pilot Press

© Pilot Press

HEINKEL He 111H

below Five-seat medium bomber powered by two Junkers Jumo 211 12-cylinder liquid-cooled engines. Armament was one 7.9mm MG 15 mounted in the nose, dorsal, ventral and beam positions. Bomb load four 250kg (551lb) mounted nose-up internally and one or two 500kg (1102lb) carried on external racks. Maximum speed 415 km/hr (258mph); service ceiling 7800m (25,590ft); range about 1200km (745 miles). Wing span 22.6m (74ft 2in), length 16.4m (53ft 9½in).

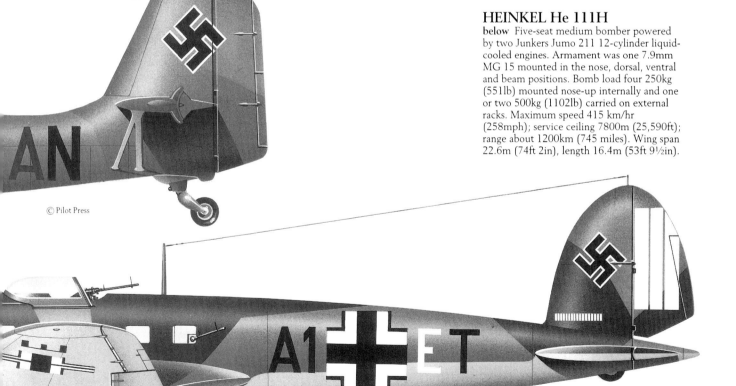

© Pilot Press

AIRCREW OF THE BATTLE OF BRITAIN

Aircrew who fought under Fighter Command operational control in the Battle of Britain, July 10th – October 31st, 1940. List of names.

* Personnel killed during the Battle of Britain.
Personnel marked killed but without an asterisk are those killed during the war but after the battle.

ADAIR, Sgt. H. H. British. 213–151. Killed
ADAMS, F/O D. A. British. 611–41
ADAMS, P/O H. C. British. 501. Killed*
ADAMS, F/Lt. J. S. British. 29
ADAMS, Sgt. R. T. British. 264. Killed
ADAMS, Sgt. E. H. British. 236
ADDISON, Sgt. W. N. British. 23
AEBERHARDT, P/O R. A. C. British. 19. Killed*
AGAZARIAN, P/O N. le C. British. 609. Killed
AINDOW, AC 2 C. R. British. 23
AINGE, Sgt. E. D. British. 23
AINSWORTH, Sgt. S. British. 23
AITKEN, Sgt. A. British. 219
AITKEN, Sgt. H. A. British. 54
AITKEN, S/Ldr. J. W. M. British. 601
AKROYD, P/O H. J. British. 152. Killed*
ALBERTINI, Sgt. A. V. British. 600
ALDOUS, P/O E. S. British. 610–41. Killed
ALDRIDGE, P/O F. J. British. 610–41
ALDRIDGE, P/O K. R. British. 32–501
ALDWINCLE, P/O A. J. M. British. 601
ALEXANDER, P/O J. W. E. British. 151
ALEXANDER, Sgt. E. A. British. 236. Killed
ALLAN, F/O J. H. L. N/Zealander. 151. Killed*
ALLARD, P/O G. British. 85. Killed
ALLCOCK, P/O P. O. D. British. 229
ALLEN, P/O J. L. British. 54. Killed*
ALLEN, P/O H. R. British. 66
ALLEN, Sgt. J.W. British. 266
ALLEN, Sgt. L. H. British. 141
ALLEN, Sgt. K. M. British. 43–257–253
ALLGOOD, P/Sgt. H. H. British. 85–253. Killed*
ALLISON, Sgt. J. W. British. 611–41. Killed

ALLSOP, S/Ldr. H. G. L. British. 66
ALLTON, Sgt. L. C. British. 266–92. Killed*
AMBROSE, P/O C. F. British. 46
AMBROSE, P/O R. British. 25. Killed*
AMBRUS, S/Ldr. J. K. Czech. 312
ANDERSON, P/O D. J. British. 29
ANDERSON, AC 2 J. D. British. 604
ANDERSON, S/Ldr. M. F. British. 604
ANDERSON, Sgt. J. A. British. 253
ANDREAE, P/O C. J. D. British. 64. Killed*
ANDREW, Sgt. S. British. 46. Killed*
ANDREWS, Sgt. M. R. N/Zealander. 264
ANDREWS, P/O S. E. British. 32–257. Killed
ANDRUSZKOW, Sgt. T. Polish. 303. Killed*
ANGUS, Sgt. R. A. British. 611. Killed
ANGUS, Sgt. J. G. C. British. 23
APPLEBY, P/O M. J. British. 609
APPLEFORD, P/O A. N. R. L. British. 66
ARBER, Sgt. I. K. British. 602
ARBON, P/O P. W. British. 85
ARBUTHNOT, Sgt. J. British. 1–229. Killed
ARCHER, Sgt. H. T. British. 23. Killed
ARCHER, Sgt. S. British. 236
ARIES, Sgt. P. O E. W. British. 602
ARMITAGE, F/Lt. D. L. British. 266
ARMITAGE, Sgt. J. F. British. 242. Killed
ARMSTRONG, P/O W. British. 54–74. Died
ARNFIELD, Sgt. S. J. British. 610
ARTHUR, P/O I. R. British. 141
ARTHUR, P/O C. J. British. 248. Killed*
ASH, F/Lt. R. C. V. British. 264. Killed*
ASHCROFT, Sgt. A. E. British. 141. Killed
ASHFIELD, F/O G. British. F.I.U. Killed
ASHTON, P/O D. G. British. 266. Killed*
ASHTON, Sgt. D. K. British. 32. Killed

ASHWORTH, Sgt. J. British. 29
ASLETT, Sgt. A. T. R. British. 235
ASLIN, Sgt. D. J. British. 257–32
ASSHETON, P/O W. R. British. 222
ATKINS, Sgt. F. P. J. British. 141. Killed*
ATKINSON, P/O R. British. 242–600–111–213. Killed*
ATKINSON, F/Lt. M. R. British. 43. Killed
ATKINSON, Sgt. G. British. 151. Killed
ATKINSON, P/O H. D. British. 213. Killed*
ATKINSON, P/O G. B. British. 248
ATKINSON, P/O A. A. British. 23. Killed*
AUSTIN, P/O. British. 151
AUSTIN, Sgt. A. T. British. 29
AUSTIN, LAC A. L. British. 604. Killed*
AUSTIN, F/O F. British. 46. Killed
AUSTIN, Sgt. S. British. 219. Killed
AYERS, Sgt. D. H. British. 600–74. Killed*
AYLING, Sgt. C. A. H. British. 42–92–421 Flt. Killed*

BABBAGE, Sgt. C. F. British. 602
BACHMANN, P/O J. H. British. 145. Killed
BACON, P/O C. H. British. 610. Killed*
BADDELEY, Sgt. D. H. British. 25. Killed
BADER, S/Ldr. D. R. S. British. 242
BADGER, F/Sgt. I. J. British. 87
BADGER, S/Ldr. J. V. C. British. 43. Died of wounds
BAILEY, P/O . G. British. 152
BAILEY, Sgt. G. J. British. 234–603
BAILEY, P/O J. C. L. D. British. 46. Killed*
BAILEY, P/O J. R. A. British. 264–85
BAILEY, P/O G. G. British. 79–56. Killed*
BAILEY, P/O H. N. D. British. 54
BAILEY, AC 2 C. British. 23
BAILLON, P/O P. A. British. 609. Killed
BAIN, P/O G. S. P. British. 111
BAINES, S/Ldr. C. E. J. British. 238
BAIRD, P/O G. H. New Zealander. 248
BAKER, P/O P. British. 600
BAKER, F/O H. C. British. 19–41–421 Flt.
BAKER, Sgt. A. C. British. 610–41
BAKER, Sgt. R. D. British. 56. Killed*
BAKER, P/O S. British. 54–66. Killed
BAKER, Sgt. B. British. 264. Killed*
BAKER, Sgt. E. D. British. 145. Killed*
BAKER, P/O C. C. M. British. 23
BAKER, Sgt. L. V. British. 236
BALL, F/Lt. G. E. British. 242
BAMBERGER, Sgt. C. S. British. 610–41
BANDINEL, P/O J. J. F. H. British. 3. Killed
BANHAM, F/Lt. A. J. British. 264–229
BANISTER, Sgt. T. H. British. 219
BANKS, Sgt. W. H. British. 245–32–504
BANN, Sgt. E. S. British. 238. Killed*
BARALDI, P/O F. H. R. British. 609

BARANSKI, F/Lt. W. Polish. 607
BARBER, P/O R. H. British. 46
BARCLAY, F/O R. G. A. British. 249. Killed
BARKER, Sgt. J. K. British. 152. Killed*
BARKER, P/O G. L. British. 600. Killed
BARKER, Sgt. F. J. British. 264
BARNARD, Sgt. E. C. British. 600
BARNES, P/O W. British. 504
BARNES, Sgt. L. D. British. 257–615–607
BARNES, F/O J. G. C. British. 600
BARNETT, S/Ldr. R. E. British. 234
BARON, P/O R. V. British. 219. Killed*
BARRACLOUGH, Sgt. S. M. British. 92
BARRACLOUGH, Sgt. R. G. V. British. 266
BARRAN, F/Lt. P. H. British. 609. Killed*
BARRETT, Sgt. W. W. British. 25
BARRON, Sgt. N. P. G. British. 236
BARROW, Sgt. H. J. R. British. 607–43–213. Killed
BARRY, P/O N. J. M. S/African. 3–501. Killed*
BARTHROPP, F/O P. P. C. British. 602
BARTLETT, Sgt. L. H. British. 17
BARTLEY, P/O A. C. British. 92
BARTON, P/O A. R. H. British. 32–253. Killed
BARTON, F/Lt. R. A. Canadian. 249
BARTOS, P/O J. Czech. 312. Killed
BARWELL, P/O E. G. British. 264
BARWELL, Wg/Com. P. R. British. 242. Killed
BARY, P/O R. E. British. 229. Killed
BASHFORD, Sgt. H. British. 248
BASSETT, F/O F. B. British. 222. Killed
BATCHELOE, P/O G. H. British. 54. Killed
BATT, Sgt. L. G. British. 238
BAXTER, Sgt. S. British. 222. Killed*
BAYLES, F/O I. N. British. 152
BAYLEY, Sgt. E. A. British. 32–249. Killed*
BAYLISS, P/O D. British. 604
BAYLISS, Sgt. E. J. British. 248. Killed
BAYLY, Sgt. J. N/Zealander. 111
BAYNE, P/O A. W. A. British. 17
BAYNE, S/Ldr. D. W. British. 257
BAYNHAM, P/O G. T. British. 234–152
BAZIN, F/Lt. J. M. British. 607
BAZLEY, F/Lt. S. H. British. 266. Killed
BEAKE, P/O P. H. British. 64
BEAMISH, Wg/Com. F. V. Irish. 151–249. Killed
BEAMISH, Sgt. R. British. 601
BEAMONT, F/O R. P. British. 87
BEARD, Sgt. J. M. B. British. 249
BEARDMORE, F/O E. W. B. Canadian. 1 (Can.) (401)
BEARDSLEY, Sgt. R. A. British. 610–41
BEATTY, Sgt. M. A. British. 266
BEAUMONT, P/O W. British. 152. Killed*
BEAUMONT, F/Lt. S. G. British. 609

CAPEL, Sgt. B. British. 23
CAPON, P/O C. F. A. British. 257. Killed
CAPSTICK, P/O H. Jamaican. 236. Died
CARBURY, P/O B. J. G. N/Zealander. 603
CARDELL, P/O P. M. British. 603. Killed*
CARDNELL, P/O C. F. British. 23. Killed*
CAREY, P/O F. R. British. 43
CARLIN, P/O S. British. 264. Killed
CARNABY, F/O W. F. British. 264–85. Killed
CARNALL, Sgt. R. British. 111
CARPENTER (F.A.A.), Sub/Lt. J. C. British. 229–46. Killed*
CARPENTER, P/O J. M. V. British. 222
CARR, F/Lt. J. British. 235
CARR-LEWTY, Sgt. R. A. British. 41
CARRIERE, P/O J. C. Canadian. 219
CARSWELL, F/Lt. M. K. N/Zealander. 43
CARTER, P/O V. A. British. 607
CARTER, Sgt. L. R. British. 66–601–41. Killed
CARTER, P/O C. A. W. British. 611
CARTER, P/O P. E. G. British. 73–302. Killed*
CARTHEW, P/O G. C. T. Canadian. 85– 253–145
CARVER (F.A.A.), Lt. R. H. P. British. 804
CARVER, P/O K. M. British. 29–229
CARVER, F/O J. C. British. 87. Killed
CASE, P/O H. R. British. 64–72. Killed*
CASSIDY, F/O E. British. 25–249
CASSON, P/O L. H. British. 616
CASTLE, Sgt. C. E. P. British. 219. Killed
CAWSE, P/O F. N. British. 238. Killed*
CAVE, F/Lt. J. G. British. 600–242
CEBRZYNSKI, F/O Polish. 303. Killed*
CHABERA, Sgt. F. Czech. 312
CHADWICK, Sgt. D. F. British. 64
CHAFFE, P/O R. I. British. 245–43. Killed
CHALDER, P/O H. H. British. 266–41. Killed*
CHALUPA, P/O S. J. Polish. 302
CHAMBERLAIN, P/O J. T. R. British. 235
CHAMBERLAIN, Wg/Com. G. P. British. F.I.U.
CHANDLER, Sgt. H. H. British. 610
CHAPMAN, Sgt. V. R. British. 246
CHAPPELL, P/O A. K. British. 236
CHAPPELL, P/O C. G. British. 65–609
CHAPPLE, Sgt. D. W. E. British. 236. Killed
CHARD, Sgt. W. T. British. 141
CHARLES, F/O E. F. J. Canadian. 54
CHARNOCK, Sgt. G. British. 25
CHARNOCK, Sgt. H. W. British. 64–19
CHATER, F/Lt. G. F. S/African. 3–247
CHEETHAM, Sgt. J. C. British. 23. Killed
CHELMECKI, P/O M. Polish. 17–56
CHESTERS, P/O P. British. 74. Killed
CHETHAM, P/O C. A. G. British. 1. Killed
CHEVRIER, P/O J. A. Canadian.

1–(1 Can.)–(401)
CHEW, Sgt. C. A. British. 17. Killed
CHIGNELL, S/Ldr. R. A. British. 145. Killed
CHILTON (F.A.A.), Sub/Lt. P. S. C. British. 804
CHIPPING, Sgt. D. J. British. 222
CHISHOLM, F/O R. A. British. 604
CHLOPIK, F/Lt. T. P. Polish. 302. Killed*
CHOMLEY, P/O J. A. G. British. 257. Killed*
CHORON, Adj. M. P. C. French. 64. Killed
CHRISTIE, Sgt. J. McBean. British. 152. Killed*
CHRISTIE, F/Lt. G. P. British. 66–242. Killed
CHRISTMAS, P/O B. E. British. 1 (Can.) (401)
CHRYSTALL, Sgt. C. British. 235
CHURCHES, P/O E. W. G. N/Zealander. 74. Killed
CHURCHILL, S/Ldr. W. M. British. 605. Killed
CIZEK, P/O E. Czech. 1. Killed
CLACKSON, F/Lt. D. L. British. 600
CLANDILLON, F/O J. A. British. 219. Killed
CLARK, P/O H. D. British. 213
CLARK, Sgt. W. T. M. British. 219
CLARK, P/O C. A. G. S/African. F.I.U. Killed
CLARK, Sgt. G. P. British. 604
CLARKE, S/Ldr. D. de B. British. 600
CLARKE, Sgt. H. R. British. 610–66
CLARKE, S/Ldr. R. N. British. 235. Killed
CLARKE, P/O A. W. British. 504. Killed*
CLARKE, Sgt. G. S. British. 248. Killed*
CLARKE, F/O R. W. British. 79–238. Killed
CLARKE, Sgt. G. T. British. 151
CLEAVER, F/O G. N. S. British. 601
CLENSHAW, Sgt. I. C. C. British. 253. Killed*
CLERKE, F/Lt. R. F. H. British. 79–32
CLIFT, F/O D. G. British. 79
CLIFTON, P/O J. G. K. British. 253. Killed*
CLOUSTON, S/Ldr. A. E. N/Zealander. 219
CLOUSTON, F/Lt. W. G. N/Zealander. 19
CLOWES, P/O A. V. British. 1.
CLYDE, F/O W. P. British. 601
COATES (F.A.A.), Lt. J. P. British. 808. Killed
COBDEN, P/O D. G. N/Zealander. 74. Killed*
COCHRANE, P/O A. C. Canadian. 257. Killed
COCK, P/O J. R. Australian. 87
COCKBURN (F.A.A.), Lt/Com. J. C. British. 804
COCKBURN (F.A.A.), Sub/Lt. R. C. British. 808

COGGINS, P/O J. British. 235. Killed
COGHLAN, F/O J.H. British. 56. Killed
COKE, F/O The Hon. D. A. British. 257. Killed
COLE, Sgt. C. F. J. British. 236
COLEMAN, P/O E. J. British. 54. Killed
COLEBROOK, P/O C. British. 54. Killed
COLLARD, F/O P. British. 615. Killed*
COLLETT, Sgt. G. R. British. 54. Killed*
COLLINGRIDGE, P/O L. W. British. 66
COLLINS, S/Ldr. A. R. British. 72–46
COLLYNS, P/O B. G. N/Zealander. 238. Killed
COMLEY, P/O P. W. British. 87. Killed*
COMERFORD, F/Lt. H. A. G. British. 312
COMPTON, Sgt. J. W. British. 25
CONNELL, P/O W. C. British. 32
CONNOR, F/O F. H. P. British. 234
CONNORS, F/Lt. S. D. P. British. 111. Killed*
CONSIDINE, P/O B. B. Irish. 238
CONSTABLE MAXWELL, F/O M. H. British. 56
CONSTANTINE, F/O A. N. British. 141. Killed
COOK, Sgt. A. W. British. 604
COOK, Sgt. H. British. 66–266
COOK, Sgt. R. V. British. 219
COOKE, P/O C. A. British. 66
COOKE, Sgt. H. R. British. 23
COOMBES, Sgt. E. British. 219
COOMBS, Sgt. R. J. British. 219
COONEY, F/Sgt. C. J. British. 56. Killed*
COOPE, S/Ldr. W. E. British. 17. Killed
COOPER, AC 2 C. F. British. 600. Killed*
COOPER, Sgt. T. A. British. 266
COOPER, Sgt. S. F. British. 253
COOPER, Sgt. D. C. British. 235
COOPER, Sgt. J. E. British. 610. Killed
COOPER, Sgt. R. N. British. 610
COOPER-KEY, P/O A. M. British. 46. Killed*
COOPER-SLIPPER, P/O T. P. M. British. 605
COOTE, Sgt. L. E. M. British. 600. Killed
COPCUTT, Sgt. R. British. 248. Killed*
COPELAND, Sgt. P. British. 616–66–73. Killed
COPELAND, Sgt. N. D. British. 235
COPEMAN, P/O J. H. H. British. 111. Killed*
CORBETT, F/Lt. V. B. Canadian. 1 (Can.) (401). Killed
CORBETT, P/O G. H. Canadian. 66. Killed*
CORBIN, P/O W. J. British. 610–66
CORCORAN, Sgt. H. British. 236. Killed*
CORDELL, Sgt. H. A. British. 64–616
CORFE, Sgt. D. F. British. 73–66–610. Killed
CORK (F.A.A.), Sub/Lt. R. J. British. 242. Killed
CORKETT, P/O A. H. British. 253
CORNER, P/O M. C. British. 264. Died

CORY, P/O G. W. British. 41
CORY, P/O. British. 25
COSBY, Sgt. E. T. British. 3–615
COSBY, P/O I. H. British. 610–72–222
COTES-PREEDY, P/O D. V. C. British. 236
COTTAM, Sgt. G. British. 25
COTTAM, P/O H. W. British. 213. Killed
COURTIS, Sgt. J. B. N/Zealander. 111
COURTNEY, F/O R. N. H. British. 151
COUSSENS, Sgt. H. W. British. 601
COUZENS, P/O G. W. British. 54
COVERLEY, F/O W. H. British. 602. Killed*
COVINGTON, P/O A. R. British. 238
COWARD, F/Lt. J. B. British. 19
COWEN, Sgt. W. British. 25
COWLEY, Sgt. J. British. 87
COWSILL, Sgt. J. R. British. 56. Killed*
COX, Sgt. D. G. S. R. British. 19
COX, P/O G. J. British. 152
COX, P/O K. H. British. 610. Killed*
COX, P/O P. A. N. British. 501. Killed*
COX, Sgt. C. R. R. British. 248. Killed*
COX, Sgt. G. P. British. 236
COX, Sgt. W. E. British. 264. Killed
COXON, Sgt. J. H. British. 141. Killed
CRABTREE, Sgt. D. B. British. 501. Killed
CRAIG, Sgt. J. T. British. 111. Killed
CRAIG, F/O G. D. British. 607
CRANWELL, Sgt. E. W. British. 610
CRAWFORD, P/O H. H. N/Zealander. 235. Killed
CRESWELL, Sgt. D. G. British. 141. Killed
CREW, F/O E. D. British. 604
CRISP, Sgt. J. L. British. 43. Killed
CROCKETT, P/O R. F. British. 236. Killed
CROFTS, F/O P. G. British. 615–605. Killed*
CROKER, Sgt. E. E. N/Zealander. 111. Killed
CROMBIE, Sgt. R. British. 141. Killed*
CROOK, P/O D. M. British. 609. Killed
CROOK, Sgt. V. W. J. Australian. 264
CROOK, Sgt. H. K. British. 219
CROSKELL, Sgt. M. E. British. 213
CROSSEY, F/O J. T. British. 249
CROSSLEY, F/Lt. M. N. British. 32
CROSSMAN, Sgt. R. G. British. 25. Killed
CROSSMAN, P/O J. D. Australian. 46. Killed*
CROWLEY, P/O H. R. British. 219–600
CROWLEY-MILLING, P/O D. W. British. 242
CRUICKSHANKS, P/O I. J. A. British. 66. Killed
CRUTTENDEN, P/O J. British. 43. Killed*
CRYDERMAN, P/O L. E. Canadian. 242. Killed
CUDDIE, P/O W. A. British. 141. Killed
CUKR, Sgt. V. Czech. 43–253
CULLEN, Sgt. R. W. British. 23
CULMER, Sgt. J. D. British. 25

CULVERWELL, Sgt. J. H. British. 87. Killed*
CUMBERS, Sgt. A. B. British. 141
CUNNINGHAM, F/Lt. J. L. G. British. 603. Killed*
CUNNINGHAM, F/Lt. W. British. 19
CUNNINGHAM, F/Lt. J. British. 604
CUNNINGHAM, Sgt. J. British. 29
CUNNINGTON, Sgt. W. G. British. 607. Killed
CUPITT, Sgt. T. British. 29
CURCHIN, P/O J. D. Australian. 609. Killed
CURLEY, Sgt. A. G. British. 141. Killed*
CURRANT, P/O C. F. British. 605
CURTIS, Sgt. F. W. British. 25
CUTTS, F/O J. W. British. 222. Killed*
CZAJKOWSKI, P/O F. Polish. 151. Killed
CZERNIAK, P/O J. M. Polish. 302. Killed
CZERNIN, P/O Count M. B. British. 17
CZERNY, F/Lt. H. Polish. 302
CZERWINSKI, F/O T. Polish. 302. Killed
CZTERNASTEK, P/O. Polish. 32. Killed

DAFFORN, F/O R. C. British. 501. Killed
DALTON, Sgt. R. W. British. 604
DALTON-MORGAN, F/Lt. T. F. British. 43
DALY, Sgt. J. J. British. 141
DANN, Sgt. J. E. British. 23
DANNATT, Sgt. A. G. British. 29
D'ARCY-IRVINE, F/O B. W. J. 257. Killed*
DARGIE, Sgt. A. M. S. British. 23. Killed
DARLEY, S/Ldr. H. S. British. 609
DARLING, Sgt. A. S. British. 611–603. Killed
DARLING, Sgt. E. V. British. 41. Killed
DARWIN, P/O C. W. W. British. 87. Killed
DASZEWSKI, P/O J. Polish. 303. Killed
DAVEY, P/O B. British. 257–32. Killed
DAVEY, P/O J. A. J. British. 1. Killed*
DAVID, P/O W. D. British. 87–213
DAVIDSON, Sgt. H. J. British. 249. Killed
DAVIES, P/O R. B. British. 29
DAVIES, P/O A. E. British. 222. Killed*
DAVIES, P/O G. G. A. British. 222
DAVIES, Sgt. M. British. 1–213
DAVIES, F/Lt. J. A. British. 604. Killed*
DAVIES, F/O P. F. M. British. 56
DAVIES, Sgt. L. British. 151
DAVIES-COOK, P/O P. J. British. 72–610. Killed*
DAVIS, Sgt. P. O. British. 222. Killed
DAVIS, F/O C. R. American. 601. Killed*
DAVIS, P/O C. T. British. 238. Killed
DAVIS, Sgt. W. L. British. 249
DAVIS, Sgt. J. N. British. 600
DAVIS, Sgt. J. British. 54
DAVIS, Sgt. P. E. British. 236
DAVIS, Sgt. A. S. British. 235
DAVISON, P/O. N/Zealander. 235
DAVY, P/O T. D. H. British. 72–266. Killed

DAW, P/O V. G. British. 32
DAWBARN, P/O P. L. British. 17
DAWICK, Sgt. K. N/Zealander. 111
DAWSON, Sgt. T. British. 235
DAY, P/O R. L. F. British. 141. Killed
DAY, Sgt. F. S. British. 248. Killed
DEACON, Sgt. A. H. British. 85–111
DEANSELY, F/Lt. E. C. British. 152
DEBENHAM, P/O K. B. L. British. 151. Killed
DEBREE, P/O. British. 264
DEE, Sgt. O. J. British. 235. Killed
DEERE, F/Lt. A. L. N/Zealander. 54
DE GRUNNE, P/O R. G. C. Belgian. 32. Killed
DE JACE, P/O L. J. Belgian. 236. Killed
DE LABOUCHERE, Adj. F. H. Free French. 85. Killed
DE LA PERRELE, P/O V. B. N/Zealander. 245
DELLER, Sgt. A. L. M. British. 43
DE MANCHA, P/O R. A. British. 43. Killed*
DEMETRIADI, F/O R. S. British. 601. Killed*
DEMOULIN, Sgt. R. J. G. Belgian. 235. Killed
DE MOZAY, 2nd Lt. J. E. French. 1
DENBY, P/O G. A. British. 600. Killed
DENCHFIELD, Sgt. H. D. British. 610
DENHOLM, S/Ldr. G. L. British. 603
DENISON, F/Lt. R. W. British. 236
DENTON, Sgt. D. A. British. 236. Killed
DERBYSHIRE, P/O J. M. British. 236
DERMOTT, P/O. British. 600
DE SCITIVAUX, Capt. C. J. M. P. French. 245
DESLOGES, F/O Canadian. 1 (Can.) (401). Killed
DE SPIRLET, P/O F. X. E. Belgian. 87. Killed
DEUNTZER, Sgt. D. C. British. 79–247
DEVITT, S/Ldr. P. K. British. 152
DEWAR, W/C J. S. British. 87–213. Killed*
DEWAR, P/O J. M. F. British. 229. Killed
DEWEY, P/O R. B. British. 611–603. Killed*
DEWHURST, P/O K. S. British. 234
DEXTER, P/O P. G. British. 603–54. Killed
DIBNAH, P/O R. H. Canadian. 1–242
DICKIE, P/O W. G. British. 601. Killed*
DICKINSON, Sgt. J. H. British. 253. Killed*
DIEU, P/O G. E. F. Belgian. 236
DIFFORD, F/O I. B. S/African. 85–607. Killed*
DIGBY-WORSLEY, Sgt. M. P. British. 248. Killed*
DITZEL, Sgt. J. W. British. 25
DIXON, Sgt. F. J. P. British. 501. Killed*
DIXON, P/O J. A. British. 1
DIXON, Sgt. C. A. W. British. 601

DIXON, Sgt. G. British. F.I.U.
DIXON, Sgt. L. British. 600
DOBREE, F/O N. R. British. 264
DODD, P/O J. D. British. 248. Killed
DODGE, Sgt. C. W. British. 219
DOE, P/O R. F. T. British. 234–238
DOLEZAL, P/O F. Czech. 19
DOMAGALA, Sgt. M. Polish. 238
DON, P/O R. S. British. 501. Killed
DONAHUE, P/O A. G. American. 64. Killed
DONALD, F/O I. D. G. British. 141. Killed*
DONALDSON, S/Ldr. E. M. British. 151
DOSSETT, Sgt. W. S. British. 29
DOUGHTY, F/O N. A. R. British. 247
DOUGLAS, P/O W. A. British. 610
DOULTON, P/O M. D. British. 601. Killed*
DOUTHWAITE, P/O B. British. 72
DOUTREPONT, P/O G. L. J. Belgian. 229. Killed*
DOWDING, F/O The Hon. D. H. T. British. 74
DOWN, Sgt. J. K. British. 64–616
DOWN, P/O P. D. M. British. 56
DRABY, Sgt. British. 25
DRAKE, P/O G. J. S/African. 607. Killed*
DRAKE, F/Lt. B. British. 421 Flight
DRAPER, P/O B. V. British. 74. Killed
DRAPER, P/O G. G. F. British. 41–610
DRAPER, Sgt. R. A. British. 232
DREDGE, Sgt. A. S. British. 253. Killed
DREVER, F/O N. G. British. 610
DREW, S/Ldr. P. E. British. 236. Killed*
DROBINSKI, P/O B. H. Polish. 65
DRUMMOND, F/O J. F. British. 46–92. Killed*
DUART, P/O J. H. British. 219
DUBBER (F.A.A.), P/O R. E. British. 808
DUCKENFIELD, P/O B. L. British. 501
DUDA, P/O J. Czech. 312
DUFF, P/O S. S. British. 23
DUKE-WOOLLEY, F/Lt. R. M. B. D. British. 253–23
DULWICH, Sgt. W. H. British. 235. Killed
DUNCAN, Sgt. British. 29
DUNDAS, F/O J. C. British. 609. Killed
DUNDAS, F/O H. S. L. British. 616
DUNMORE, Sgt. J. T. British. 266–222. Killed
DUNN, Sgt. I. L. British. 235
DUNNING-WHITE, F/O P. W. British. 145
DUNSCOMBE, Sgt. R. D. British. 213–312. Killed
DUNWORTH, S/Ldr. F. P. R. British. 66–54
DUPEE, Sgt. O. A. British. 219
DURRANT, Sgt. C. R. N/Zealander. 23. Killed
DURYASZ, F/O M. Polish. 213
DUSZYNSKI, Sgt. S. Polish. 238. Killed*
DUTTON, F/Lt. R. G. British. 145

DUTTON, Sgt. G. W. British. 604
DUVIVIER, P/O R. A. L. British. 229. Killed
DU VIVIER, P/O D. A. R. G. Belgian. 43. Killed
DVORAK, Sgt. A. Czech. 310. Killed
DYE, Sgt. B. E. British. 219. Killed
DYER, Sgt. N/Zealander. 600. Killed
DYGRYN, Sgt. J. Czech. 1. Killed
DYKE, Sgt. L. A. British. 64. Killed*
DYMOND, Sgt. W. L. British. 111. Killed*

EADE, Sgt. A. W. British. 266–602
EARP, Sgt. R. L. British. 46
EASTON, Sgt. D. A. British. 248
ECKFORD, F/Lt. A. F. British. 32–253–242
EDGE, F/Lt. G. R. British. 253–605
EDGE, F/Lt. A. R. British. 609
EDGLEY, Sgt. A. British. 601–253
EDMISTON, P/O G. A. F. British. 151
EDMOND, P/O N. D. Canadian. 615. Killed
EDMUNDS, P/O E. R. N/Zealander. 245–615
EDRIDGE, P/O H. P. M. British. 222. Killed*
EDSALL, P/O E. F. British. 54–222. Died
EDWARDS, F/O R. L. Canadian. 1 (Can.) (401). Killed*
EDWARDS, P/O H. D. Canadian. 92. Killed*
EDWARDS, Sgt. F. British. 29
EDWARDS, Sgt. A. J. British. 604
EDWARDS, P/O K. C. British. 600
EDWARDS, Sgt. H. H. British. 248
EDWARDS, P/O I. H. British. 234
EDWARDS, F/Lt. R. S. J. Irish. 56
EDWARDS, Sgt. British. 247
EDWORTHY, Sgt. G. H. British. 46
EDY, F/O A. L. Canadian. 602. Killed
EGAN, Sgt. E. J. British. 600–501–615. Killed*
EIBY, P/O W. T. N/Zealander. 245
EKINS, Sgt. V. H. British. 111–501
ELCOME, Sgt. D. W. British. 602. Killed*
ELEY, Sgt. F. W. British. 74. Killed*
ELGER, P/O F. R. C. Canadian. 248
ELIOT, P/O H. W. British. 73. Killed
ELKINGTON, P/O J. F. D. British. 1
ELLACOMBE, P/O J. L. W. British. 151
ELLERY, P/O C. C. British. 264
ELLIOTT, F/O G. J. Canadian. 607
ELLIOTT, P/O R. D. British. 72
ELLIS, Sgt. R. V. British. 73
ELLIS, F/Lt. J. British. 610
ELLIS, Sgt. J. H. M. British. 85. Killed*
ELLIS, Sgt. W. T. British. 92–266
ELLIS, P/O G. E. British. 64
ELSDON, F/O T. A. F. British. 72
ELSDON, Sgt. H. D. B. British. 236. Killed*
ELSE, Sgt. P. British. 610
EMENY, Sgt. C. S. N/Zealander. 264

GRANT, P/O S. B. British. 65
GRANT, Sgt. I. A. C. N/Zealander. 151.Killed
GRANT (F.A.A.), Sub/Lt. D. British. 804
GRASSICK, F/O R. D. Canadian. 242
GRAVES, Sgt. E. A. British. 235. Killed*
GRAVES, P/O R. C. British. 253
GRAY, F/O A. P. British. 615
GRAY, F/O C. F. N/Zealander. 54
GRAY, P/O C. K. British. 43
GRAY, P/O D. Mc.T. British. 610. Killed
GRAY, Sgt. M. British. 72. Killed*
GRAY, Sgt. K. W. British. 85. Killed
GRAY, P/O T. British. 64
GRAYSON, F/Sgt. C. British. 213
GREEN, F/Lt. C. P. British. 421 Flt.
GREEN, Sgt. W. J. British. 501
GREEN, P/O M. D. British. 248. Killed*
GREEN, P/O A. W. V. British. 235. Killed*
GREEN, Sgt. H. E. British. 141
GREEN, Sgt. G. G. British. 236
GREEN, Sgt. F. W. W. British. 600
GREENWOOD, P/O J. P. B. British. 253
GREENSHIELDS (F.A.A.), Sub/Lt. H. la Fore. British. 266. Killed*
GREGORY, P/O F. S. British. 65. Killed*
GREGORY, Sgt. A. E. British. 219
GREGORY, Sgt. A. H. British. 111. Killed
GREGORY, Sgt. W. J. British. 29
GRELLIS, P/O H. E. British. 23
GRESTY, Sgt. K. G. British. 219. Killed
GRETTON, Sgt. R. H. British. 266–222
GRIBBLE, P/O D. G. British. 54. Killed
GRICE, P/O D. H. British. 32
GRICE, P/O D. N. British. 600. Killed*
GRIDLEY, Sgt. R. V. British. 235. Killed
GRIER, P/O T. British. 601. Killed
GRIFFEN, Sgt. J. J. British. 73. Killed
GRIFFITHS, Sgt. G. British. 17
GRIFFITHS, Sgt. British. 32
GROGAN, P/O G. J. Irish. 23
GROSZEWSKI, F/O. Polish. 43. Killed
GROVE, Sgt. H. C. British. 501–3. Killed
GRUBB, Sgt. E. G. British. 219
GRUBB, Sgt. H. F. British. 219
GRUSZKA, F/O F. Polish. 65. Killed*
GRZESZAK, F/O S. Polish. 303. Killed
GUERIN, Adj. C. Free French. 232. Killed
GUEST, P/O T. F. British. 56–79
GUNDRY, P/O K. C. British. 257. Killed
GUNN, P/O H. R. British. 74. Killed
GUNNING, P/O P. S. British. 46. Killed*
GUNTER, P/O E. M. British. 43–501. Killed*
GURTEEN, P/O J. V. British. 504. Killed*
GUTHRIE (F.A.A.), Sub/Lt. G. C. M. British. 808
GUTHRIE, Sgt. N. H. British. 604
GUY (F.A.A.), Mid/Ship. P. British. 808. Killed
GUY, Sgt. L. N. British. 601. Killed
GUYMER, Sgt. e. N. L. British. 238

HACKWOOD, P/O G. H. British. 264. Killed
HAIG, P/O J. G. E. British. 603
HAIGH, Sgt. C. British. 604. Killed*
HAINE, P/O R. C. British. 600
HAINES, F/O L. A. British. 19. Killed
HAIRE, Sgt. J. K. British. 145. Killed
HAIRS, P/O P. R. British. 501
HALL, P/O R. M. D. British. 152
HALL, F/Lt. N. M. British. 257. Killed*
HALL, P/O R. C. British. 219
HALL, Sgt. British. 235
HALL, Sgt. British. 29
HALL, P/O W. C. British. 248. Killed
HALLAM, F/O I. L. Mc.G. British. 222
HALLIWELL, P/O A. B. British. 141
HALLOWES, P/O H. J. L. British. 43
HALTON, Sgt. D. W. British. 615. Killed*
HAMALE, Sgt. R. E. de C. d'. Belgian. 46. Killed
HAMAR, P/O J. R. British. 151. Killed*
HAMBLIN, Wg/Com. R. K. British. 17
HAMER, Sgt. R. C. British. 141. Killed
HAMILL, P/O J.W. N/Zealander. 229. Killed
HAMILTON, F/Lt. H. R. Canadian. 85. Killed*
HAMILTON, Sgt. J. S. British. 248. Killed
HAMILTON, Sgt. C. B. British. 219. Killed
HAMILTON, P/O A. L. Australian. 248
HAMILTON, P/O A. C. British. 141. Killed*
HAMILTON, P/O C. E. British. 234. Killed
HAMLYN, Sgt. R. F. British. 610
HAMMERTON, Sgt. J. British. 3–615. Killed
HAMMOND, P/O D. J. British. 253–245–54
HAMPSHIRE, Sgt. C. E. British. 85–111–249–422 Flt.
HANBURY, P/O B. A. Canadian. 1 (1 Can.)–(401). Killed
HANBURY, P/O O. V. British. 602. Killed
HANCOCK, P/O N. P. W. British. 1
HANCOCK, P/O N. E. British. 152–65
HANCOCK, P/O E. L. British. 609
HANNAN, P/O G. H. British. 236. Killed
HANSON, P/O D. H. W. British. 17. Killed*
HANUS, P/O J. Czech. 310
HANZLICEK, Sgt. O. Czech. 312. Killed*
HARDACRE, F/O J. R. British. 504. Killed*
HARDCASTLE, Sgt. J. British. 219. Killed
HARDIE, Sgt. British. 232
HARDING, Sgt. N. D. British. 29
HARDING, F/O N. M. British. 23. Killed
HARDMAN, P/O H. G. British. 111
HARDWICK, Sgt. W. R. H. British. 600
HARDY, P/O R. British. 234
HARDY, Sgt. O. A. British. 264
HARE, Sgt. M. British. 245. Killed
HARGREAVES, P/O F. N. British. 92. Killed*

HARKER, Sgt. A. S. British. 234
HARKNESS, S/Ldr. H. Irish. 257
HARNETT, F/O T. P. Canadian. 219. Killed
HARPER, F/O W. J. British. 17
HARRIS, P/O P. A. British. 3. Killed
HARRISON, P/O A. R. J. British. 219. Killed
HARRISON, P/O J. H. British. 145. Killed*
HARRISON, P/O D. S. British. 238. Killed*
HARROLD, P/O F. C. British. 151–501. Killed*
HART, F/O J. S. Canadian. 602–54
HART, P/O K. G. British. 65. Killed
HART, P/O N. Canadian. 242. Killed
HARTAS, P/O M. Mc.D. British. 603–421 Flt. Killed
HARVEY, Sgt. L. W. British. 54–245
HASTINGS, P/O D. British. 74. Killed*
HATTON, Sgt. British. 604
HAVERCROFT, Sgt. R. E. British. 92
HAVILAND, P/O J. K. American. 151
HAVILAND, P/O R. H. S/African. 248. Killed
HAW, Sgt. C. British. 504
HAWKE, Sgt. P. S. British. 64–19
HAWKE, Sgt. S. N. British. 604. Killed
HAWKINGS, Sgt. R. P. British. 601. Killed*
HAWLEY, Sgt. F. B. British. 266. Killed*
HAWORTH, F/O J. F. J. British. 43. Killed*
HAY, F/O I. B. D. E. S/African. 611
HAY (F.A.A.), Lt. R. C. British. 808
HAYDEN, Sgt. L. H. British. 264
HAYES, S/Ldr. H. L. British. 242
HAYES, F/Lt. T. N. British. 600
HAYLOCK, Sgt. R. A. British. 236
HAYSOM, F/Lt. G. D. L. British. 79
HAYTER, F/O J. C. F. N/Zealander. 605–615
HAYWOOD, Sgt. D. British. 504–151
HEAD, Sgt. F. A. P. British. 236. Killed*
HEAD, Sgt. G. M. British. 219. Killed
HEAL, P/O P. W. D. British. 604
HEALY, Sgt. T. W. R. British. 41–611. Killed
HEATH, F/O B. British. 611
HEBRON, P/O G. S. British. 235
HEDGES, P/O A. L. British. 245–257
HEIMES, Sgt. L. British. 235
HELCKE, Sgt. D. A. British. 504. Killed*
HELLYER, F/Lt. R. O. British. 616
HEMINGWAY, P/O J. A. Irish. 85
HEMPTINNE, P/O B. M. G. de. Belgian. 145. Killed
HENDERSON, P/O J. A. Mc.D. British. 257
HENDRY, Sgt. D. O. British. 219
HENN, Sgt. W. B. British. 501
HENNEBERG, F/O Z. Polish. 303. Killed
HENSON, Sgt. B. British. 32–257. Killed

HENSTOCK, F/Lt. L. F. British. 64
HERON, P/O H. M. T. British. 266–66
HERRICK, P/O M. J. N/Zealander. 25. Killed
HERRICK, P/O B. H. N/Zealander. 236. Killed
HESLOP, Sgt. V. W. British. 56
HESS, P/O Z. Czech. 310
HETHERINGTON, Sgt. E. L. British. 601. Killed
HEWETT, Sgt. G. A. British. 607
HEWITT, P/O D. A. Canadian. 501. Killed*
HEWLETT, Sgt. C. R. British. 65. Killed
HEWSON, F/Lt. J. M. Australian. 616
HEYCOCK, S/Ldr. G. F. W. British. 23
HEYWOOD, P/O N. B. British. 32–607–257. Killed*
HEYWORTH, S/Ldr. J. H. British. 79
HICK, Sgt. D. T. British. 32
HIGGINS, Sgt. W. B. British. 253–32. Killed*
HIGGINSON, F/Sgt. F. W. British. 56
HIGGS, F/O T. P. K. British. 111. Killed*
HIGHT, P/O C. H. N/Zealander. 234. Killed*
HILES, P/O A. H. British. 236. Killed
HILKEN, Sgt. C. G. British. 74
HILL, P/O H. P. N/Zealander. 92. Killed*
HILL, S/Ldr. J. H. British. 222
HILL, P/O S. J. British. 609. Killed
HILL, P/O M. R. S/African. 266. Killed
HILL, Sgt. C. R. British. 141
HILL, P/O A. E. British. 248. Killed
HILL, Sgt. A. M. British. 25
HILL, Sgt. G. British. 65
HILL, P/O G. E. British. 245. Killed
HILLARY, P/O R. H. British. 603. Killed
HILLCOAT, F/Lt. H. B. L. British. 1. Killed*
HILLOCK, P/O F. W. 1 (Can) (401)
HILLMAN, Sgt. R. W. British. 235. Killed
HILLWOOD, Sgt. P. British. 56
HIMR, P/O J. J. Czech. 56–79. Killed
HINDRUP, Sgt. F. G. N/Zealander. 600. Killed
HINE, Sgt. M. H. British. 65. Killed
HIRD, Sgt. L. British. 604. Killed
HITCHINGS, F/O R. A. H. British. 3
HITHERSAY, Sgt. A. J. B. British. 141
HLAVAC, Sgt. J. Czech. 56. Killed*
HLOBIL, P/O A. Czech. 312
HOARE-SCOTT, P/O J. H. British. 601. Killed
HOBBIS, P/O D. O. British. 219. Killed
HOBBS, Sgt. S. J. British. 235. Killed
HOBBS, P/O J. B. British. 3–232. Killed
HOBSON, P/O C. A. British. 600. Killed*
HOBSON, S/Ldr. W. F. C. British. 601
HOBSON, F/Lt D. B. British. 64
HODDS, Sgt. W. H. British. 25
HODGE, Sgt. J. S. A. British. 141. Killed
HODGKINSON, Sgt. A. J. British. 219. Killed

KELSEY, Sgt. E. N. British. 611. Killed
KEMP, P/O J. R. N/Zealander. 141. Killed*
KEMP, P/O N. L. D. British. 85–242
KEMP, P/O J. L. British. 54
KENDAL, P/O J. B. British. 66. Killed
KENNARD, F/O H.C. British. 66
KENNARD-DAVIS, P/O P. F. British. 64. Killed*
KENNEDY, Sgt. R. W. British. 604. Killed
KENNEDY, F/Lt. J. C. Australian. 238. Killed*
KENNER, P/O P. L. British. 264. Killed*
KENNETT, P/O P. British. 3–605. Killed
KENSALL, Sgt. G. British. 25. Killed
KENT, F/Lt. J. A. Canadian. 303
KENT, P/O R. D. British. 235
KEOUGH, P/O V. C. American. 609. Killed
KEPRT, Sgt. J. Czech. 312
KER-RAMSAY, F/Lt. R. G. British. 25–F.I.U.
KERSHAW, P/O A. British. 1. Killed
KERWIN, F/O B. V. Canadian. 1 (Can) (401)
KESTIN (F.A.A.), Sub/Lt. I. H. British. 145. Killed*
KESTLER, Sgt. O. Czech. 111. Killed
KEYMER, Sgt. M. British. 236. Killed*
KEYNES, Sgt. J. D. British. 236. Killed
KIDSUN, P/O R. N/Zealander. 141. Killed*
KILLICK, Sgt. P. British. 245
KILLINGBACK, Sgt. F. W. G. British. 249
KILMARTIN, F/Lt. J. I. Irish. 43
KILNER, Sgt. J. R. British. 65
KINDER, P/O M. C. N/Zealander. 85–607–92
KINDER, P/O D. S. British. 73–615
KINDERSLEY (F.A.A.), Lt. A. T. J. British. 808. Killed
KING, S/Ldr. E. B. British. 249–151. Killed*
KING, F/O P. J. C. British. 66. Killed*
KING, P/O F. H. British. 264. Killed*
KING, F/O L. F. D. British. 64. Killed
KING, P/O M. A. British. 249. Killed*
KING, P/O W. L. British. 236. Killed
KINGABY, Sgt. D.E. British. 266–92
KINGCOMBE, F/Lt. C. B. F. British. 92
KINGS, P/O R.A. British. 238
KIRK, Sgt. T. B. British. 74. Killed*
KIRKPATRICK, P/O J. C. Belgian. 235. Killed*
KIRKWOOD, P/O M. T. British. 610. Killed
KIRTON, Sgt. D. I. British. 65. Killed*
KITAL, Sgt. S. Polish. 85–253
KITSON, P/O T. R. British. 245. Killed
KLELZKOWSKI, P/O S. Polish. 302
KLEIN, Sgt. Z. Polish. 234–152. Killed
KNIGHT, F/Lt. T. A. L. British. 23. Killed
KNOCKER, P/O W. R. A. British. 264

KOMAROFF, Sgt. L. A. British. 131. Killed
KOMINEK, F/Sgt. J. Czech. 310. Killed
KOPECKY, Sgt. V. A. Czech. 111–253
KOPRIVA, Sgt. J. Czech. 310
KORBER, Sgt. Czech. 32. Killed
KORDULA, Sgt. Czech. 17–1
KOSARZ, Sgt. Polish. 302. Killed
KOSINSKI, F/Lt. Polish. 32. Killed
KOUKAL, Sgt J. Czech. 310
KOWALSKI, P/O J. Polish. 302
KOWALSKI, , Sgt. J. Polish. 303
KOZLOWSKI, P/O F. Polish. 501. Killed
KRAMER, P/O M. British. 600 Killed
KRASNODEBSKI, S/Ldr. Z. Polish. 303
KRATKORUKY, Sgt. B. Czech. 1. Killed
KREDBA, F/Lt. M. Czech. 310. Killed
KREPSKI, P/O W. Polish. 54. Killed*
KROL, P/O J. Polish. 302
KRUML, P/O T. Czech. 312
KUCERA, Sgt. J. V. 111
KUCERA, Sgt.J. Czech. 245. Killed
KUMIEGA, P/O L. Polish. 17
KUSTRZYNSKI, F/O Z. Polish. 607
KUTTLEWASCHER, Sgt. K. M. Czech. 1
KWIECINSKI, Sgt. J. Polish. 145. Killed

LACEY, Sgt. J. H. British. 501
LACEY, Sgt. E. R. British. 219
LACKIE, Sgt. W. L. British. 141
LAPONT, Adj. Henrie G. Free French. 615–245
LAGUNA, F/Lt. P. Polish. 302. Killed
LAING, F/O A. J. A. British. 64
LAING, Sgt. A. British. 151
LAKE, F/O D. M. British. 219. Killed
LAMB, P/O R. L. British. 600
LAMB, Sgt. A. British. 25
LAMB (F.A.A.), Sub/Lt. R. R. British. 804. Killed
LAMB, F/O P. G. British. 610
LAMB, P/O O. E N/Zealander. 151. Killed
LAMBERT, F/Lt. H. M. S. British. 25. Killed*
LAMBIE, P/O W. G. M. British. 219. Killed
LAMMER, P/O A. British. 141
LANDELS, P/O L. N. British. 32–615. Killed
LANDESDELL, Sgt. J. British. 607. Killed*
LANE, F/Lt. B. J. E. British. 19. Killed
LANE, P/O R. British. 43. Killed
LANGDON, P/O C. E. N/Zealander. 43. Killed
LANGHAM-HOBART, P/O N. C. British. 73
LANGLEY, Sgt. L. British. 23
LANGLEY, P/O G. A. British. 41. Killed*
LANNING, P/O F. C. A. British. 141
LAPKA, P/O S. Polish. 302
LAPKOWSKI, P/O W. Polish. 303. Killed
LARBALESTIER, P/O B. D. British. 600
LARICHELIERE, P/O J. E. P. Canadian. 213. Killed*

LATTA, P/O J. B. Canadian. 242. Killed
LAUDER, Sgt. A. J. British. 264
LAUGHLIN, F/O J. H. British. 235
LAURENCE, Sgt. G. British. 141. Killed
LAW, P/O K. S. British. 605
LAWFORD, Sgt. D. N. British. 247
LAWLER, Sgt. E. S. British. 604
LAWRENCE, Sgt. N. A. British. 54
LAWRENCE, P/O K. A. N/Zealander. 603–234–421 Flt.
LAWRENCE, P/O J. T. British. 235
LAWS, Sgt. G. G. S. British. 501–151. Killed
LAWS, P/O A. F. British. 64. Killed*
LAWSON, P/O W. J. British. 19. Killed
LAWSON, P/O R. C. British. 601. Killed
LAWSON-BROWN, P/O. British. 64. Killed
LAWTON, F/O P. C. F. British. 604
LAYCOCK, P/O H. K. British. 79–56. Killed
LAYCOCK, F/O. British. 87
LAZORYK, F/Lt. W. Polisyh. 607
LEARY, P/O D. C. British. 17. Killed
LEATHART, S/Ldr. J. A. British. 54
LEATHAM, P/O E. G. C. British. 248
LEATHER, F/Lt. W. J. British. 611
LE CHEMINANT, Sgt. J. British. 616
LECKRONE, P/O P.H. american. 616. Killed
LECKY, P/O J. G. British. 610–41. Killed*
LE CONTE, Sgt. E. F. British. F.I.U.
LEDGER, Sgt. L. British. 236
LE DONG, Sgt. E. British. 219. Killed
LEE, P/O K. N. T. British. 501
LEE, Sgt. M. A. W. British. 72–421 Flt. Killed
LEE, F/Lt. R. H. A. British. 85. Killed*
LEES, S/Ldr. R. B. Australian. 72
LEES, P/O A. F. Y. Britisyh. 236
LE FEVRE, , P/O P. W. British. 46. Killed
LEGG, P/O R. J. British. 601
LEGGETT, P/O P. G. 245–615–46
LEIGH, S/Ldr. R. H. A. British. 66
LEIGH, Sgt. A. C. British. 64–72
LE JEUNE, Sgt. O. G. Belgian. 235
LENAHAN, P/O J. D. British. 607. Killed*
LENG, Sgt. M. E. British. 73
LENNARD (F.A.A.), Mid/Ship. P. L. British. 501. Killed
LENTON, P/O E. C. British. 56
LE ROUGETEL, F/O S. P. 600
LE ROY DU VIVIER, P/O D. A. R. G. Belgian. 43
LERWAY, Sgt. F. T. British. 236
LESLIE, Sgt. G. M. British. 219. Killed
LEVENSON, Sgt. S. A. British. 611. Killed
LEVISON, Sgt. S. A. British. 611. Killed
LEWIS, P/O A. G. S/African. 85–249
LEWIS, Sgt. W. G. British. 25. Killed
LEWIS, Sgt. C. S. British. 600
LEWIS, P/O R. G. Canadian. 1 (Can) (401). Killed
LEYLAND, Sgt. R. H. British. F.I.U.

LILLE, Sgt. British. 264
LILLEY, Sgt. R. British. 29. Killed
LIMPENNY, Sgt. E. R. British. 64
LINDSAY, P/O A. I. British. 72. Killed
LINES, F/O A. P. British. 17
LINGARD, F/O J. G. British. 25
LINNEY, P/O A. S. British. 229
LIPSCOMBE, Sgt. A. J. British. 600. Killed
LISTER, S/Ldr. R. C. F. British. 92–41
LITCHFIELD, P/O P. British. 610. Killed*
LITSON, Sgt. F. W. R. British. 141
LITTLE, F/O B. W. British. 609
LITTLE, P/O A. G. British. 235
LITTLE, Sgt. R. British. 238. Killed*
LITTLE, F/O T. B. Canadian. 1 (Can) (401). Killed
LITTLE, S/Ldr. J. H. British. 219. Killed
LITTLE, S/Ldr. P. British. 600
LLEWELLYN, Sgt. R. T. British. 213
LLEWELLYN, F/O. A. J. A. British. 29. Killed
LLOYD, Sgt. D. E. British. 19–64. Killed
LLOYD, Sgt. P. D. British. 41. Killed
LLOYD, P/O J. P. British. 72–64
LLOYD, Sgt. British. 29
LOCKHART, P/O J. British. 85–213. Killed
LOCHNAN, F/O P. W. Canadian. 1 (Can) (401). Killed
LOCK, P/O E. S. British. 41. Killed
LOCKTON, Sgt. E. E. British. 236. Killed*
LOCKWOOD, Sgt. J. C. British. 54. Killed
LOFTS, P/O K. T. British. 615–249
LOGAN, P/O C. British. 266. Killed
LOGIE, P/O O. A. British. 29
LOKUCIEWSKI, P/O W. Polish. 303
LONG, Sgt. British. 236
LONSDALE, Sgt. R. V. H. British. 242–501–46
LONSDALE, P/O J. British. 3. Killed
LOOKER, P/O D. J. British. 615
LOUDON, F/Lt. M. J. British. 141
LOVELL, P/O A. D. J. British. 41
LOVELL-GREGG, S/Ldr. T. G. N/Zealander. 87. Killed*
LOVERSEED, Sgt. J. E. British. 501
LOVETT, F/Lt. R. E. British. 73. Killed*
LOWE, Sgt. British. 236
LOWETH, P/O P. A. British. 249
LOWTHER, Sgt. W. British. 219
LOXTON, S/Ldr. W. W. British. 25
LUCAS, P/O R. M. M. D. British. 141
LUCAS, Sgt. S. E. British. 32–257
LUKASZEWICZ, F/O K. Polish. 501. Killed*
LUMSDEN, P/O D. T. M. British. 236
LUMSDEN, Sgt. J. C. British. 248
LUND, P/O J. W. British. 611–92. Killed
LUSK, P/O H. S. N/Zealander. 25
LUSTY, P/O K. R. British. 25
LYALL, F/Lt. A. Mc. L. British. 25
LYALL, P/O A. British. 602. Killed
LYNCH, Sgt. J. British. 25. Killed
LYONS, P/O E. B. British. 65

MITCHELL, Sgt. G. British. 23
MITCHELL, P/O G. T. M. British. 609. Killed*
MITCHELL, Sgt. R. R. British. 229
MITCHELL, Sgt. H. R. N/Zealander. 3. Killed
MITCHELL, Sgt. P. M. British. 65. Killed
MOBERLEY, F/O G. E. British. 616. Killed*
MOLSON, F/O H. de. M. Canadian. 1 (Can) (401)
MONK, P/O E. W. J. British. 25. Killed
MONK, Sgt. D. A. British. 236
MONTAGU, S/Ldr. G. W. British. 236. Killed
MONTAGUE-SMITH, F/Lt. A. M. British. 264
MONBRON, Sgt. Xavier de. Free French. 64–92
MONTGOMERY, Sgt. H. F. British. 43. Killed*
MONTGOMERY, P/O C. R. British. 614. Killed*
MOODY, P/O H. W. British. 602. Killed*
MOODY, Sgt. D. G. British. 604
MOORE, Sgt. A. R. British. 245–615–3
MOORE, P/O W. British. 264
MOORE, Sgt. P. J. British. 253. Killed
MOORE, F/O W. S. British. 236. Killed
MORE, S/Ldr. J. W. C. British. 73. Killed
MOREWOOD, F/Lt. R. E. G. British. 248
MORFILL, F/Sgt. P. F. British. 501
MORGAN, P/O P. J. British. 238–79
MORGAN-GRAY, P/O H. 46. Killed
MORRIS, P/O E. J. S/African. 79
MORRIS, P/O G. E. British. F.I.U.
MORRIS, P/O J. British. 248
MORRISON, Sgt. N. British. 54–74–72. Killed
MORRISON, Sgt. J. P. British. 46–43. Killed*
MOROGH-RYAN, P/O O. B. British. 41. Killed
MORTIMER, P/O P. A. British. 257. Killed
MORTON, P/O J. S. British. 603
MOSS (F.A.A.), Sub/Lt. W. J. M. British. 213. Killed*
MOSS, Sgt. R. C. British. 29
MOTT, Sgt. W. H. British. 141
MOTTRAM, P/O R. British. 92. Killed
MOUCHOTTE, Adj. R. G. O. J. Free French. 615. Killed
MOULD, Sgt. E. A. British. 74. Killed
MOULTON, Sgt. E. W. British. 600
MOUNSDON, P/O M. H. British. 56
MOUNT, F/O C. J. British. 602
MOWAT, F/Lt. N. J. N/Zealander. 245
MOWAT, Sgt. R. I. British. 248
MOYNHAM, Sgt. H. F. J. British. 248. Killed
MRAZEK, P/O K. Czech. 46
MUDIE, P/O M. R. British. 615. Killed*
MUDRY, Sgt. M. Polish. 79
MUIRHEAD, F/Lt. I. J. British. 605. Killed*

MUMLER, S/Ldr. M. Polish. 302
MUNGO-PARK, F/O J. C. British. 74. Killed
MUNN, F/Sgt. W. S. British. 29
MURCH, F/O L. C. British. 253. Killed
MURLAND, Sgt. W. J. N/Zealander. 264
MURRAY, Sgt. J. British. 610
MURRAY, P/O T. B. British. 616
MURRAY, S/Ldr. A. D. British. 73–501–46
MURRAY, Sgt. P. H. British. 23. Killed

NAISH, Sgt. K. E. British. 235
NARUCKI, P/O A. R. Polish. 607. Killed
NAUGHTIN, Sgt. H. T. British. 235. Killed
NEER, Sgt. British. 29
NEIL, P/O T. F. British. 249
NELSON, F/O W. H. Canadian. 74. Killed
NELSON, F/Sgt. D. British. 235
NELSON-EDWARDS, P/O G. H. British. 79
NESBITT, F/O A. D. Canadian. 1 (Can) (401)
NEVILLE, Sgt. W. J. British. 610. Killed*
NEWBURY, P/O J. C. British. 609
NEWBURY, P/O M. A. British. 145. Killed
NEWHAM, Sgt. E. A. British. 235
NEWLING, P/O M. A. British. 145. Killed
NEWPORT, Sgt. D. V. British. 235
NEWTON, Sgt. H. S. British. 111
NEWTON, Sgt. E. F. British. 29
NICHOLAS, F/O J. B. H. British. 65
NICHOLLS, Sgt. T. G. F. British. 23. Killed
NICHOLLS, Sgt. D. B. F. British. 151
NICHOLS, Sgt. D. H. British. 56
NICHOLSON, F/Lt. J. B. British. 249. Killed
NICHOLSON, Sgt. P. B. British. 232. Killed
NIEMIEC, F/O P. Polish. 17
NIGHTINGALE, P/O F. G. 219. Killed
NIVEN, P/O H. G. British. 601–602
NIXON, Sgt. W. British. 23. Killed
NOBLE, Sgt. W. J. British. 54
NOBLE, P/O B. R. British. 79
NOBLE, Sgt. D. British. 43. Killed*
NOKES-COOPER, F/O B. British. 236. Killed*
NORFOLK, P/O N. R. British. 72
NORRIS, F/O R. W. Canadian. 1 (Can) (401)
NORRIS, F/Lt. S. C. British. 610
NORRIS, Sgt. P. P. British. 213. Killed*
NORTH, P/O G. British. 257. Killed
NORTH, P/O H. L. N/Zealander. 43. Killed
NORTH-BOMFORD, Sgt. D. J. British. 17–229–111
NORWELL, Sgt. J. K. British. 54–41
NORWOOD, P/O R. K. C. British. 65
NOSOWICZ, P/O Z. Polish. 56

NOWAK, P/O T. Polish. 253. Killed
NOWAKIEWICZ, Sgt. E. J. A. Polish. 302
NOWELL (F.A.A.), Sub/Lt. W. R. British. 804
NOWIERSKI, P/O T. Polish. 609
NUNN, P/O S. G. British. 236
NUTE, Sgt. R. R. J. British. 23. Killed
NUTTER, Sgt. R. C. British. 257
OAKS, Sgt. T. W. N/Zealander. 235
O'BRIAN, F/O P. G. St. G. Canadian. 247–152
O'BRIEN, S/Ldr. J. S. British. 92–234. Killed*
O'BRYNE, Sgt. P. British. 73–501
O'CONNELL, P/O A. British. 264
OELOFSE, P/O J. R. S. S/African. 43. Killed*
ODBERT, S/Ldr. N. C. British. 64
OFFENBERG, P/O J. H. M. Belgian. 145. Killed
OGILVIE, P/O D. B. British. 601
OGILVIE, F/O A. K. Canadian. 609
OLDFIELD, Sgt. T. G. British. 64–92. Killed*
O'LEARY, Sgt. A. A. British. 604
OLENSEN, P/O W. P. British. 607. Killed
OLENSKI, P/O Z. Polish. 234–609
OLEWINSKI, Sgt. B. Polish. 111. Killed
OLIVE, F/Lt. C. G. Australian. 65
OLIVER, P/O P. British. 611
OLIVER, Sgt. G. D. British. 23. Killed
OLVER, P/O. British. 603
O'MALLEY, F/O D. K. C. British. 264. Killed*
OMMANEY, Sgt. R. J. British. 229. Killed
O'MEARA, P/O J. J. British. 421 Flt.–64–72
O'NEILL, F/O D. H. British. 611–41. Killed*
O'NEILL, F/Lt. J. A. British. 601–238
ORCHARD, Sgt. H. C. British. 65. Killed
ORGIAS, P/O E. N/Zealander. 23. Killed*
ORTMANS, P/O V. M. M. Belgian. 229.
ORZECHOWSKI, F/Lt. J. Polish. 607
OSMAND, P/O A. G. British. 3–213. Killed
OSTASZEWSKI-OSTOJE (now Raymond), F/O P. Polish. 609
OSTOWICZ, F/O A. Polish. 145. Killed*
OVERTON, F/O C. N. British. 609
OWEN, Sgt. A. E. British. 600. Killed
OWEN, Sgt. H. British. 219
OWEN, Sgt. W. G. British. 235
OXSPRING, F/O R. W. British. 66

PAGE, P/O A. G. British. 56
PAGE, Sgt. W. T. British. 1. Killed
PAGE, Sgt. V. D. British. 610–601
PAGE, Sgt. A. J. British. 257. Killed
PAGE, F/Lt. C. L. British. 234–145
PAGE, Sgt. A. D. British. 111–257. Killed
PAIN, P/O J. F. British. 32. Killed
PAISEY, Sgt. F. G. British. 235

PALAK, Sgt. J. Polish. 303–302
PALLISER, Sgt. G. C. C. British. 249–43–17
PALMER, Sgt. N. N. British. 248. Killed
PALUSINSKI, P/O J. H. Polish. 303
PANKRATZ, F/Lt. W. Polish. 145. Killed*
PANNELL, Sgt. G. C. N/Zealander. 3. Killed
PARKE (F.A.A.), Sub/Lt. T. R. V. British. 804. Killed
PARKER, Sgt. K. B. British. 64–92. Killed*
PARKER, P/O T. C. British. 79
PARKER, Sgt. D. K. British. 66–616
PARKER, P/O V. Australian. 234
PARKER, Wg/Com. I. R. British. 611
PARKES, Sgt. E. G. British. 501
PARKIN, P/O E. G. British. 501
PARKINSON, Sgt. C. British. 238. Killed*
PARNALL, P/O S. B. British. 607. Killed*
PARNALL, F/Lt. D. G. British. 249. Killed*
PARR, Sgt. L. A. British. 79
PARR, Sgt. D. J. British. 29. Killed
PARROTT, F/O D. T. British. 19. Killed
PARROTT, F/O P. L. British. 145–605
PARROTT, Sgt. R. J. British. 32. Killed
PARRY, Sgt. M. E. British. 604
PARRY, Sgt. E. British. 23. Killed
PARSONS, Sgt. E. E. N/Zealander. 23
PARSONS, Sgt. C. A. British. 66–610. Killed
PARSONS, F/O P. T. British. 504. Killed
PARSONS, Sgt. J. G. British. 235
PASSY, F/O C. W. British. 605
PASZKIEWICZ, F/O L. W. Polish. 303. Killed*
PATEREK, Sgt. E. Polish. 302–303. Killed
PATERSON (F.A.A.), Lt. B. British. 804
PATERSON, F/O J. A. N/Zealander. 92. Killed*
PATRICK, Sgt. L. F. British. 222
PATSON, LAC. A. G. British. 604
PATTEN, F/O H. P. F. British. 64
PATTERSON (F.A.A.), Mid/Ship. P. J. British. 242. Killed*
PATTERSON, P/O R. L. British. 235. Killed*
PATTERSON (F.A.A.), Sub/Lt. N. H. British. 804. Killed
PATTERSON, Sgt. L. J. British. 501. Killed
PATTINSON, F/O A. J. S. British. 616–23–92. Killed
PATTISON, Sgt. K. C. British. 611. Killed*
PATTISON, F/O J. D. Canadian. 1 (Can) (401)
PATTISON, F/O J. G. N/Zealander. 266–92
PATTULLO, P/O W. B. British. 151–249–46. Killed*
PAUL (F.A.A.), Sub/Lt. F. D. British. 64. Killed*
PAVITT, Sgt. H. J. British. 235
PAVLU, Sgt. O. Czech. 1. Killed
PAYNE, Sgt. A. D. British. 610

ROBINSON, Sgt. P. T. British. 257
ROBINSON, S/Ldr. M. British. 616
ROBSHAW, P/O F. A. British. 229
ROBSON, P/O N. C. H. British. 72. Killed
RODEN, Sgt. H. A. C. British. 19
ROFE, P/O B. J. British. 25. Killed
ROGERS, F/O B. A. British–85. 242. Killed
ROGERS, Sgt. G. W. British. 234. Killed
ROGERS, P/O E. B. British. 501–615
ROGOWSKI, Sgt. J. Polish. 303. Killed
ROHACEK, P/O R. B. Czech. 238–601. Killed
ROLLS, Sgt. W. T. E. British. 72
ROMAN, P/O C. L. Belgian. 236
ROMANIS, Sgt. A. L. British. 25. Killed
ROOK, F/Lt. A. H. British. 504
ROOK, F/O M. British. 504
ROSCOE, F/O G. L. British. 87–79. Killed
ROSE, F/O J. British. 32–3
ROSE, P/O S. N. British. 602
ROSE, Sgt. J. S. British. 23. Killed
ROSE-PRICE, P/O A. T. British. 501. Killed*
ROSIER, F/Lt. F. E. British. 229
ROSS, P/O J. K. British. 17. Killed
ROSS, P/O A. R. British. 610. Killed
ROTHWELL, P/O J. H. British. 601–605–32. Killed
ROUND, P/O J. H. British. 248. Killed*
ROURKE, Sgt. J. British. 248
ROUSE, Sgt. G. W. British. 236
ROWDEN, P/O J. H. British. 64–616. Killed
ROWELL, Sgt. P. A. British. 249
ROWLEY, F/O R. M. B. British. 145. Killed
ROYCE, F/O M. E. A. British. 504
ROYCE, F/Lt. W. B. British. 504
ROZWADOWSKI, P/O M. Polish. 151. Killed*
ROZYCKI, P/O W. Polish. 238
RUDDOCK, Sgt. W. S. British. 23
RUDLAND, Sgt. C. P. British. 263
RUSHMER, F/Lt. F. W. British. 603. Killed
RUSSEL, F/O B. D. Canadian. 1 (Can) (401)
RUSSELL, F/Lt. H. a'b. British. 32
RUSSELL, Sgt. L. P. N/Zealander. 264. Killed
RUSSELL, P/O G. H. British. 236
RUSSELL, Sgt. A. G. British. 43
RUSSELL, P/O. British. 141
RUSSELL (F.A.A.), Lt. G. F. British. 804. Killed
RUST, Sgt. C. A. British. 85–249
RUSTON, F/Lt. P. British. 604
RUTTER, P/O R. D. British. 73
RYALLS, P/O D. L. British. 29–F.I.U. Killed
RYDER, F/Lt. E. N. British. 41
RYPL, P/O F. Czech. 310

SADLER, P/O N. A. British. 235. Killed
SADLER, F/Sgt. H. S. British. 611. Killed
ST. AUBIN, F/Lt. E. F. British. 616. Killed
ST. JOHN, P/O P. C. B. British. 74. Killed*
SALMON, F/O H. N. E. British. 1–229. Killed
SALMOND, P/O W. N. C. British. 64
SALWAY, Sgt. E. British. 141. Killed
SAMOLINKSKI, P/O W. M. C. Polish. 253. Killed*
SAMPLE, S/Ldr. J. British. 504. Killed
SAMPSON, Sgt. A. British. 23
SANDERS, S/Ldr. P. J. British. 92
SANDERS, F/Lt. J. G. British. 615
SANDIFER, Sgt. A. K. British. 604
SARGENT, Sgt. R. E. B. British. 219
SARRE, Sgt. A. R. British. 603
SASAK, Sgt. W. Polish. 32. Killed
SATCHELL, S.Ldr. W. A. J. British. 302
SAUNDERS, P/O C. H. British. 92
SAUNDERS, F/Lt. G. A. W. British. 65
SAVAGE, Sgt. T. W. British. 64. Killed
SAVILL, Sgt. J. E. British. 242–151–501
SAWARD, Sgt. C. J. British. 615–501
SAWICZ, P/O T. Polish. 303
SAWYER, S/Ldr. H. C. British. 65. Killed*
SAYERS, F/Sgt. J. E. British. 41
SCHOLLAR, P/O E. C. British. 248
SCHUMER, P/O F. H. British. 600. Killed
SCHWIND, F/Lt. L. H. British. 257–213. Killed*
SCLANDERS, P/O K. M. Canadian. 242. Killed*
SCOTT, Sgt. A. E. British. 73–422 Flt. Killed
SCOTT, Sgt. G. W. British. 64–19
SCOTT, Sgt. W. J. N/Zealander. 264
SCOTT, Sgt. E. British. 222. Killed*
SCOTT, Sgt. J. A. British. 611–74. Killed*
SCOTT, F/Lt. D. R. British. 605. Killed
SCOTT, P/O A. M. W. British. 3–607–605. Killed
SCOTT, P/O D. S. British. 73
SCOTT, F/O W. J. M. British. 41. Killed*
SCOTT, P/O R. H. British. 604
SCOTT-MALDEN, P/O F. D. S. British. 611–603
SCRASE, F/O G. E. T. British. 600. Killed
SEABOURNE, Sgt. E. W. British. 238
SEARS, P/O L. A. British. 145. Killed*
SECRETAN, P/O D. British. 72–54
SEDA, Sgt. K. Czech. 310
SEDDON, P/O W. J. British. 601. Killed
SEGHERS, P/O E. G. A. Belgian. 46–32. Killed
SELLERS, Sgt. R. F. British. 46–111
SELWAY, F/O J. B. British. 604
SENIOR, Sgt. J. N. British. 23. Killed
SENIOR, Sgt. B. British. 600
SEREDYN, Sgt. A. Polish. 32
SERVICE, Sgt. A. British. 29. Killed
SEWELL, Sgt. D. A. British. 17. Killed

SHANAHAN, Sgt. M. M. British. 1. Killed*
SHAND, P/O M. M. N/Zealander. 54
SHARMAN, P/O H. R. British. 248
SHARP, P/O M. British. 111. Killed
SHARP, Sgt. B. R. British. 235. Killed*
SHARP, Sgt. R. J. British. 236
SHARPLEY, Sgt. H. British. 234. Killed
SHARRATT, Sgt. W. G. British. 248. Killed
SHAW, P/O R. H. British. 1. Killed*
SHAW, F/O I. G. British. 264. Killed*
SHAW (F.A.A.), Petty/Off. F. J. British. 804. Killed
SHEAD, Sgt. H. F. W. British. 257–32
SHEARD, Sgt. H. British. 236. Killed
SHEEN, F/Lt. D. F. B. Australian. 72
SHEPHERD, Sgt. F. W. British. 264. Killed
SHEPHLEY, P/O D. C. British. 152. Killed*
SHEPPARD, Sgt. W. J. P. British. 236
SHEPHERD, Sgt. J. B. British. 234
SHEPPERD, Sgt. G. E. British. 219. Killed*
SHEPPERD, Sgt. E. E. British. 152. Killed*
SHEPHERD, Sgt. F. E. R. British. 611. Killed*
SHERIDAN, Sgt. S. British. 236
SHERRINGTON, P/O T. B. A. British. 92
SHEWEL, Sgt. British. 236
SHIPMAN, P/O E. A. British. 41
SHIRLEY, Sgt. S. H. J. British. 604. Killed
SHORROCKS, P/O N. B. British. 235. Killed*
SHUTTLEWORTH, F/O Lord R. U. P. KAY-. British. 145. Killed*
SIBLEY, Sgt. F. A. British. 238. Killed*
SIKA, Sgt. J. Czech. 43
SILK, Sgt. F. H. British. 111
SILVER, Sgt. W. G. British. 152. Killed*
SILVESTER, Sgt. G. F. British. 229
SIM, Sgt. R. B. British. 111. Killed*
SIMMONDS, P/O V. C. British. 238
SIMPSON, F/O G. M. N/Zealander. 229. Killed*
SIMPSON, F/Lt. J. W. C. British. 43
SIMPSON, P/O P. J. British. 111–64
SIMPSON, P/O L. W. British. 141–264
SIMS, Sgt. I. R. British. 248. Killed
SIMS, P/O J. A. British. 3–232
SINCLAIR, F/Lt. G. L. British. 310
SINCLAIR, P/O J. British. 219
SING, F/Lt. J. E. J. British. 213
SIUDAK, Sgt. A. Polish. 302–303. Killed*
SIZER, P/O W. M. British. 213
SKALSKI, P/O S. Polish. 501–302
SKILLEN, Sgt. V. H. British. 29. Killed
SKINNER, Sgt. W. M. British. 74
SKINNER, F/Lt. C. D. E. British. 604
SKINNER, F/Lt. S. H. British. 604. Killed
SKOWRON, Sgt. H. Polish. 303. Killed
SLADE, Sgt. J. W. British. 64
SLATTER, P/O D. M. British. 141. Killed*
SLEIGH (F.A.A.), Lt. J. W. British. 804

SLOUF, Sgt. V. Czech. 312
SLY, Sgt. O. K. British. 29. Killed*
SMALLMAN, AC2 J. British. 23
SMART, F/O T. British. 65. Killed
SMITH, Sgt. A. British. 600. Killed
SMITH, Sgt. A. D. British. 66. Killed*
SMITH, P/O D. N. E. British. 74. Killed*
SMITH, P/O E. British. 229
SMITH, F/O D. S. British. 616. Killed*
SMITH, F/Lt. A. T. British. 610. Killed*
SMITH, F/Lt. E. B. B. British. 610
SMITH, F/Lt. F. M. Canadian. 72
SMITH, P/O I. S. N/Zealander. 151
SMITH, P/O J. D. Canadian. 73. Killed
SMITH, F/Lt. R. L. British. 151
SMITH, Sgt. K. B. British. 257. Killed*
SMITH, P/O R. R. Canadian. 229
SMITH, F/O W. A. British. 229
SMITH, P/O P. R. British. 25. Killed
SMITH, F/Lt. C. D. S. British. 25. Killed
SMITH, P/O A. W. Canadian. 141. Killed
SMITH (F.A.A.), Sub/Lt. F. A. British. 145. Killed*
SMITH, P/O A. J. British. 74
SMITH, Sgt. R. C. British. 236. Killed
SMITH, P/O E. L. British. 604
SMITH, Sgt. W. B. British. 602
SMITH, F/Lt. E. S. British. 600
SMITH, Sgt. L. E. British. 234
SMITH, Sgt. St. James. British. 600. Killed
SMITH, AC2 F. British. 604. Killed
SMITH, Sgt. G. E. British. 264
SMITH, AC2 L. British. 219
SMITH, Sgt. P. R. British. 236. Killed
SMITH, P/O N. H. J. British. 235
SMITH, Sgt. E. C. British. 600
SMITH, F/Lt. W. O. L. British. 263. Killed
SMITHERS, P/O J. L. British. 601. Killed*
SMITHER, F/O R. Canadian. 1 (Can) (401). Killed*
SMITHSON, Sgt. R. British. 249. Killed
SMYTH, Sgt. R. H. British. 111
SMYTHE, Sgt. G. British. 56
SMYTHE, F/O R. F. British. 32
SMYTHE, P/O D. M. A. British. 264
SNAPE, W/O O. V. R. British. 501–151
SNELL, F/O V. R. British. 213. Killed
SNOW, P/O W. G. British. 236
SNOWDEN, Sgt. E. G. British. 213. Killed
SOARS, Sgt. H. J. British. 74
SOBEY, Sgt. P. A. British. 235. Killed
SODEN, P/O J. F. British. 266–603. Killed
SOLAK, P/O J. J. Polish. 151–249
SOLOMON, P/O N. D. British. 17. Killed*
SONES, Sgt. L. C. British. 605
SOUTHALL, Sgt. G. British. 23. Killed
SOUTHORN, Sgt. G. A. British. 235
SOUTHWELL, P/O J. S. British. 245. Killed
SPEARS, Sgt. A. W. P. British. 222–421 Flt.

VERITY, P/O V. B. S. N/Zealander. 229
VESELY, P/O V. Czech. 312
VICK, S/Ldr. J. A. British. 607
VIGORS, P/O T. A. British. 222
VILES, Sgt. L. W. British. 236
VILLA, F/Lt. J. W. British. 72–92
VINCENT, G/Capt. S. F. British. 229
VINDIS, Sgt. F. Czech. 310
VINYARD, Sgt. F. F. British. 64. Killed*
VLAD, P/O. Czech. 501
VOKES, P/O A. F. British. 19. Killed
VOPALECKY, W/O. Czech. 310
VRANA, F/O A. Czech. 312
VYBIRAL, P/O T. Czech. 312
VYKOURAL, P/O K. J. Czech. 111–73.
   Killed

WADDINGHAM, F/O J. British. 141.
   Killed
WADE, P/O T. S. British. 92.
WADHAM, Sgt. J. V. British. 145–601.
   Killed*
WAGHORN, Sgt. P. H. British. 249–111.
   Killed
WAGNER, Sgt. A. D. British. 151. Killed
WAINWRIGHT, P/O A. G. British. 151.
   Killed
WAINWRIGHT, P/O M. T. British. 64
WAKE, Sgt. F. W. British. 264
WAKEFIELD, P/O H. K. British. 235
WAKEHAM, P/O E. C. J. British. 145.
   Killed*
WAKELING, Sgt. S. R. E. British. 87.
   Killed*
WALCH, F/Lt. S. C. Australian. 238.
   Killed*
WALKER, Sgt. S. British. 236. Killed
WALKER, Sgt. J. I. B. N/Zealander. 600
WALKER, F/O J. H. G. British. 25. Killed
WALKER, Sgt. N. Mc. D. British. 615.
   Killed
WALKER, P/O W. L. B. British. 616
WALKER, P/O J. A. Canadian. 111.
   Killed
WALKER, P/O J. R. Canadian. 611–41.
   Killed
WALKER, P/O W. L. B. British. 616
WALKER, Sgt. G. A. British. 232
WALKER, P/O R. J. British. 72
WALKER-SMITH, Sgt. F. R. British. 85.
   Killed
WALLACE, P/O C. A. B. Canadian. 3.
   Killed
WALLACE, Sgt. T. Y. S/African. 111.
   Killed
WALLEN, F/Lt. D. S. British. 604
WALLENS, F/O R. W. British. 41
WALLER, Sgt. J. A. British. 29
WALLEY, Sgt. P. K. British. 615. Killed*
WALLIS, Sgt. D. S. British. 235. Killed
WALMSLEY, Sgt. H. W. British. 248
WALSH, Sgt. E. British. 141
WALSH, P/O J. J. Canadian. 615. Killed

WALSH (F.A.A.), Sub/Lt. R. W. M.
   British. 111
WALTON, Sgt. H. British. 87
WANT, Sgt. W. H. British. 248. Killed*
WAPNIAREK, P/O S. Polish. 302. Killed*
WARD, Sgt. R. A. British. 66–616.
   Killed*
WARD, Sgt. W. B. British. 604
WARD, F/O D. H. N/Zealander. 87.
   Killed
WARD, P/O J. L. British. 32. Killed
WARD, S/Ldr. The Hon. E. F. British.
   601
WARDEN, Sgt. N. P. British. 610. Killed
WARD-SMITH, Sgt. P. British. 610
WARE, Sgt. R. T. British. 3. Killed
WAREHAM, P/O M. P. British. 1–242.
   Killed
WAREING, Sgt. P. T. British. 616
WARING, Sgt. W. British. 23
WARNER, F/Lt. W. H. C. British. 610.
   Killed*
WARREN, Sgt. S. British. 1. Killed*
WARREN, Sgt. T. A. British. 236
WARREN, Sgt. J. B. W. British. 600.
   Killed
WARREN, P/O C. British. 152
WARREN, P/O A. P. British. 248. Killed
WATERSTON, F/O R. McGregor. British.
   603. Killed*
WATKINS, F/O D. H. British. 611
WATKINSON, P/O A. B. S/African. 66
WATLING, P/O W. C. British. 92. Killed
WATSON, Sgt. J. G. British. 604
WATSON, P/O A. R. British. 152. Killed
WATSON, P/O E. J. British. 605. Killed
WATSON, P/O L. G. British. 29
WATSON, F/O R. F. British. 87
WATSON, P/O. British. 64
WATSON, P/O F. S. Canadian. 3. Killed
WATTERS, P/O J. N/Zealander. 236
WATTS, P/O F. British. 253
WATTS, Sgt. E. L. British. 248. Killed
WATTS, Sgt. R. D. H. British. 235.
   Killed*
WAY, P/O L. B. R. British. 229
WAY, F/Lt. B. H. British. 54. Killed*
WCZELIK, P/O A. Polish. 302. Killed
WEAVER, F/Lt. P. S. British. 56. Killed*
WEBB, F/O P. C. British. 602
WEBBER, P/O W. F. P. British. 141
WEBBER, Sgt. J. British. 1–145
WEBER, P/O F. Czech. 145
WEBSTER, F/Lt. J. T. British. 41. Killed*
WEBSTER, P/O F. K. British. 610. Killed*
WEBSTER, Sgt. H.G. British. 73. Killed
WEBSTER, Sgt. E. R. British. 85
WEDGEWOOD, F/Lt. J. H. British. 253.
   Killed
WEDLOCK, Sgt. G. V. British. 235
WEDZIK, Sgt. M. Polish. 302
WEIR, P/O A. N. C. British. 145. Killed
WELCH, Sgt. E. British. 604. Killed
WELFORD, P/O G. H. E. British. 607

WELLS, P/O E. P. N/Zealander. 41–266
WELLS, F/O P. H. V. British. 249
WELLS, P/O M. L. British. 248
WELSH, P/O T. D. British. 264
WELLUM, P/O G. H. A. British. 92
WENDEL, P/O K. V. N/Zealander. 504.
   Killed*
WEST, S/Ldr. H. British. 151–41
WEST, P/O D. R. British. 141
WESTCOTT, Sgt. W. H. J. British. 235
WESTLAKE, P/O G. H. British. 43–213
WESTLAKE, P/O R. D. British. 235
WESTMACOTT, F/O I. B. British. 56
WESTMORELAND, Sgt. T. E. British. 616.
   Killed*
WHALL, Sgt. B. E. P. British. 602. Killed*
WHEATCROFT, P/O N. R. British. 604.
   Killed
WHEELER, P/O N. J. British. 615–600
WHELAN, Sgt. J. British. 64–19
WHINNEY, P/O M. T. British. 3
WHIPPS, Sgt. G. A. British. 602. Killed
WHITBREAD, P/O H. L. British. 222.
   Killed*
WHITBY, Sgt. A. W. British. 79
WHITE, P/O B. E. G. British. 504. Killed
WHITE, Sgt. J. W. British. 3–F.I.U.
WHITE, S/Ldr. F. L. British. 74
WHITE, Sgt. J. British. 72. Killed
WHITE, Sgt. British. 604
WHITE, Sgt. R. British. 235
WHITE, Sgt. J. British. 248. Died
WHITE, Sgt. J. S. British. 32
WHITEHEAD, Sgt. C. British. 56. Killed
WHITEHEAD, Sgt. R. O. British. 253–151
WHITEHOUSE, P/O British. 32
WHITEHOUSE, Sgt. S. A. H. British. 501
WHITFIELD, Sgt. J. J. British. 56. Killed*
WHITLEY, S/Ldr. E. W. N/Zealander.
   245
WHITLEY, P/O D. British. 264. Killed*
WHITNEY, P/O D. M. N/Zealander. 245
WHITSON, Sgt. A. D. British. 236. Killed
WHITTICK, Sgt. H. G. British. 604
WHITTINGHAM, F/O C. D. British. 151
WHITTY, F/O W. H. R. British. 607
WHITWELL, Sgt. P. C. N/Zealander. 600.
   Killed
WICKINGS-SMITH, P/O P. C. British. 235.
   Killed*
WICKINS, Sgt. A. S. British. 141
WICKS, F/O B. J. British. 56. Killed
WIDDOWS, S/Ldr. S. C. British. 29
WIGG, P/O R. G. N/Zealander. 65
WIGGLESWORTH, P/O J. S. British. 238.
   Killed
WIGHT, F/Lt. R. D. G. British. 213.
   Killed*
WIGHTMAN (F.A.A.), Mid/Ship. O. M.
   British. 151. Killed
WILCOCK, Sgt. C. British. 248. Died
WILCOX, P/O E. J. British. 72. Killed*
WILDBLOOD, P/O T. S. British. 152.
   Killed*

WILDE, P/O D. C. British. 236
WILKES, Sgt. G. N. British. 213. Killed*
WILKINSON, S/Ldr. R. L. British. 266.
   Killed*
WILKINSON, Sgt. W. A. British. 501
WILKINSON, Sgt. K. A. British. 616–19
WILKINSON, F/O R. C. British. 3
WILLANS, P/O D. A. British. 23. Killed
WILLCOCKS, Sgt. P. H. British. 610–66.
   Killed
WILLCOCKS, Sgt. C. P. L. British. 610
WILLIAMS, S/Ldr. C. W. British. 17.
   Killed*
WILLIAMS, P/O D. G. British. 92. Killed*
WILLIAMS, F/Sgt. E. E. British. 46.
   Killed*
WILLIAMS, F/O T. D. British. 611
WILLIAMS, P/O W. D. British. 152
WILLIAMS, P/O S. N/Zealander. 266.
   Killed*
WILLIAMS, Sgt. G. T. British. 219
WILLIAMS, P/O D. C. British. 141. Killed
WILLIAMS, P/O M. A. British. 604
WILLIS, Sgt. W. A. N/Zealander. 600
WILLIS, Sgt. R. F. British. 219. Killed
WILLS, Sgt. W. C. British. 73–3. Killed
WILSCH, P/O British. 141
WILSDON, Sgt. A. A. British. 29. Killed
WILSON, F/Lt. D. S. British. 610
WILSON, P/O R. R. Canadian. 111.
   Killed*
WILSON, P/O D. F. N/Zealander. 141
WILSON, Sgt. W. C. British. 29
WILSON, Sgt. W. British. 235
WILSON-MACDONALD, F/Lt. D. S.
   British. 213
WINGFIELD, Sgt. V. British. 29. Killed
WINN, P/O V. British. 29
WINSKILL, P/O A. L. British. 603–72
WINSTANLEY, Sgt. J. British. 151
WINTER, P/O D. C. British. 72. Killed*
WINTER, P/O R. A. British. 247
WISE, Sgt. J. F. British. 141. Killed*
WISEMAN, P/O W. D. British. 600
WISSLER, P/O D. H. British. 17. Killed
WITHALL, F/Lt. L. C. Australian. 152.
   Killed*
WITORZENC, F/O S. Polish. 501
WLASNOWOLSKI, P/O B. Polish.
   607–32–213. Killed
WOJCICKI, Sgt. A. Polish. 213. Killed*
WOJCIECHOWSKI, Sgt. M. Polish. 303
WOJTOWICZ, Sgt. S. Polish. 303. Killed*
WOLFE, S/Ldr. E. C. British. 141–219
WOLTON, Sgt. R. British. 152
WOOD, Sgt. S. V. British. 248
WOOD, Sgt. K. R. British. 23. Killed
WOODGATE, Sgt. J. E. British. 141.
   Killed
WOODGER, P/O D. N. British. 235.
   Killed*
WOODLAND, Sgt. N. N. British. 236
WOODS-SCAWEN, P/O C. A. British. 43.
   Killed*

ACKNOWLEDGEMENTS
FOR PHOTOGRAPHS

Lufthansa, Group Captain J. Kent, *Kent Messenger*, Vickers-Armstrongs, Air Commodore P. M. Brothers, The Press Association, Central Press Photos, Hawker Siddeley, British Lion Films, Imperial War Museum, Crown Copyright, AEI, Dr. Gaertner, London News Agency Photos, Fox Photos, Wing Commander Havercraft, Bundesarchivs, Lt. Col. Aviateur BEM M. Terlinden, Group Captain Wilson, Westland Aircraft, Royal National Lifeboat Institution, Hodder and Stoughton, Dennis Knight, Air Commodore Donaldson, Syndication International, Associated Press, Field Marshal Milch, T. Angelle Weisse, A. W. Capel, R.A.C. Tank Museum, Topix, Lalouette, Wing Commander R. P. Beamont, The Museum of British Transport, Captain J. H. Mann, Associated Newspapers, Short Brothers and Harland, Force Aerienne Belge, British Leyland Motor Corporation, T. H. McLellan, A. Wilson, Hutton-Deutsch Collection, Barratt's Photo Press.